DANCE WITH AN ANGEL

The true story of an eight-year-old hero

By

Robyn V. Accetturo, L.C.S.W.

2009
Dear Sabine,
Love is the answer...
Let my Buddy show you
how. Light & Love,
Robyn

This book is a work of non-fiction. Names have been changed to protect the privacy of all individuals, except where permission was given. The events and situations are true. The dialogue contained within was not recorded at the time of occurrence, but after-the-fact, during the re-creation of the story.

ISBN: 1-4107-8397-9 (e-book)
ISBN: 1-4107-8398-7 (Paperback)

Library of Congress Control Number: 2003095495

This book is printed on acid free paper.

Printed in the United States of America
Bloomington, IN

1stBooks – rev. 11/11/03

PRAISE FOR *DANCE WITH AN ANGEL*

Robyn did everything she could within the rules of the system, as a professional social worker, to protect Jeremy. When the system continued to fail them, she turned to her spiritual guidance to do the job. You don't always look to a child to find the meaning of life, but in this true story, you find an unexpected gem. I highly recommend this book to everyone. Open your heart and let its wisdom sink in.

Jeffrey Pollack, R.N.C., M.S.W., L.C.S.W.

Three Oaks, Michigan

Dance With An Angel is an amazing story of the love and commitment it took to protect an abused child from his own mother. In her role, which far exceeded that of a traditional social worker, the author was guided by a Higher Power to make decisions on behalf of this young boy. Often times her greatest inspiration came from this very child, who showed the world true unconditional love, despite his own tragic circumstances. The relationship that develops between the author and child is a "dance" between TWO very special "Angels!"

Marsha McKay, M.S. in ED., Elementary School Teacher

Lisle, Illinois

In the story, *Dance With An Angel,* Robyn is a signpost that Miracles do happen. She has given us the Blessed Assurance that God leads us through every valley, no matter how difficult the obstacle, onward to victory. Your Soul will be touched and your Spirit renewed. Thank you, Robyn, for being the channel of God's love.

Reverend Sally Wales, The First Temple of Universal Law

Chicago, Illinois

ABOUT THE COVER

Two years ago, I bound my manuscript and allowed several copies to circulate within my community. A lot of people had been asking to read it. My children's art teacher, Nancy Staszak, read a copy. The story really moved her, and she asked to purchase several copies. I told her that once it was published, I'd be honored. She had never seen a picture of Jeremy, but he had made quite an impression on her. Last fall in 2002, my family attended one of Nancy's art shows at a local library. We had purchased a monotype of hers at a previous show. She is very talented, and we have been blessed to have her teach our children.

We walked into the area where Nancy's art was on display, I looked up on the wall, and my eyes immediately went to three angel prints. I froze in my steps. Tears welled up in my eyes as I gasped. Our son, Stephen, looked at me and looked up at the wall as I declared, "Look, Stephen, it's Jeremy. He's an angel!" Jim, my husband, and Kathryn, our daughter, heard and came over. We were absolutely astounded. Nancy joined us to see what all the commotion was about. When I told her, I'm not sure she really believed me, it was kind of hard to fathom. But when I sent three photos of Jeremy to Nancy at school the following day, she couldn't believe it. She shared the story behind the three angels.

The first and third prints were in ink. They represented the Old Testament and the New Age respectively. The angel in the center represented the time of Christ. It was Jeremy! His eyes, nose, mouth, neck, and locks of hair on top of his head were so real. Even his skin tone was exactly the same color as his skin.

Nancy explained that her intention was to make the center angel a Native American Indian. Then Nancy kept getting the feeling that it wasn't quite right, she needed to change it to an African American angel. So she erased the face of the Native American angel and replaced it with an African American one. And when she actually had it in her printing press, during the etching process, the face changed even more from what she had line drawn, to look like Jeremy.

Nancy's daughter, JoAnne, was home on break from college, where she's an art major. She'd seen the center angel and asked her mom if she could color it in. And without ever seeing a picture of him, she chose the exact tone of Jeremy's skin color, using Prismacolor ® pencils as her medium. We purchased our "Jeremy Angel," and he hangs proudly in our living room. We are so thankful.

Several months later, as I was preparing my manuscript for 1st Book Library, I mustered up the courage to ask Nancy for permission to use our angel in my book. She said she'd be honored.

Our angel appears on the cover. It's title is "Surely Goodness and Mercy," from the 23rd Psalm. God does indeed work in mysterious ways. Thank you Nancy and JoAnne for this phenomenal gift of seeing Jeremy, as he truly is, a real life Angel.

CONTENTS

DEDICATION

I could not, and would not, have taken one step with Jeremy if I didn't have the support and wisdom of my husband, Jim. When things got so tough, Jim held me together like glue. I am so grateful for his strength and his spirituality. And to our children, Kathryn and Stephen, you are both incredible souls. I am so thankful for your presence in our life. I dedicate this book to all of us as a family, including big brother Jeremy. Thank you, Jeremy, for having the courage to walk this incredible journey. We love ya, Buddy! Say hi to Chief Yellow Sports Car!

I would also like to dedicate this book to my Mom, who graduated to higher ground Christmas of 1993. Her incredible strength, courage, and fun-loving nature have helped me to become who I am today. Without the experiences I've had, and knowledge I gained through her, I would not have undertaken this seemingly impossible task of seeing Jeremy through to the end. I love you, Mom. Thank you.

To the promises of God that I stood on and that saw us through each and every moment, I am forever humble and grateful. May Divine Order reign over our story, Amen.

PREFACE

The miracles in the making of this whole experience continue to this day. That's what happens when you have an Angel in your life. *Dance With An Angel* is a timeless, true story, written from my heart, of my twenty-two month journey with the most courageous child and hero I have ever known, "Jeremy Miller." As I started to share Jeremy's story verbally with friends, I got encouragement to write it down, so it could reach more people. Thus, *Dance With An Angel* began as a way to honor Jeremy and to share his love with the world.

Writing helped me to heal. After all, I had carried Jeremy's burden of darkness and fear with me for so long alone, without the proper authorities taking responsibility for keeping him safe, his story had become my life. My entire being needed to heal. Honoring my promise to Jeremy that I would keep him safe, without much of a system to back me up, and with a mother who could have played the character of Glenn Close in the movie, Fatal Attraction, brought challenges and obstacles that were humanly impossible to overcome. Jeremy's mom could have easily fled and taken Jeremy with her, or lost impulse control, and in her moment of uncontrollable rage, she had the capabilities of killing her son, our beautiful Jeremy.

But with the help of God and the Universe, and Divine Order declared over every part of our lives, our mission was accomplished. I realized I needed to also write about our journey together as a part of my healing process from all of the human tragedy that I witnessed, and to show the glory of All That Is.

When I was pregnant with my son, Stephen, and my daughter, Kathryn, was two years old, my husband, Jim, and I, made a commitment that I would write *Dance With An Angel.* For the next five years, Jim often took our children on weekend outings, so I could have chunks of time alone to write. He also put the children to bed many nights, and I would write well into the morning.

I joined the Lisle Library Writer's Group and did my best to unravel all of the layers of the story inside of me. Early on, the group members made fun of me, they said they didn't want to read a big social work report. They wanted to live it with me, in my shoes. I'd have to "bleed onto the page," as "show don't tell," was their mantra.

So I did my best to relive our journey. As traumatic as parts of it were, the triumphant parts made up for it. "Jeremy" continues to work miracles in my life. My hope is that he will also work them in yours.

And with humble adoration, I give you Jeremy Miller, the brightest star in the Universe in a long, long time.

"WE ARE NOT HUMAN BEINGS SHARING OUR SPIRITUAL
EXPERIENCE,

WE ARE SPIRITUAL BEINGS SHARING OUR HUMAN
EXPERIENCE"

(AUTHOR UNKNOWN)

INTRODUCTION

There are people who enter our lives and we are never the same. They set us on a journey, teach us a lesson, test our limits, and help us to grow.

Jeremy Miller, whom I called "My Little Buddy," was one of those people. He was much wiser than his age. Jeremy watched us all without judgement, giving only unconditional love. One of the greatest lessons that I learned from Jeremy was that *the only way out of darkness is through the Light.* May Jeremy teach you as much as he has taught me.

"Life has meaning only in the struggle. Triumph or defeat is in the hands of the gods. Let us celebrate the struggle...."

A Swahili Warrior Song

CHAPTER ONE -- THE JOB

In the fall of 1992, Delilah Miller refrained from suffocating her two-year-old son, Simon, with a pillow. She then, for the first time in her life, signed herself into a psychiatric hospital. I can't help but think, had I reached her sooner, the fate of her eight-year-old son, Jeremy, may have been different, and I might not be telling you this story. Yet, every cell of my being knows that my journey with them was not by accident.

It was mid-January, 1990. I telephoned Joan, my co-worker, to tell her I'd be giving my two-week notice at work the following day. I had accepted a job working with families afflicted by AIDS. As I explained a little about the position, she interrupted. "Are you out of your mind? What possessed you to take this job? Going into Robert Taylor Homes and Cabrini Green? Gang bangers shoot people there almost every day! What does Jim say about it?"

"Jim knows that even if I have to go into some of Chicago's worst housing projects, I'll be safe and protected. He also knows that when I have a strong conviction about something, it's pretty hard to change my mind."

"You guys and your spirituality stuff... I don't know about you. If I accepted a job like that, Robert would kill me first, then he'd forbid me to go."

"Yeah, a lot of guys probably would. But I married a guy who's kinda weird, like me... we rely a lot on our spirituality. If we didn't, I don't think I'd be taking the job."

"More power to ya, Sister. I'm happy for you, I think. Congratulations. You'll be greatly missed on the unit."

As I hung up, part of me wanted to shrug off her response. Another part understood where she was coming from. Even when I told my family, I sensed their concern and apprehension for my safety, and I appreciated their respect for my decision. I had a strong belief, an internal knowing; this was the path I had to take. My Dad always said, "If it's meant to be, it'll work out." So I figured, if getting the position was meant to be, then the Universe wouldn't let any harm come to me while performing it.

I anticipated great things happening while serving these families. I hoped I'd be able to reach people on a very deep level. I'd be helping families through the most difficult crises of all; the death of one or more of its members. And not only that, I might be able to help make a difference in a kid's life. The families would only be referred if they were involved with the state for child abuse or neglect.

So I quit my job as a social worker on the adult in-patient psychiatric unit to respond to the push I felt inside. Whatever drove me to make this lateral move, one thing was certain: The feeling inside of me was so strong, I couldn't live with myself if I didn't take the job. I call it my spiritual calling. Jim shared my excitement and had as much faith and assurance that everything would work out for me, and for us, as I began my new job.

My supervisor at the new job, Connie, was in charge of the private contract to provide case management and counseling services to the state child welfare department's "intact families with AIDS." This meant that for each case I would carry, the parents had allegedly abused and/or neglected their children, yet still had custody of them. Also one or more of the family members were HIV positive or had full-blown AIDS. In some cases, the parent(s) had it, in some cases the children had it, and in others the whole family was HIV positive.

The program was designed with the hope of preventing further child abuse and neglect. It was also created with the hope of assisting the families in coming to terms with their terminal illnesses and planning for the future of their children. My coworker, Carolyn Mitchell, whose title was Community Worker, and I would do anything and everything we could to help these families cope. Whatever they needed – therapy, emotional support, food, shelter, clothing, transportation, we'd provide it for them. If we couldn't, we'd find someone who could. Often, Carolyn and I were their last hope.

The freedom of the job intrigued me. The job was really mine to create. Connie's contract stated *what* the program would provide for the families. *How* to carry it out was up to me. The lack of direction turned out to be anxiety producing at times.

Most of our work was provided in the family's home or in the community. My role was to help each family deal with their diagnoses, their lives, and ultimately their deaths, while always keeping a watchful eye for child abuse or neglect. Carolyn, who had a lifetime of experience working with impoverished families in Chicago's inner city, attended to more of their physical needs; transportation to and from appointments, or obtaining clothing for the children, for example. She helped me keep watch over the children as well.

As Carolyn and I got to know each other, it became apparent to us why the Universe had placed us together. Carolyn is an incredibly spiritual African - American woman almost thirty years my senior, although you'd never know it by looking at her. She is a certified teacher in the Unity School of Christianity. Carolyn had a way of taking me under her wing and of supporting and inspiring me, which I had never experienced before. She has an innate ability to trust God and listen with an open heart for answers, and a way of sharing her knowledge and inspiration which could calm even the most restless of hearts. As we worked on some incredibly difficult and often surprisingly frightening cases together, we both tapped into our spirituality to survive. There was no other way to get through such darkness.

Soon after I started the job, we visited a heroin-addicted mother and her two children in their apartment on the city's West Side. The apartment happened to be in an abandoned building. Often Carolyn and I would drive together for safety. On this occasion however, due to different client visits, we were in separate cars. It was a blistering afternoon near the end of summer. I arrived before Carolyn and sat in my car, blasting the air conditioner.

I said a prayer of protection. Carolyn and I had a ritual for ourselves, which we performed faithfully whether alone or together on a visit. We'd say aloud a prayer of protection. We'd also pray for

God's will to be done, which we called "Divine Order," not our will or our needs. We would also ask for the highest possible good, of all the players involved, to be served as well. Even if the player wasn't a person, but an entire political system.

As I looked around and checked out the area, I was surprised by the lack of activity around the client's apartment building. It was deserted except for four African - American men leaning up against a late model, royal blue Cadillac with a gold plated ram's head hood ornament, and wide, whitewall tires. They were parked kitty corner from my car. A young boy came out from a basement apartment, which had music blaring so loudly from the barred windows I heard it over the roar of my air. The boy approached the men, stuck his head in the car, and then ran back inside the apartment. This happened several times. I noticed three of the men wearing beepers. Perspiration trickled down my temples, not from the heat, but from the tension I felt. They had glanced over at me several times, probably trying to figure out what the heck this white woman was doing, sitting there in her car.

I did my best not to look at them.

The huge red, brick apartment building had a courtyard in front. I felt sad as I imagined what the place must have looked like at one time. The building had beautifully carved, heavy oak doors, and elaborate architecture under the eaves. The majority of the building now covered in gangs' graffiti, stood silent, most of its windows broken. Every area of the ground was strewn with garbage and broken glass.

Finally, Carolyn drove up. We both got out and said a quick prayer of protection together. The four men snickered at us as we walked by, our arms filled with bags of clothing for the family. Carolyn and I both chuckled after we were out of their space, knowing that not only would we be protected throughout this visit, but our cars would be as well. After all, we had been in worse areas, and so far our prayers had always been answered. We felt like soldiers of goodness.

As we walked up four flights of stairs to the client's apartment, the stench of stale, hot urine permeated the air. Carolyn knocked hard several times to no avail. She yelled the client's name, and what sounded like a very sleepy voice answered from behind the locked door.

"Yes?"

"It's Carolyn and Robyn. Let us in, please."

"Who?"

"You know me. Carolyn, the caseworker that brought you clothes the other day. I've brought Robyn, the social worker, with me for our meeting. Remember?" Carolyn said with exasperation in her voice.

"Carolyn..." her voice trailed off. "Oh yeah, Carolyn." She unlocked the door and let us in.

After sitting down on a filthy couch, covered in dust, loud hammering began from somewhere outside the building. Carolyn commented, "Oh good, they must be finally fixing something around here." The client didn't say a word.

When our visit ended and we left, Carolyn walked ahead of me as we climbed back down the filthy stairwell. She reached her hand up to open the heavy oak door to the outside. The door wouldn't budge. It had a small window, which Carolyn looked through. Looking back at her was, as she said, "A pair of big, black eyes and some dark black skin...." In her panic she yelled, "Oh my God, we're dead. There's a gang out there and they're gonna kill us!"

The man behind the face yelled to us, "You're locked in. I have orders to board up the building. You can't get out."

"We can't get out, what does that mean?" I thought aloud to myself. Thinking that he'd give us some preferential treatment, Carolyn yelled to him, "We're social workers from an agency. We made a home visit to help a family upstairs. You *have* to let us out."

The man, unimpressed, yelled back, "Go up to her apartment and use her fire escape." It seemed strange that he knew she was up there, yet still proceeded with his orders.

Having no choice, we trudged back up the four flights of stairs, combating the urine fumes and the waves of heat, and knocked on the client's door. She eventually let us back in, after Carolyn reminded her a couple of times who we were. She showed us to her back door.

The refrigerator was pushed in front of the door for security. We pulled it out only to find a thick board, nailed tightly to the floor, a few inches in front of the door. We tried everything to get the board up, but it wouldn't budge.

As desperate as we were, we decided to try and force our bodies through the small opening to freedom. Carolyn whispered to me, "Sister, I'll go first, cuz if you go first and you make it out but I don't... well... here it goes!" She tried to get one leg through and use her weight to force the door open. No way, she was stuck. She finally squeezed her way back into the kitchen.

Feeling rather panicky, we ran to the window and screamed to the man again. He was so busy boarding up every window in the place, he didn't hear us. We were trapped. No calling for help, no phones. We ran back downstairs and banged on a hall window that was still free, until we got his attention. He yelled to us, "Go into the apartment on the third floor, the door is open. Use that fire escape."

Okay, I thought to myself, *there's hope yet. We'll get out soon.*

Carolyn and I couldn't get into the stupid apartment. It was locked. We ran back down, screaming at the man as loud as we could. I stepped back, pulled my soaked hair off of my face, and began fanning vigorously. Carolyn, also dripping with perspiration, looked at me. We burst out laughing. Tears streamed down our cheeks. Once we regained our composure, we yelled even louder. After a few minutes, the man heard us and came over. He obviously saw our distress. "I'll go up the back fire escape, and get you out. Go back up to the third floor and wait for me." He broke through a window and door to find us. We were finally free.

When we reached our cars, my knees turned instantly to rubber. Our audience of four onlookers laughed at us and applauded as we passed by. From that time on, Carolyn named us, "Lethal Weapon III." She, of course, was Danny Glover, and I was Mel Gibson. We found out later that the family had received several orders to vacate the premises because the building had been condemned. They had chosen to stay.

This was just one experience that I went through while on this job. This was a new endeavor for me; I had not worked with child abuse before. In fact, I really knew nothing about it except that I was a "mandated reporter." In other words, if I learned of an abuse or witnessed one first hand, the law would require me to report what I saw to the appropriate authorities. My graduate school training had been in mental health.

Jeremy and Delilah were only the second case Carolyn and I had received. Who would have ever thought, this child, Jeremy, would have such a profound impact on my life?

CHAPTER TWO -- OUR FIRST ENCOUNTER

After two weeks of intensive, on the job HIV/AIDS training, and very little child abuse training except how to fill out the required paperwork, I sat at my desk, picked up the file marked Delilah and Jeremy Miller, and began reading.

Reason for state intervention:
Case reported to state when 6 y/o Jeremy fell from second story window of homeless shelter. Child placed in full body cast due to severity of leg injury. Incident considered unfounded. (That basically meant that there was not enough evidence to prove it was truly child abuse because there were no witnesses except Jeremy, and he did not tell what really happened.) **Accident seen as result of inadequate supervision. Referred to private program for counseling, assistance with parenting issues, coping with Jeremy's chronic illness and other stresses, and for concrete services** (such as help with food, clothing, housing and financial assistance.)

Identifying information:
Delilah Miller, 26 y/o African American female, presents as reserved, highly controlled, and gracefully polite. Recently diagnosed with HIV, she is four months pregnant. Lives alone in apartment with only son, Jeremy, who was just diagnosed with full-blown AIDS, due to condition known as wasting syndrome. Mother's boyfriend, father of baby, tested negative for HIV. Jeremy's father presumed dead. No evidence of illicit drug usage by mother who recently learned her birth certificate showed a

8

birth mother she never knew. **She states family abused her since childhood. Doesn't want anyone to know about HIV diagnoses. Quit full-time job few weeks ago as office worker due to Jeremy's frequent hospitalizations. Family extremely isolated - no support system. Mother relies heavily on hospital staff.** (That concerned me.)

Immediate needs/Treatment planning:
   Food, clothing, housing, $, assistance applying for Public Aid and disability for Jeremy. Help mother find alternative ways for coping with stress and handling anger. Increase support system. Help mother discuss future plans for children/permanency planning.
   I put the file down. My heart felt sorrowful and heavy, and I had only read their story, not lived it. What would I do if I were in her shoes? Permanency planning was the last thing I'd want to do with this poor woman... ask what she wants to happen to her children if she dies before they do.
   My heart instantly went out to her... a single working mom, pregnant, both she and her son just diagnosed... and now she wonders where will their next meal come from? How will she pay their rent?
   So many feelings filled my being... sadness, compassion, and anger at the disease, and at them getting it. I feared that I might not be able to find them enough help... *My first case with a child with AIDS, and he's being physically abused...oh my... the mom has got to be stressed out from just finding out... I can help her cope with all of this so she won't hurt her son... I know I can help her to not hit him ever again....*
   Underneath, I felt a strong connection to them from deep down inside of me. No logic to it. Purely emotional, intuitive, spiritual. The more I tried to put them out of my mind, the stronger the feeling became.
   When I got home from work, I called my mom, who lived in Florida. "Got my second case, Mom. Something's up with this one. There's some sort of bigger connection going on. I can't even find the words to explain what I'm experiencing."
   She gave me helpful advice. "Trust yourself. Your hunches are good. This is going to be interesting to watch as everything unfolds."

"That's a really neat way to describe it, unfolding. Thanks." I knew she was right.

Shauna, the state worker assigned to the Miller family scheduled our initial home visit with Delilah. During the first visit, we needed to introduce ourselves, our program, and try to convince her to work with us. She could choose not to, although the state certainly didn't want that to happen. Her caseworker from the state regularly carried anywhere from 50 to 100 cases. Carolyn and I would be limited to around 20. We would be able to give them the special attention they needed.

If Delilah accepted our services, we could visit as often as we found necessary, and Shauna would reduce her visits to once a month. I'd keep Shauna posted with phone calls and quarterly reports.

Early Monday morning, Carolyn and I pulled in front of a well - kept, old, gray stone, three - flat building bearing Delilah's address. We were impressed. I guess we expected it to be worse. Our first case certainly was. There even appeared to be a flower garden in Delilah's front yard, although it was hard to tell in February. We had been instructed to wait for the state worker before attempting to go in alone. Our appointment was for 9:00.

So we waited. And waited. At 9:45, we decided to go in without her, assuming she had an emergency. We found no doorbell and discovered the entrance unlocked. Delilah lived in the third floor apartment. The unlit stairwell wound around at an awkward angle. As we passed the second floor apartment, children greeted us while playing with their door open. We continued our ascent to Delilah's door and knocked. No answer. I knocked louder using my car key. No answer. One more try… nothing.

"Huh, what do you think's going on?" asked Carolyn.

"I'm not sure," I responded. "Hope everything's all right though." We left.

When we got back to the office there were no messages on my desk. I telephoned Shauna. She wasn't in. I left a message for her to please call me. Delilah had a phone, but I was reluctant to call her. It was Shauna's responsibility to make the first contact. Shauna telephoned me later in the day. "I'm sorry. Delilah *had* to go to the doctor first thing this morning. I rescheduled for this Thursday at 9:00. I had no way to get a hold of you."

"If it happens again, please call the office anytime. We have an answering machine." I also gave her my home phone number and asked her to please call if something came up before the next visit. She agreed.

As I hung up, a part of me felt a little leery about what had taken place. I wasn't so sure if Delilah made the doctor's appointment because she actually needed to, or if she did it to avoid meeting us. I thought she'd want to meet us. I talked myself out of it and gave her the benefit of the doubt. Shauna didn't seem to have a problem with it. I felt guilty for having my suspicions.

On Thursday, Carolyn and I drove to Delilah's again. Shauna arrived 15 minutes late. She led us upstairs to meet Delilah and knocked hard on the door. A petite black woman answered. Shauna greeted her, "Good morning. Do you know if Delilah's home?"

"No Ma'am. Left early this morning with her son, probably around 7:00." As I glanced in the door, I saw another door behind the woman, padlocked. "If you see her, please tell her Shauna came by. I'll call her tonight. Thanks."

Back at our cars, I asked Shauna about the arrangements upstairs. "The woman who answered the door is Delilah's neighbor. She and Delilah share the third floor apartment. It's illegally divided into two residences. They share a bathroom in the hallway of the neighbor's apartment. Delilah's door is the padlocked one. It opens to a kitchen adjoined by another small room, which they use as a living/bedroom area. The neighbor has a small, one bedroom apartment."

Shauna appeared extremely sympathetic to Delilah. "I'm absolutely sure something must have happened to Jeremy. Delilah would've been here," she kept repeating wholeheartedly. "She's very responsible."

Again, I had to take a couple of steps back to think about this one. The emphasis Shauna put on her words made my little voice begin to whisper again. This felt too strange. She disappears to the doctor for our second scheduled appointment with her? I was beginning to get the impression that Delilah had Shauna wrapped

11

around her little finger. I had to let this go, after all, I hadn't even met her, yet. Again, I had a hard time trusting that skeptical part of myself. I didn't want to trust it. I wasn't quite as hard on myself for having second thoughts this time, though.

Shauna agreed to call the office the following day to let me know what happened and to reschedule. The next day the only thing her message said was, "Jeremy's fine. We'll meet next Thursday at 2:00 p.m." So much for her conviction that something must have happened to him. Since the appointment was in the afternoon, I hoped to meet Jeremy when he came home from school. As far as my hunches went? Time would tell.

The next Thursday, Carolyn and I again drove to Delilah's. We waited only a few minutes for Shauna, who laughed as she led the way upstairs. "I know she's home today, I just dropped her off a little while ago from the food pantry. I'm surprised she let me take her. She's very reluctant to accept charity from anyone." *Oh great*, I thought to myself as I took a deep breath. And with that comment, she knocked on the door.

A tall and slender, but pregnant, dark-skinned woman answered. "Hi Delilah. I'd like to introduce you to Robyn and Carolyn, the women I've been telling you about."

"Nice to meet you," I said, extending my hand toward hers. She softly shook my hand without making any eye contact.

"Please, come in and sit down." She motioned toward the living/bedroom area and closed the padlocked door behind us. We walked through an immaculate, cheery kitchen. The sun shined brightly through the yellow curtains. The living room was furnished with what looked like a brand new, soft gray checkered couch with a matching love seat. A gray tapestry rug accentuated the hard wood floor, which had a square wooden table in the center of it. Toy dinosaurs of every shape and size filled the table.

"Would you care for something to drink?" Delilah asked politely.

"No, thanks." Carolyn and I answered in sync.

Shauna asked for a glass of water. Delilah's tone of voice changed as she asked her to drink it in the kitchen because she "does not allow food in the living room." Carolyn and I exchanged a glance.

Delilah was beautiful; very distinguished looking. She had huge, brown eyes and long curly eyelashes, which stood out against her high cheekbones and flawless skin. But even with all this stunning beauty, the coldness and aloofness coming from her eyes froze a little piece of my heart.

She wore a brown plaid, corduroy jumper and trendy brown leather granny boots. Her beautifully braided hair placed carefully in a bun on her head emphasized her striking features.

I made small talk, trying to break the ice. Her apprehension toward us was apparent. I sensed she felt frightened and alone, yet she tried to project an air of confidence and properness about her. I gently asked questions about her health, the baby, and her needs for the baby. Obviously, her own health was a subject she wanted us to avoid. She answered only about the baby, giving an elaborate explanation of her desire for a crib, changing table, stroller, and newborn clothing. She had nothing for the baby, so far.

"A friend of mine has baby clothes and other items she wants to give away. May I get them for you? I know she has an infant carrier, a changing table, layette sets, and baby toys."

"Could I see them first and then decide?" she asked.

"Sure," I responded with suppressed shock. If I were in her shoes, I would have jumped at the opportunity.

I tried to take her lead in the conversation, depending upon the answers she gave and how she gave them. This was my gauge to decide whether or not I'd explore things further with her, or if she'd be more comfortable keeping them on the surface.

Since Jeremy's name had not yet come up, I decided to ask about him and see how she'd respond. "How's Jeremy doing?"

"Just fine."

That didn't do much. So I inquired further, "What grade is he in this year?"

"First."

"How does he feel about the baby coming?"

"He's excited. He wants a brother."

Now we're getting somewhere. I heard myself take another deep breath.

"How about you? Would you prefer one sex over the other?"

"Yes."

13

She didn't elaborate, so I asked, "Have you had an ultrasound yet? Sometimes they tell you the sex of the baby then."

"Yes, I have," she stated with little affect.

"Would you like to know if they offer to tell you?" I asked, trying to show a hint of excitement.

"I'm supposed to find out at my next ultrasound." Her tight control over her emotions filled the room with an eerie calm.

After some exhausting dialogue, enough of an initial connection was made with Delilah. It was time to explain our program.

"This is probably a good time to tell you about why we're here and what we can offer you," I said.

"That would be nice." I wasn't sure how to take that comment… sounded a little standoffish.

"One of the biggest things we can do is provide you with whatever type of support you might need. If we can't give it to you ourselves, we'll do our best to find someone who can."

Delilah remained silent, staring at the floor.

"Do you know what I mean by support?" I asked gently.

"Sort of."

"Support can come in many forms. It can be physical, emotional, or even spiritual, for example. We can take you to and from doctor appointments, or any other appointment you might have. We can help you find clothing, food, or housing assistance. We can be an advocate for you with anyone you need, Public Aid, Social Security, or a food pantry. We have access to attorneys and a lot of other networks specifically designed for people with HIV. We'll do our best to get you the most help."

Delilah quickly added, "Please don't say that word around Jeremy. He doesn't know about it," she said curtly, folding her arms tightly against her chest.

"Which word," I asked, "HIV?"

"Yes."

"I'm sorry. I'll pay more attention." Obviously it made her very uncomfortable, too. I couldn't be sure she heard anything I said, except HIV.

I waited a minute before I continued. "We'll do our best to support you and your children emotionally, as well. The more we get to know each other, the easier it will become to open up and talk about things." I paused for a minute and looked into her eyes. "Have you ever been in counseling before?"

"No."

"What do you think about the possibilities of it?"

"I'm not sure. I really don't think there's anything I have to talk about," she said as she coughed and then tightly refolded her arms.

"That's fine. If you decide along the way that there is, we'll be here. Shauna tells us you've been under incredible pressure and have a lot coming down on you at once. I'd imagine you feel pretty overwhelmed."

She didn't respond, so I said, "Shauna told me that one of your doctors has been pressuring you to terminate your pregnancy. If you ever want to talk about it, I'm here to listen."

Delilah continued her silence, her cold stare.

"One of the things we can work on is healthy ways to cope with all the stress you're dealing with. You won't have to walk your path alone anymore. We'll share your burdens with you, if you let us."

Still, no response. This poor woman has just had her whole world shattered. I was sure she needed some time to digest what had happened to her and her family.

Shauna jumped in, "Delilah, are these some things you think you would want help with?"

Delilah answered without looking up. Her arms remained fixed in the same position. "I'm not sure. I've never needed help before."

"We won't push ourselves on you. We'll let you take the lead and respond as you need us," I said in a quiet voice. "How does that sound?"

"Okay."

"Great. There is one more thing I need to make clear though," I said as I took a deep breath. "Our program is involved because of the reports made to the state hotline about things which have happened to Jeremy. I need to let you know that I'm a mandated reporter. Part of my job is to report to Shauna any abusive or neglectful behaviors I see toward your children. Remember though,

15

the state hired us to work with you **in hopes of keeping your family together**, not tearing it apart. Neither Carolyn nor I have the authority to remove Jeremy from your custody. Does this sound reasonable?"

"I suppose," Delilah answered, looking put off.

I was concentrating so hard on Delilah that I had almost forgotten Carolyn still sat next to me. I glanced over at her, and as our eyes met, Carolyn gave me her look of, "She's gonna be a tough one to crack."

Carolyn wrote both of our home phone numbers down for Delilah and explained that she could call either of us anytime in an emergency. Unfortunately, this was a job requirement for both of us. We didn't have a pager in our budget.

"Can we talk a minute about the pressure from your doctor to have an abortion?" I asked.

"What's there to talk about? I'm not going to do it."

"Has anyone told you about the chances your baby has of being born healthy?"

"One of them did. The others are still pushing me to change my mind, and quickly."

"I didn't know that a baby could be born healthy from an HIV mom," blurted Shauna. "How can that be?"

"Carolyn and I had to take a lot of specialized training for this job. We learned that with HIV positive moms, the baby always tests positive in the beginning because of the mom's antibodies in their system. At around eighteen months, approximately 70% of all the children shed their HIV status when they shed the mom's antibodies and go on to live normal, healthy lives. Approximately 30% keep the virus and eventually develop AIDS."

"Wow, that's great," blurted Shauna again. "It's too bad they don't advertise that anywhere. Most people think if the mom has it, the kid doesn't have a chance." I couldn't help but think this woman must be totally oblivious to Delilah's plight.

I quickly looked at Delilah to see her response to Shauna's statement. She continued her blank, cold stare, so I held my response in check.

"Yeah, I didn't know it either," added Carolyn. "There's a lot we had to learn about HIV before we started seeing our families."

Jeremy was one of the 30%. He wasn't the only one who didn't know of his HIV status. The father of Delilah's baby did not know until recently, when Delilah had to ask him to get tested himself.

Just then, the front door flew open. A very thin boy entered the room, taking long, swift strides toward all of us, as if he had a mission ahead of him. The huge welt and bruise around his right eye momentarily stunned me, and my heart became heavy. He wore a long-sleeved, blue oxford shirt, heavily starched khakis and brightly polished pennyloafers. I noticed he even wore color -coordinated argyle socks. Every soft black curl on his head was arranged perfectly around his beautiful, brown, silky skin. I soon became lost in his rich, brown eyes as they searched the room and stopped the second they met mine. I felt an instant connection to him from deep within my soul. It was like something in me opened up.

He came right over to me, took my hand in his and said, "Hi! I'm Jeremy. Who are you?" He wore an enormous, impish grin on his face and looked at me knowingly.

"Hi, I'm Robyn," I said, feeling the warmth of his hand in mine. "I'm very pleased to meet you, Jeremy."

"I got my report card today. Here, why don't you look at it?" He handed it to me.

"I'd love to, if it's all right with your mom. Why don't you ask her first? Maybe she'd like to see it too," I responded, trying to include Delilah.

He glanced over at her. She looked at him and sternly responded, "You can show her first, that's fine." She folded her arms tightly across her chest, clenching her teeth. From the tone of her voice, I wasn't sure if she even wanted me near her child, never mind reading his report card.

With report card in hand, I approached Delilah to share it with her. Jeremy's grades were average to above average. A hand written comment, "Jeremy is unable to stay in his seat for long periods of time without being disruptive to others," appeared at the bottom. He was absent a lot.

I commented, "Good report card, Kiddo."

Delilah ignored my comment and said, "He's disruptive and doesn't listen like he could. And he forgets his homework, too." Not a word of praise escaped her lips.

Jeremy seemed to let her comments roll off his back. He already seemed older than his six years.

Carolyn and Shauna went into the kitchen with Delilah. I sat on the couch with Jeremy and took time to observe him more closely. He had started playing Nintendo.

His eyes, the window to the soul, oh my, his incredibly large, brown, puppy dog eyes, told a story in and of themselves. He seemed to see right through me. Brightness, depth, and power exuded from within his meager, little frame. He was very present in the room, as though he had nothing to hide. Every part of him said, "Here I am world. Take me as I am." I could literally feel the love pouring out from every cell of his being. I've met people with good vibes before, but this sensation was much more powerful than anything I had ever experienced.

I teased him about his Nintendo. "Could I learn something like that? It looks really hard."

"If you had a teacher like me, you could!" Jeremy glowed with pleasure.

"I'd love to take you up on it. Another time, though. Right now, I need to go in the kitchen to talk with the grown ups."

"Okay, but only if you promise to let me teach you another time. We will see each other again, right?"

"I sure hope we will. I'd be honored if you taught me another time."

"Honored? You're silly. It'd be great!" He gleamed from ear to ear.

I excused myself from Jeremy, entered the kitchen and quietly asked Delilah about Jeremy's eye, since I hadn't read about it in any of the reports I had from the state.

Before she could answer, Shauna piped in, "Yeah, the school made a hotline report, but we kept it low key since we knew she'd be accepting your services."

I wasn't even sure she'd accept our services. This meant we had another unfounded incident. That still didn't explain what had happened. So I asked again.

"Delilah, will you please tell me what happened?"

She responded abruptly, "The belt I whupped him with accidentally backlashed, and the buckle hit him in the face."

"Backlashed from where?" I asked, trying to hide my emotion.

"His behind."

"What happened that you chose to 'whup' him with a belt?"

"He forgot his homework at school. How's he going to pass his spelling test if he doesn't bring home his practice sheet? The belt's a good way to discipline him."

I cringed when I heard her say those words. *How could she?*

I had to step back a minute and think — *Okay, she's under an incredible amount of stress. Is this another unusual incident or is this how she acts all of the time, AIDS or no AIDS?*

Time would tell.

I immediately responded, "Hitting Jeremy with a belt is no longer an option for you. Using corporal punishment on a child is against the law. Carolyn and I will help you find other ways to cope and to discipline Jeremy."

I stressed as delicately, yet as firmly as possible, that she needed to begin making different choices. She now could reach out to us. I knew I was treading on thin ice.

I set up our next visit for the following week. Since Jeremy and Delilah had no more questions, we left. Frankly, I was surprised she even agreed to work with us.

Despite my compassion for her, I had the feeling this was going to be a formidable assignment.

CHAPTER THREE -- THE "WHUPPIN"

If I wanted to help Delilah learn new ways of coping so she wouldn't hurt Jeremy anymore, I needed to be successful at quickly forming a bond with her — a connection of trust. Jeremy was quite ill, and the seriousness of the allegations of child abuse really concerned me. Her pattern for coping had already become apparent. She completely isolated herself and Jeremy, severed all ties to her family and friends, and didn't have one person to whom she could turn for support. So afraid of HIV and AIDS, their names never crossed her lips. I was careful not to put any pressure on Delilah so that I wouldn't overwhelm her more. If I did, I was sure she'd push me away as well. And if she didn't allow Carolyn and I to help her, she really had no place else to turn.

I gently and carefully began to build our relationship. Carolyn and I did everything we could to meet Delilah's, Jeremy's and the baby's basic needs for food, shelter, and clothing. It was a good way to get Delilah to trust us: to help make her world a more safe and secure place. The first few weeks we saw her, Carolyn and I brought her baby clothes and items, maternity clothes, and a changing table. Delilah liked them all, but wanted white baby furniture. So one afternoon, Delilah and I cleaned and spray painted the changing table together. Some of the items we brought she politely accepted, while others she didn't care for. She'd hold those items aside, just in case she was able to save up enough money to purchase the ones she liked. At least in this regard, Delilah felt optimistic.

Carolyn helped Delilah apply for AFDC (Aid to Families with Dependent Children) and Social Security Disability for Jeremy. Each was eventually approved. In the meantime, an agency came forth voluntarily to pay one month's rent for Delilah, and I found two other agencies, which each paid her rent for one month until their money started coming in. We obtained a brand new high chair and used crib and mattress for the baby. Delilah loved the high chair, but didn't care for the crib and mattress. So she put them aside, just in case she couldn't obtain one she did care for, and eventually did save enough money each month to buy new ones. She gave me the used ones back.

In a short time, we had accomplished quite a bit, for which Delilah seemed grateful. A bond of trust had at least been established between us, as much as Delilah would allow it to be.

After helping Delilah get most of her own and her family's physical needs met, it was time to focus on counseling and the emotional support that was needed. Since our caseload was growing rapidly, and we had no other child abuse cases, just child neglect, Carolyn lessened her involvement with Delilah and Jeremy and increased her involvement with our other families.

As Delilah and I got to know each other, the more she showed me just how dispirited she really felt. Besides keeping herself completely isolated, she barely ate, began losing weight even though she was five months pregnant, and became sullen and withdrawn. Delilah gave very mixed messages. On the one hand, she rebuffed each attempt I made to emotionally support her and help her to open up and begin talking about her feelings and her situation. I was often met with hostility. Yet underneath her rage and defensiveness, on a deeper level, she desperately wanted to connect with someone... with me.

One night in early March, after only knowing Delilah for a few weeks, the ring of our telephone startled and awakened Jim and me around 11:30 p.m.

"Hi. It's Delilah." I hardly recognized her voice.

"Is everything all right?"

"Not really..."

When I heard her words, my heart leapt from my chest as I thought *Oh my God, it's Jeremy...* (At this point she wouldn't have been calling about her own physical needs, she had no symptoms from the HIV, as of yet, and her pregnancy had been going well. Or maybe she was reaching out in a time of rage so she wouldn't hurt Jeremy, as I had suggested for her to do.)

My grief quickly shifted as I heard her words, "I'm ready to talk now." As I gazed at the clock, and at my husband lying next to me in bed trying to get some sleep, part of me wondered why she chose this exact time to call me. I spent many an hour trying to help her to open up, to get her to talk, but wound up adhering to the distance she wished to keep. Although it didn't sound like an emergency, she did reach out and call me in a time of need. So I checked in with my gut and made a decision to continue talking with her, even though I felt somewhat ambivalent about it. That same voice that doubted her missing our first two appointments went on alert, in case this was another game or another of her tests.

Part way through the call, my gut instinct was confirmed when she said she felt like "walking in front of a moving bus, just to get this over with." I asked if she would act on her feeling and she said she wouldn't. Even so, I made a verbal suicide contract with her on the spot. She promised to call me anytime, day or night, if she felt like she wanted to hurt herself and promised not to act out her feelings.

As we ended our call, again, part of me wasn't sure if Delilah really felt like killing herself, or if she was using it to connect with me in some strange sort of way. My gut said she was testing my reaction to, "How much do you care about me?"

During the next few weeks, this behavior became more clear to me. Delilah tried several different times to call the shots by telephoning me at home, despite the fact that I saw her several times per week, at this point, and allowed her every opportunity to open up and connect with me each visit. She knew the rule we had set at our first meeting — only call Carolyn or I at home in a medical emergency, or when she felt like lashing out at her children, or herself.

The first time I had to set limits by telephone with her was very awkward for me. It was on a Sunday afternoon. Jim was working on a paper for school, and I was cooking dinner.

I answered the phone. "Hello?"

A vague, almost inaudible voice answered, "Hi." I didn't recognize the voice on the other end.

So I said, "I'm sorry, I don't know who this is."

"It's me," the voice announced louder and more cheerfully. Now I knew who it was.

"Delilah? Is everything all right?"

"Yes. I just called to see how your day is." I quickly had to regroup.

What's she up to? Okay, she's taking a risk, reaching out and calling me — a coping mechanism new to her, but she's talking like we're friends. My home phone is off limits except for emergencies. If I don't set a limit this time, she'll keep doing it. She broke a boundary, which needed to remain fixed. This was one rule I wouldn't break.

"That's thoughtful of you," I responded, "but are you calling me within the phone rules we set, Delilah?"

An awkward void filled the air. I could feel her discontent through the phone wires.

I waited a moment before I asked, "Are you still there?"

She didn't answer. So I added, "If this isn't an emergency, I'll be happy to call you from my office first thing in the morning and we can talk then."

She continued her silence.

"Will you be home in the morning?"

"I'm busy tomorrow," she snapped.

"Oh. Well, I'll try anyway. You can call me at work when you get home then. Please call me here only under the conditions we set; if you feel like you will harm your children or yourself, in a medical emergency, or if there is pertinent information I need to know that came up after office hours."

She didn't say anything.

So I said, "I'm sorry, Delilah, it has to be this way. Why don't you write down what you wanted to talk about, just in case you might forget, and we can talk tomorrow."

An awkward silence hung heavily between us. "Talk to you tomorrow. I'm going to have to end our call now. Bye."

I felt terrible, but I had to hang up on her. I was shaking and felt sick to my stomach. Delilah had quickly figured out how to get to me — through my heart. Here she is, completely isolated, and finally reaching out to someone, to me, and I had to hang up on her because it was important for her to learn about limit setting and boundaries.

23

A picture began to form in my mind. Delilah was showing more and more symptoms of what is called borderline personality disorder. Someone with this disorder is extremely distrustful and protective of anyone coming close to him or her. If they do let someone in, they become possessive and demanding, wanting attention all of the time. But if they become displeased with the person they let in, they completely withdraw and often terminate the relationship.

I could tell by Delilah's behavior that if I didn't set good limits and boundaries at this early stage of our relationship, she would have the tendency to try to engulf me, wanting more and more of me to fill up the emptiness she felt inside. No matter how difficult it was, or how bad I felt for limiting myself with her, I knew this was the right path.

I never reached Delilah the following day. Power and control is a tough game. I certainly wasn't going to call her from home, after work, just to chitchat, then I'd be breaking the boundary. She had an appointment with me in a few days.

It took a few sessions for Delilah to warm up to me again. Once she did, she started opening up about her life ever so slightly. She continued to call my home, but in a more appropriate fashion. She'd inform me of changes in our appointment times, or give other pertinent news that I needed that had come up after our visits. At times, it felt like she created obstacles just so she could call me.

Unable to reach me at the office, she called one evening to ask if I would go with her to inform the nurse and principal at Jeremy's school of "Jeremy's health status." The hospital suggested that Delilah speak with them because Jeremy had missed a lot of classes.

"Sure, I'll go with you, Delilah. I'll help you every way I can." It would be excruciating for her to admit that she and her son had "it."

"I appreciate that," she answered.

"What role do you want me to have while we're there?"

"I'm not sure. Hannah will be there. I don't think either of us will need to do much talking. Hannah said she'd handle things. I just want you to be there for me." Hannah, the pediatric nurse practitioner from Jeremy's hospital, worked with Jeremy and Delilah a few months before I came into the picture.

24

I sensed Delilah's apprehension and fear. This was a big step for her. She couldn't acknowledge their illness to herself, and now she was being asked to tell someone else. It surprised me she had agreed.

When the day to inform the school had arrived, I went alone with Delilah. Carolyn was in court with another of our families. Delilah and I stopped at the principal's office and were instructed to meet in a room down the hall. We entered the quiet room. Three women sat around a long, rectangular table. Delilah sat in the empty chair next to Hannah, and I sat beside Delilah. The principal, Ms. Jones, and the school nurse, Mrs. Little, sat across from us. The meeting began. We all introduced ourselves. As Delilah had hoped, Hannah did most of the talking. Hannah informed both school personnel of Jeremy's HIV status and shared what to expect as Jeremy got sicker. I grabbed Delilah's hand under the table and gave it a squeeze. She held on to my hand and didn't let go.

Ms. Jones appeared shocked and saddened by the news. Tears welled up in her eyes as she shared how much she enjoyed spending time with Jeremy when he came to her office to lie down. When the nurse wasn't in, children were sent to the principal's office to rest. She added that her concern increased recently when the episodes of resting had become more frequent. Jeremy's weight loss also stunned her, as well as his latest bout with listlessness. "Jeremy is always so lively and fun loving. He's so engaging with the faculty. I just can't believe it." For a moment, she covered her face in her hands.

The atmosphere quickly changed as we heard the nurse's reaction. Her voice sounded robotic. "I knew it must have been that disease. What a shame," she stated coldly, as she straightened her posture in the chair and folded her hands on the table. Then she asked, "How did you and Jeremy become infected?" I was appalled. That wasn't any of her business. Hannah responded by saying that it really was not an appropriate question to be asking, but that didn't stop her. She didn't let up and asked again, adding she thought it was a very appropriate question.

Hannah kept her cool and politely stated, "It's really none of your business."

Delilah, ashamed, head hanging low, made no eye contact during the rest of the meeting. I squeezed Delilah's hand, took a deep

25

breath, consciously sent love out from my heart to Delilah, and held her in prayer.

As Delilah and I left the meeting escorted out by the nurse, we passed through a pod full of faculty and students putting up a bulletin board. The nurse, acting as though she and I were chums, completely ignored Delilah, then stated loudly, "You'd be surprised how fast this devastating disease is spreading among children." Heads turned, staring at us. Delilah looked like a wounded animal ready to lunge. I felt the same way.

We left as quickly as possible and afterwards nicknamed the woman, "Nurse Ratchet." This helped Delilah lighten up a bit.

Nurse Ratchet gave Delilah an agenda of what she needed to do to process this information through "appropriate channels." I thought to myself, *wasn't this enough to put this woman through?*

Delilah needed to disclose Jeremy's condition to two physicians at the Board of Education's headquarters. She wanted to get it over with, so we called from my office and made an appointment for that afternoon. I treated Delilah to lunch and we drove to the appointment. (I would be reimbursed from our budget.)

We entered the crowded waiting room. The secretary gave Delilah forms to fill out and informed us that the doctors were waiting for her. Delilah finished the forms, and we waited for them over 45 minutes. The secretary escorted us to their office. Both physicians greeted me before Delilah. I introduced Delilah and myself. They began by asking me questions. I politely responded, "Ms. Miller is quite capable of answering any questions you might have." The way they treated her saddened me.

They read rule after rule, policy after policy to us. After what seemed like an eternity of listening to their bureaucratic mumbo jumbo, including when Jeremy needed to be excluded from school due to certain symptoms he might have, the meeting ended, but not before they informed Delilah they'd be keeping tabs on Jeremy's behavior and health status.

One week after this meeting, Jeremy got into a scuffle with a little girl in his class who took his seat. When he attempted to reclaim it from her, she scratched him. He retaliated by biting her lightly on the arm, without breaking the skin. The girl didn't get suspended, but Jeremy did for three days.

I worked hard at getting to know Delilah more deeply and letting her know me.

Since she was so leery of trusting anyone, I had to prove my trustworthiness to her on an emotional level, if I hoped to help her change. I tried being as gentle as possible, not pushing anything at this point. I hoped and prayed she'd confide in me and lean on me, so she didn't have to go through what lay ahead of her alone. I wanted her to let me through her wall of protection, so I could support her and teach her to stop hurting Jeremy.

I thought that if she'd learn to lash out at me, or with me, and deal with her rage in another way, allowing me to help her learn new ways to cope, **maybe** Jeremy would be safe and could live out the rest of his life with her.

As the days flew by, I kept one eye on Jeremy and one on Delilah, watching to see if she allowed any of my counsel, support, and kindness to sink in, even just a little bit. I continued to support Delilah through all of the difficulties facing her. I took her to and from her own doctor appointments and any other appointment I could help her with.

I usually took her out to lunch, which work continued to pay for, after each doctor's visit. The only way I knew how to really break down Delilah's defenses and penetrate her wall of rage and fear was to try and connect with her on a heart to heart level. I wanted her to feel something positive, instead of remaining closed off and isolated. But with Delilah, feeling like another human being cared deeply about you, while keeping good boundaries with that person was next to impossible.

On several occasions, I shared with Delilah the importance of telling Jeremy about his illness, which she opposed every time. On one particular visit, and since the incident at school, I really stressed the importance of it. "It would help Jeremy if he knew about his illness. He needs to know how it can spread and how to protect himself from other people's germs. And for his peace of mind, Delilah. I'm sure it would ease his burden if he understood why he gets so sick."

"You're right, Robyn. Let's tell him next time you're here. Can you come here after school next time for our appointment?"

"Sure. You're doing the right thing, Delilah. I'll be right here with you when you tell him, I promise." She appreciated my gesture.

When the next visit rolled around, as soon as I walked in the door, I sensed Delilah's resistance. She wouldn't look at me. Her arms, tightly folded against her chest, signaled her opposition and extremely frigid vibes. So I gave it my best shot. "So, Delilah," I asked as neutrally as I could, "have you thought about how we might tell Jeremy about his illness?"

"He will not be told," she stated caustically. "I do not want him to know."

"I thought we agreed. That was the purpose for my visit."

"I changed my mind."

"After the biting incident at school, don't you think Jeremy needs to know he can't do that?"

"It won't happen again."

"What does that mean?" My body tensed.

"Just that," she replied curtly.

"I don't understand," I responded. "Please explain what you mean."

She remained silent. I didn't want to push her too far; after all, I didn't want to lose her, so I tried to appeal to her warmer side.

"There are other reasons for telling him, too," I went on. "Jeremy's a bright kid. On some level, he knows something serious is happening. If you share the truth with him, it can bring the two of you closer and make things less scary for him. You can help him make sense of what he's been going through."

"NO, NO, NO. He will not be told."

I tried one more time. "What if there's something going around at school and they send him home? Remember, they said they'd have to if there were an outbreak of something, like measles or chicken pox? Don't you think it would help him if he knew he wasn't in school for his own protection, rather than leading him to believe he may have done something wrong?"

"No. He will not be told. That's final."

What could I say? I had no right to tell him. "Because you're his mom, I have to respect your decision."

Once I said that, she began to soften a little. To my surprise, she opened up as never before.

"Can we talk about something?" she asked.

"Sure."

"You've probably been wondering why I split away from my family, especially at a time like this…"

I remained silent, looking into her eyes.

"When the state got involved with me, I had to go to city hall to get my birth certificate. I was totally shocked when I saw it. My mother, or shall I say the woman I thought all this time was my mother, wasn't on it. My father's name was, along with a woman by the name of Miller, Shari Miller. That's why I changed my name from Thomas, my dad's name and her name, to my real mother's name. All those years, I never felt like I belonged. My dad died when I was thirteen. My brothers, I should say stepbrothers, always picked on me. My dad protected me. But after he died, she'd throw things at me and hit me in the head with whatever she found handy at the time. She became very mean to me. I remember one time…"

Suddenly, the front door banged open. Jeremy walked in, limping. He seemed scared, apprehensive. He walked into the living room, glanced at his mom, looked at me, and asked to sit on my lap. I could see he was in pain.

"What's wrong, Jeremy?" I asked, putting my arm around him.

He glanced at her again with that look, of not understanding, not knowing how to handle my question for fear of retaliation. And she spoke.

"Go ahead. Tell Robyn what happened."

"She whupped me."

Devastated, I said nothing. Dead silence filled the room. My heart raced so fast and my stomach tied in knots.

Oh Dear God, what do I do? I've been working my hardest to open my heart to this woman, warmly inviting her to trust me, share with me, be with me, unconditional love and acceptance so that she would, in turn, open her heart… and she goes and beats him again, even when I told her it's unlawful. Nothing is getting through to her.

29

"What do you mean she whupped you, Jeremy?" I watched his eyes shift as he surveyed her, his teeth clenched, waiting for some sort of clue from her as to how he should respond.

"Go ahead. Tell Robyn why I did it."

"She beat me with the belt yesterday cuz I went potty when she took me to the bathroom."

What? Bathrooms are places that you go potty. I don't understand. I fought back the flood of feelings in my heart, in my soul - the disbelief, the rage, the betrayal.

"Please, tell me what happened, Sweetie." He looked at her again with fear in his eyes.

She began to speak, glaring at him with her threatening cold stare. "Tell the *whole* story, Jeremy. Tell her what *you* were doing."

I interrupted. "Delilah, you please tell me."

"He was playing Nintendo, jumping up and down with his legs crossed like he had to go to the bathroom. So I asked if he had to go, and he said no. He kept playing and jumping up and down again, so I asked again. He said no. I told him to go to the bathroom and he said he didn't have to. So I *made* him go into the bathroom with me. I told him if he was lying, if he went, he was in big trouble."

I sat there, feeling dumbfounded. I didn't know what to say. Normal behavior for a six year old, to be having so much fun he won't take time out to go to the bathroom, and Jeremy got beaten for it. Jeremy tightened his grip on me while I gathered my wits.

"So you hit him?"

"Yes."

"With your hand?"

"No."

"With what?"

"The belt."

I wanted to grab Jeremy and run as fast and as far as I could. Part of me wanted to shake her. I knew I had to be extremely careful with what I said and did next. I didn't want to alienate her more that would be defeating my purpose. I couldn't blemish the relationship I had worked so hard to develop. I feared what could happen when I left, if she became angry with me. Overcome with feeling, I had to hold it together. This was too important.

I held Jeremy. Lovingly but firmly I asked if she had remembered what I told her when her caseworker was there for our first meeting, when Jeremy had the welt on his face. After a brief interlude of silence, I took a deep breath and began.

"From my heart, I tell you this, Delilah. No more belt. No more corporal punishment. You have to start calling for help, for support." I felt the veins in my neck sticking out. "Do not act on your rage and take it out on your son. Please, reach to us for help. You cannot beat Jeremy with a belt ever again. It's against the law. Please, please, call Carolyn or me anytime, day or night, when you feel the urge to hit Jeremy. We will help you through whatever is happening. It's our job to keep Jeremy safe and to help you find other ways to cope with what's going on. Please use us. Stop hurting your son." My voice cracked, filled with so much emotion.

"Okay, okay. I won't ever use a belt again."

And from that day forward, she never did.

I reaffirmed my commitment to her, our program's commitment. I assured her we'd be available to her anytime, to help her not hurt her son. Jeremy looked so relieved that I knew what happened. His truth had been told. She seemed comfortable with my firmness, my pledge to help her.

I left their apartment totally overwhelmed and frightened — unsure that what I had done was right. Had I called my supervisor, Delilah's caseworker, or the child abuse hotline, I didn't think anything would have been done differently. At least it hadn't been up to this point. Jeremy's falling from the second story window was unfounded, and when I met them, the caseworker let the huge welt on his face and black eye slide, so that Delilah would accept our services. Already referred by the state to help, I vowed in my heart to do my best. I left, carrying Jeremy's burden of darkness and fear and made it my quest to protect this angel. The only way I could do that 100% of the time was to be with him 100% of the time, and that was impossible.

When I got to work on Monday, Connie said **I blew it.** I didn't know I was supposed to pull down Jeremy's pants right then and there to examine him. I should've called the hotline.

Oh God...

CHAPTER FOUR -- THE PROMISE

I always think of spring as a new beginning. The month of April brought me this renewed energy, so I worked even more passionately helping Delilah and Jeremy. I was still absolutely convinced I could get through to her so she'd stop hurting him.

Over the next couple of weeks, Delilah seemed more comfortable with me. One afternoon, while sitting alone together at her kitchen table, Delilah brought up a very difficult subject for her. "I want someone I trust to take care of the baby... to become its guardian." Her voice trailed off as she turned away and hid her face from me. She walked to her kitchen window, breathing as though she was crying. "I don't have anyone. Just you and Hannah, and Hannah's not even married...."

I sat in silence to see if she would say anything else. She remained with her back to me.

"It would be better if you knew who'd be the guardian," I said. I felt uneasy. She was getting at something here, but I didn't think she'd be able to ask directly. So I waited a minute. Delilah remained with her back to me and continued crying in silence. Then I asked, "Are you asking if Jim and I would take your child?"

"Well..." she took a deep breath, turned toward me and stared anxiously at the floor. "Would you at least think about it?"

Oh boy... I took a deep breath. "Parenting's the hardest job on earth. We'd really have to think about it."

"That's all I'm asking." She shrugged her shoulders and wiped her tears.

Jim and I hadn't even decided firmly that we wanted children of our own, yet.

When I got home that evening, I told Jim what Delilah had asked of us. We had a long talk about Delilah's request. I had just graduated the year before, and Jim was going to school full time, earning his Masters degree in Social Work, too.

We covered every possible aspect we could think of, from, "What if Delilah dies first, and what if the new baby seroconverts at eighteen months to become a healthy child?" to, "If Jeremy needs a full time caregiver toward the end, how would we make it financially if Jim is still in school, and I stayed home to care for him?"

As terrible as I felt for Delilah, I had no desire to become the baby's guardian. Neither did Jim. We both knew we didn't want children at this point in our lives. But we decided if it became necessary for his safety, both of us would adopt Jeremy in a second. We'd work out the details, somehow.

The following week, Delilah and I spent an exhausting and frustrating afternoon hunting for an affordable one bedroom apartment, since the baby's due date was coming closer. While driving her home, she asked me another painful question. "Can we move in with you?"

I guessed I had finally earned her trust. "I care deeply about you and your family, Delilah, but I don't think that would work out. I think it's great that you were able to ask me for what you wanted though." I smiled at her. She turned away.

A few days later, Jeremy's school suspended him again, "for his own good." Someone in his class had chicken pox. It turned out to be the longest chicken pox epidemic in history. Weeks went by with no firm date for his return to school. The school supposedly ordered a home tutor who never manifested. We connected Delilah to an attorney, specializing in assisting people with HIV, in order to get Jeremy reinstated. His services were free. He arranged for the tutor, who ended up not coming every day, and diligently worked on the prospect of Jeremy returning to school. Jeremy's remaining home with Delilah 24 hours a day concerned me, even though she seemed to be coping with things a little more acceptably.

Later that week, I received another late night call from Delilah. When I answered the phone, I recognized her despondent voice on the other end. "Ryan White died." That was all she said. He was the young man from Indiana whose story made the headlines of newspapers across the country, when he was not allowed to return to school after being diagnosed with AIDS. In Delilah's silence, I sensed her dread of this disease. Emptiness, a dull ache, filled the pit of my stomach. And my Little Buddy? I didn't want to think about that. Delilah had reached out again to me in her anguish, a very good sign.

The following night, the phone awakened me around midnight. "Robyn, it's Delilah." Her voice sounded shaky. "I'm sorry to be calling so late, but I started spotting. Dr. Murphy says I might lose the baby. If the bleeding gets worse tonight, I have to go to the emergency room."

"I'm so sorry. Are you in any pain?"

"No. I'm scared, though."

"Do you need me to take you if you have to go?"

"No, but I'll need someone to take Jeremy."

"Can you hold on a sec?"

"Sure." I covered the receiver with my hand. Jim and I quickly discussed a plan.

"How does this sound? If you have to go in tonight, I'll pick you guys up, drop you off at the hospital, and take Jeremy home with me till I can make emergency arrangements for him in the morning."

"That sounds good."

"Good. Call me if it gets worse. I'll be there as soon as I can."

"Robyn?"

"Yeah…"

"Thanks. I really appreciate your help."

"That's what I'm here for, Delilah. Thanks for calling me." It felt good that she had reached out again to me in a time of need. Maybe she was beginning to allow her heart to open up just a sliver. After tossing and turning forever, I finally fell back asleep. I called Delilah first thing in the morning and felt relieved when she said her bleeding had stopped. I picked them both up and took Delilah to see her doctor.

As the nurse weighed Delilah, I peeked to read the scale. Eight months pregnant, and five feet eight, her 117 pounds made me shudder. The nurse scolded her. "You need to force yourself to eat,

Ms. Miller." Delilah faked a smile and walked away. The three of us sat in the waiting room.

"We have to get you fattened up, Delilah," I said halfway joking, "How 'bout burgers and shakes after this? I'll treat."

Jeremy answered, "Yippee! I'm hungry. Can we go now? Please?"

Delilah looked at him sternly, pointing her finger at him. Before she could get a word out, I said, "I brought you a snack, Jeremy." I quickly tossed him a package of cheese and crackers. "We'll have lunch as soon as your mom's done, okay, Sweetie?"

"Sure. Can I go play, Mommy?" One corner of the waiting room was stacked full of toys.

"Yes, but be quiet. These people don't want to hear a peep out of you." Three adults sat quietly on the couch. Two, obviously very ill, smiled at Jeremy. The nurse called Delilah's name.

"Would you come with me, Robyn?" Delilah asked to my surprise.

"Sure." I asked the nurse if it was all right if Jeremy stayed in the waiting room alone. She promised to keep an eye on him.

After examining her, Dr. Murphy suggested that Delilah begin AZT and pentamidine treatments. AZT is used to slow the process of HIV and pentamidine is a breathing treatment used to prevent pneumocystis pneumonia. He had consulted with a team of physicians from other teaching hospitals on the benefits versus the risks of taking the drugs while pregnant. They all agreed that the benefits outweighed the risks and hoped the drugs would decrease the chances of her becoming ill after the baby's birth.

Delilah agreed to begin the treatments, but I could see by the look on her face, she was uncomfortable with the decision. She instantly withdrew and became sullen. I encouraged her to tell her doctor how she felt, but she didn't. She refused to talk about it.

When we got back to the waiting room, Jeremy had engaged everyone in the room. "Hi, you guys! Look! Here's a picture for you, Mommy, and one for you, Robyn. And these are my new friends, Molly, and Sam, and Tricia," he said pointing to each of them. Molly, who looked Jeremy's age, colored with him, while he played a word game with Sam, a large but frail Latino man. Evidently Jeremy had made quite an impression on Tricia, who appeared skeleton - like and pale, almost translucent. On our way out, she motioned for us to wait a minute, until she could muster enough energy to speak.

"You have quite an angel on your hands," she whispered. "Thank you, Jeremy. I haven't smiled in a long time." Jeremy approached her, placed her hand in his and kissed it.

In the elevator I asked, "How'd ya make her smile, Kiddo?"

"It's my secret," he whispered, winking at me. He was glowing. We filled Delilah's prescriptions and headed for lunch as promised.

Earth Day was over the weekend. I had an idea in mind, but didn't know if Delilah would go for it. I realized that I had never been alone with Jeremy. She watched him like a hawk when I was around. I thought it'd be a good idea to spend some time alone with him for several reasons. I wanted to further assess the abuse, and I hoped he'd tell me more if she wasn't there. I needed to let him know that I was there for him too, not just his mom. And I wanted him to be able to blow off some steam, have fun like a normal kid. Delilah didn't let him do that. I thought the zoo's celebration of Earth Day would be a good place to accomplish these things.

Connie, my supervisor, encouraged us to do special things with our families on the weekends, to help them feel more normal and have fun. She'd give us comp-time off during the week when we did.

So after escorting them up to their apartment, I asked, "Would the two of you like to go out to breakfast on Saturday? And if it's all right with you, Delilah, may I take Jeremy to Lincoln Park Zoo? They're having a special celebration for Earth Day."

She looked surprised. "Sure, that would be nice."

"Great! Jim and I'll pick you guys up around 9:00. See ya."

"See ya," shouted Jeremy, jumping up and down, giving me a high five.

On Saturday, we picked them up at 9:00. Jim hadn't met either of them in person. Before we even set foot on the front porch, Jeremy bolted through the door in pressed blue jeans and a navy and green Teenage Mutant Ninja Turtle sweater. He jumped up into my arms and kissed me on the cheek. "Good morning."

He looked over at Jim and sang, "Hi!" while he looked straight into Jim's eyes.

"Hi!" Jim sang back, mimicking Jeremy's tones. "You must be Jeremy. I've heard a lot about you." Jim shook Jeremy's hand as I continued holding him. It looked to me like they instantly became friends.

"Is your mom coming, Little Buddy? Or do I need to go up and get her?" I asked.

"She'll be down in a minute." He jumped down from my arms. Approaching Jim, he began punching and roughhousing with him. Jim ate it up. "Can I touch your hair?" he asked as he reached toward Jim's head. "It's so shiny and straight!"

Jim grabbed Jeremy's hand, placed it on his head, and messed his hair up with it. Jeremy touched the hair on Jim's mustache and arms, too. Jim began to tickle him. Jeremy giggled until he heard Delilah's voice. He froze. She came down the stairs, demanding he "behave" himself. She was dressed beautifully, as usual. Her black patent leather shoes accented her red maternity dress and her matching hair bow.

Once we got in our car, Jeremy couldn't sit still, he was so excited to see us. He continually bopped up and down on the back seat, chattering and singing away, asking Jim a thousand questions. "Can I come to your house to meet your cats?"

"Well, we ca…"

And before Jim could finish his sentence, Jeremy excitedly asked another question. "Do you know howta play baseball, Jim? Could ya teach me?"

"Jeremy, stop it right now. Jim doesn't want to answer your silly questions," Delilah demanded.

"I'm fine really," Jim said tactfully. "I enjoy talking to children."

So Jeremy continued, "Do ya go fishin', Jim? How 'bout roller skating?"

"I can't roller skate, but I love to fish…"

Delilah said again, "Jeremy, that's about enough out of you. Sit back right now and behave yourself." She yanked his coat, flinging him toward the back of the seat. "Not another word out of you. I mean it."

Delilah seemed to want Jeremy to be a perfect, nonmoving, silent object. In fact, she expected it from him. She began picking at

37

him, fixing each curl on his head, adjusting his clothes. When she finished finding fault with him physically, she began to criticize the way he fidgeted in his seat and for the sounds she heard him make. All I heard was his breathing. It was a little tense eating breakfast, but Jeremy must have felt safe because he allowed himself to relax a bit and be more of his free and uninhibited self. Jim and I tried to distract Delilah from Jeremy, engaging her in conversation and paying lots of attention to her.

After breakfast, as we drove Delilah home, the level of tension in the car increased. Delilah looked like she was pouting. I assumed it was because I hadn't asked her to come with us. Delilah had already given me the implicit message, *how much will you give to me? Fill me and never leave me. Be my friend. I need you...* I sensed that on a deep, emotional level she wanted and needed much more than I could give to her.

Keeping this in mind, before she exited the car, I made sure to add, "Okay, Jim, you're next to be dropped off."

I smiled at her and added, "Jeremy and I will be back around 3:30 or 4:00, if that's all right with you."

"That's fine. I'm not going anywhere. I'll be waiting." She slammed the car door hard on her way out.

Jeremy and I drove Jim home and the two of us headed to the zoo. Jeremy could hardly contain himself. He behaved as a perfectly normal six-year-old boy. I needed to stop and get gas for my car. Jeremy insisted on pumping it for me and washing my windshield. He also fixed the latch on my glove compartment, which had been broken for some time. The dealer couldn't even fix it and said it needed replacing. I tried to gently ask questions about his mom, his safety, but Jeremy replied, "Let's not talk about that stuff. Let's just have fun. Okay?"

So we acted like kids together all day. We sang at the top of our lungs and held hands under the noonday sun. My side ached from laughing so hard tickling each other. After joining other kids playing double dutch, we skipped our way to the children's zoo, barking like dogs and snorting like pigs. Attempting to outdo each other's cartwheels, we bumped into one another and fell down laughing. We bought some chocolate chip cookies and fed some to the ducks. A dance competition to a disc jockey prompted Jeremy to try to tackle me, and we ended up wrestling in the grass. People looked at us like we were nuts, but we didn't care.

"Can I sit on your shoulders? I'm gettin' tired," he asked.

"Sure, Sweetie. Wanna go home?"

"No way."

We walked over and watched the polar bears play. When we finished, Jeremy asked, "Can we go sit on the grass over there?" He pointed to a big, old oak tree. "I gotta ask ya somethin'."

I sat on the grass leaning against the sturdy thick tree. Jeremy climbed on my lap, turned around so he could look at me and asked, "Can you be my mommy?"

I pulled him tightly against my chest and took a deep breath. When I could, I whispered, "I'm sorry, Sweetie. You already have a mommy. I'll always be your friend, though. And you can always count on me, no matter what."

He snuggled in closer, closing his eyes. I rocked him. "I want you to know something else, Jeremy." I turned him so I could look directly into his eyes. I placed one hand on each shoulder and said, "I'll do everything in my power to make sure that no one ever hurts you again. I promise."

"You promise?" he asked, with raised eyebrows.

"I promise. I'll always be there for you. Always."

We sat and held each other for what seemed like forever. We became lost in time, in the moment. I didn't want to ever let him go. As the sun hid behind a cloud, it became chilly. I glanced at my watch again. It read 3:00. "Are you hungry, Little Buddy?"

"Yep!"

"How 'bout McDonald's on the way home?"

"Deal!"

As we started for the car, I carried him. He was exhausted. A man walked toward us carrying a French Poodle. Jeremy barked as they passed by, startling the dog, which then snapped at the owner's nose. We tried not to laugh. The owner, furious, began yelling at me, "You better control your kid, lady…"

"Your kid," Jeremy squealed, "He thinks I'm your son!" I tried to control my emotions, but my eyes filled with tears.

I wished he were.

Jeremy and I made a connection that day no one could ever take away from us, soul to soul. When we looked deeply into each other's eyes, it was as though we could surrender to God within…Total unconditional love…Total commitment…No strings attached.

We stopped and got Jeremy's favorite, a Cheeseburger Happy Meal. Returning to his home, we arrived at 3:45. I knocked on the door. The neighbor answered. "Your mom left a while ago, Jeremy. You and your friend can wait here till she gets home."

"Thanks, Annie. Can we watch cartoons?" he asked excitedly.

"Sure, if your friend wants to."

"Hi, I'm Robyn. That'd be great, thanks."

"Annie. Nice to meet you."

Jeremy went right in and made himself comfortable on her couch. He clicked on the TV to a Tom and Jerry cartoon. I sat beside him and glanced at Annie, who was cooking a heavenly smelling meal — fresh corn bread from scratch, collard greens, and catfish.

In between stirs, she ironed. "I only cook and do laundry on the weekends. Too busy working two jobs during the week," she shared, as I got up to look out the window.

At first I felt worried as we waited and waited for Delilah. My worry turned to anger as time crawled by. Finally, after almost two hours, Delilah walked in with a man carrying a VCR. Jeremy ran toward him, giving him a big hug.

"Oh, hi." Delilah stated nonchalantly, "Leonard came by and offered to take me to get our VCR fixed. I didn't think you'd mind. I wasn't sure what time you'd be back."

"You weren't?" I asked trying to remain as calm as possible. "I'm sure I said we'd be back between 3:30 and 4:00. We've been waiting almost two hours."

I was sure her passive aggressive response was done in order to get back at me for not taking her to the zoo with us.

Jeremy begged me not to leave as we hugged goodbye.

I found out later that Leonard was the husband of one of the nurses who worked with Jeremy during his hospitalization for his full body cast. Jeremy had a marvelous capacity to draw people to himself.

CHAPTER FIVE -- MAKE - A - WISH

PART ONE -- THE DECISION PROCESS

Hannah and I talked the Tuesday following Easter. She had called the Make - A - Wish Foundation to see if they could grant Jeremy a wish as quickly as possible. At Jeremy's last clinic visit, his T cell count was at an all time low. T cells measure the health of our immune system. Normal is 2000. Jeremy's was 12. His doctors weren't sure how much time he had left. They wanted him to have an opportunity to receive his wish — to go to Disney World and meet Mickey Mouse. The Make - A - Wish Foundation is a wonderful institution that grants terminally ill children their final wish, when they can.

Hannah informed me that Jeremy told Delilah he felt like he was dying. He said this while twirling and blowing dandelions on Easter Sunday. Delilah was unable to respond to him.

Later in the week, Make - A - Wish called with a tentative date for Jeremy's wish. But they added one *small* requirement... a chaperone had to accompany them. Make - A - Wish was trying to make sure that Jeremy would have fun. Since Hannah had filled them in about the urgency of the trip due to Jeremy's compromised health and Delilah's ninth month of pregnancy, they figured that if Delilah needed to rest, went into labor early, or had difficulty walking because of the severe varicose veins in her calves, the chaperone could escort Jeremy.

Who would chaperone them? Make - A - Wish didn't offer any answers. Hannah and I were their only support system, and Hannah already said she had other commitments. So if I didn't go, no one would.

My gut said, *no way, I don't do this with other clients.* Then another part of me responded, *but I've never worked with anyone who's had so much happening, with life and death in the balance. And if I don't go, Jeremy will never get his wish. Can I live with that?*

I didn't want Delilah to perceive our relationship as personal or as a friendship. I had been working hard to maintain good boundaries, doing my best to be there for her, yet trying to make sure she didn't conclude that our relationship was anything but professional. And now I'd be living under the same roof with them for six consecutive days. If we had to share a bathroom, the limits I had established with her could be damaged. My toothbrush next to hers? That isn't exactly professional. She might draw the wrong conclusions.

Delilah had already made desperate attempts to try to get me to be more than her social worker. She was cognizant of how deeply I cared for Jeremy and for her. But in her mind, that wasn't enough. I hadn't committed myself to her as her friend. Therefore, I didn't care enough. By not crossing over that line, I had failed to prove my loyalty to her. She often gave the underlying message, "You don't do what I want, so why should I do what you want?" She also knew where I was most vulnerable… Jeremy. She wouldn't hesitate to use my vulnerability to get what she wanted from me… more and more of me. She desperately wanted me to fill the incredible hole she felt inside. I felt like even if I literally jumped inside of her, it wouldn't be enough.

A feeling of uneasiness penetrated my being as I pondered this decision. If I chose not to go to Florida, she'd hate me and pull back from me even more, if not completely. I'd lose everything I had built so far with her. She wasn't court ordered to cooperate with me. I had no authority over her. The mere thought of what could happen terrified me. Delilah held all the power. She could easily flee with Jeremy, leaving me completely helpless to protect him.

My "job," to help Delilah deal with HIV, AIDS, and teach her ways to cope, rather than lashing out at her kids, didn't necessitate actually diagnosing her psychological difficulties. But if I was going to survive working with her and successfully get through to her so she would stop abusing Jeremy, I needed to think in terms of a diagnosis. Delilah suffered from borderline personality disorder.

This is a serious characterological disorder in which the core of the individual's personality and identity is disturbed. The person is often unable to control their rage and impulsiveness. Their relationships with others, if they have any, are intense but unstable. They alternate between extreme overidealization and devaluation of the other person in the relationship. They think this person can do no wrong, and hold this person in very high esteem. Should this person let them down and not live up to their expectations, which are not realistic in the first place, the person falls from their grace and becomes the object of their intense rage. People with this disorder make frantic efforts to avoid real or even imagined abandonment, and may become extremely depressed, irritable, or anxious for no apparent reason.

A good example for this disorder is from the movie, <u>Fatal Attraction</u>. The character named Alex, played by Glenn Close, fits this diagnosis. She has a hot and heavy affair with the character played by Michael Douglas. When he begins to set limits with her and chooses not to fill her every need, as she demands, she becomes volatile. Near the end of the movie, she boils his child's pet rabbit after breaking into his home, and eventually tries to kill his wife.

Putting a name to Delilah's cluster of behaviors gave me a framework from which to work, to determine how to best handle her. The state gave me no other option than to assist Delilah to make changes within herself, to stop abusing Jeremy. In the back of my mind, I didn't want to acknowledge the fact that Delilah probably had the capacity to kill Jeremy because of her lack of impulse control... her needs don't get met so she takes her underlying rage out on him.

At times, it felt like no training in the world would have been enough to prepare me, with so much at stake. Delilah knew she had all of us dangling from her strings, and I played the role of her lead marionette. I had to be very careful not to come on too strong or threatening. If Delilah felt alienated or backed into a corner, it might be enough to prompt Jeremy's death.

She wouldn't ever hurt or kill him intentionally, but she was capable of doing so because of her underlying rage and lack of impulse control. She lacked the internal control to stop herself.

I didn't know what to do. I needed to make a choice that I'd be comfortable living with. I really wanted Jeremy to have his last wish. Maybe the trip would give me the opportunity I needed to get through to her, and maybe I could break the fortress she had so vigilantly built around herself. On the other hand, I didn't know how I could go out of state with a woman I had no authority or control over, who wanted me in her clutches. I knew one thing for sure though, if Delilah continued closing herself off, as their illness progressed, Jeremy would remain in grave danger from his own mother.

After turning to my support system for help, I prayed and meditated on it. It took awhile for the dust to settle in my mind, before I could sort out all my thoughts to make my decision. But I did it. In my heart of hearts, I knew I was getting into something grievously pivotal. The dark cloud around me, which I often felt regarding Jeremy's situation, was becoming darker and heavier than ever. I felt it closing in on me.

I told Hannah my decision, and we talked about it. She was the only person who had experienced Delilah's rage as I had. I trusted her opinion. She supported my decision.

I called Jeremy and Delilah. They were ecstatic. We'd be leaving in one week. *Only one week.* I'd have to be at their apartment at 5:30 a.m. A limousine would pick us up and take us to O'Hare Airport.

PART TWO -- DAY ONE, SEA WORLD

I hardly slept the night before the trip. It was still dark outside at 5:00 a.m. when Jim drove me to Delilah and Jeremy's apartment. We walked upstairs, and before Jim could even knock on the door, it flew open and Jeremy jumped onto Jim, hanging his arms from Jim's neck.

"Hi! There's my stuff. I'm ready!" He gently punched Jim in the stomach and they began to wrestle.

Delilah came out of the bathroom. "Stop it right now, Jeremy. Sit on the couch and be quiet."

Just then the limo honked for us. Jeremy flew down the stairs in a flash. Delilah began her tirade, "Get back..."

Jim interrupted and softly stated that he'd be happy to follow Jeremy downstairs to supervise. Delilah quieted. Jim carried their luggage down as I followed with my bag.

"Yippee, you guys, what a hot car!" A brand new, black BMW limo awaited our entry. "Look at the driver with the cool hat!"

The driver with the cool hat opened the front door of the limo, asking Jeremy, "Would you like to ride in front?"

"Does it have a TV?"

"No lad, I'm sorry, it doesn't," the chauffeur chuckled.

"It's all for me, Jim," he boasted proudly as he pointed both thumbs at his chest. His eyes glistened.

"Yeah, Kiddo, it's all for you. You deserve it." Jim bent down to give Jeremy a big hug. Jeremy jumped into his arms, wrapped his legs around Jim's waist and gave him a long, hard squeeze good bye.

Delilah came down the stairs. As Jeremy climbed in the front seat, Delilah snapped, "Get in the back."

As Jeremy climbed over the seat into the back, Delilah yanked at his arm, prematurely pulling him over the seat. He smacked his face on the bottom seat cushion as he landed in the back. Delilah yelled at him for putting his feet on the leather seats.

The chauffeur, glancing in the rear view mirror, said, "It's all right, Ma'am. Don't worry about it."

I said good bye to Jim. He whispered in my ear to call him anytime if I needed a shoulder to lean on. I was grateful. I couldn't do this alone. Jim and Delilah hugged.

On the way to the airport, Jeremy got a bloody nose. Delilah explained, "He's had one on and off all week. The doctors don't know what's causing it." *Perhaps it had something to do with you yanking him off of the seat, and his face getting hit...*

Luckily, Delilah had plenty of Kleenex in her pocket. It didn't want to stop bleeding. I wanted to help but couldn't. Even though I came armed with plastic gloves, Jeremy still didn't know his body fluids were deadly. Thank goodness it stopped bleeding by the time we got to the airport.

As we exited the limo, two women volunteers from Make - Λ - Wish awaited our arrival. They gave Jeremy a Mickey Mouse helium balloon and Mickey Mouse ears, and had a birthday present for Delilah. I hadn't realized it was her birthday. After checking our baggage, we sat down to finish business.

"Delilah, this contains $400 in travelers checks." One of the women handed Delilah an envelope. "You need a picture ID to cash them. Please sign the back of them."

Delilah didn't have the proper identification. "Robyn, would you please handle the travelers checks?"

"Sure." I signed all of them.

"Here's coupons and tickets for all the different attractions. You guys can go anywhere you want, Sea World, Epcot, Disney World, MGM Studios, Water World, even Busch Gardens if you'd like. You'd have to drive there of course, it's in Tampa." The other woman continued, "We made dinner reservations for you tonight at 6:00 for a western show. Jeremy gets to participate in some of the acts on stage."

I looked over at Delilah, who feigned a smile. *If she lets him, that is.*

Then they explained everything else to us, from where to pick up our rental car, to what VIP treatment we'd be receiving wherever we went because of Jeremy's "Give Kids the World" pin, which they attached to his shirt. This notified the various merchants he was from Make - A - Wish. We had few restrictions placed upon us. All admissions would be free except Busch Gardens. Sounded like fun.

The plane ride went smoothly. I was surprised Jeremy stayed in his seat — he could hardly contain his excitement. Delilah felt sick a couple of times, but made it through successfully.

As we walked into the Orlando terminal, Jeremy spotted an elderly man holding a sign with "Jeremy Miller," printed in all different colored markers. Another volunteer from Make - A - Wish. Jeremy ran toward him. We quickly caught up. He gathered our luggage for us and took us to the rental car counter. Trying to be polite and sociable, he turned to strike up a conversation with Delilah.

"The little guy sure has a lot of energy." And then came the million - dollar question, "What illness does he have?" I could hear the words as they were coming out of his mouth as if in slow motion. It quickly changed the mood of things.

Delilah glanced at me with panic in her eyes. I held my breath, waiting to see how she'd handle it. She and I had rehearsed what she wanted to say, if anyone had asked, but we hadn't expected it so soon.

"Crohn's disease."

Jeremy stood right in front of her.

"Oh. What's that?" the man asked innocently, totally oblivious to Delilah's feelings.

"It's a blood disease," Delilah stated curtly as she quickly moved away from him, giving him a threatening look.

We got our rental car without any further problems and drove to the villas at "Give Kids the World." With Jeremy as my co-pilot, we found the villas successfully. The ride was somewhat uncomfortable as Delilah put her coat of armor back on for protection. My guess was she was preparing herself for everyone else to ask her what Jeremy was dying from.

As we turned onto the road leading to the villas, I felt my heart rate beating faster from my nervousness and excitement. As we pulled into the parking lot it seemed as though we had entered into paradise. Beauty surrounded us. Gorgeous flowering white oleanders, creeping ivy, and bushes shaped like animals captivated us. The grounds were exquisitely landscaped. We parked and walked into the office of the villas. Even that was beautifully decorated, and the staff greeted us warmly. They offered us a map of the grounds and our tickets for dinner that evening. They gave us a schedule for a support group, which met for the parents and caregivers. Babysitting would be provided for us. All three of us felt so excited, we kept our luggage in the car and quickly took a tour of the grounds and facilities.

We had a perfect day ahead of us. My watch read 10:00 which meant it was actually 11:00, Florida time. The warmth of the sun beat down on us from the bright blue sky. Jeremy was so ecstatic, our tour turned out to be a quick one. He just had to get to our villa to see his new home! He asked if we could tour again more slowly, once we got settled in.

Behind the playground full of swings, and slides, and monkey bars was a pond the size of a football field stocked with fish. A variety of turtles and ducks called it home. A pirate's plank set partially over the pond. You could actually walk on it. Not far from there was an in-ground, Olympic size swimming pool surrounded by a multilevel deck. The picnic area around the pool, filled with vending machines, led to an old train car loaded with video games and pinball machines. It really did look and feel like paradise. I sure hoped it would turn out to be.

We drove our car to our villa. As we carried our luggage up the sidewalk leading to our door, a chameleon scurried by Jeremy's foot. He squealed with delight as the chameleon hid behind the leaves of the bright, pink hibiscus flower in our garden. Delilah unlocked the front door and we all stepped into the large kitchen. A lovely, welcoming fresh fruit basket and presents wrapped in Mickey Mouse wrapping paper filled the dining room table. A note attached to the basket told us to enjoy our stay.

The villa, larger than my entire apartment, had two bedrooms, two bathrooms, one equipped with a wheelchair accessible shower, a living room with TV, VCR, and stereo, and an eat in kitchen. Jeremy raced around checking the place out, leaving the presents on the table. He was bursting with joy. I caught Delilah smiling right along with him.

"I want Robyn to share my room with me!" Jeremy grabbed my hand, dragging me into the bedroom with two twin beds. Delilah followed.

"You need to ask your mom, Sweetie."

"Please, Mommy, can she?"

"If you want to, Robyn, that would be fine."

"Then it's settled," I said, smiling at both of them.

"Did you see the master bedroom?" Delilah asked me as she walked into its doorway.

"Wow, this is really nice," I said, following her inside the room. "You can really get a good night's sleep on that bed," I teased. It was a king-sized bed full of super fluffy pillows. A beautiful wooden chest of drawers filled one wall.

"Are you sure you don't mind?" She sounded a little self-conscious.

"Thanks for asking. Please, you enjoy it." At home, they had only one twin-sized bed. One of them always slept on the couch.

As I went back into our room to unpack, Jeremy changed into shorts and got ready to go outside to do some serious exploring. We had some time, since we had decided in the car that we'd spend the afternoon at Sea World, before going to dinner. Our reservations were for 6:00 p.m.

Jeremy invited Delilah to explore with us. She said she might later. Jeremy glanced at me with disappointment in his eyes. We went outside without her while she diligently hung up all their clothes. Jeremy and I stepped into the bright morning sun. I took a deep breath to drink up the fresh morning air.

"Can we go see the pool first?"

"Sure, Sweetie. Whatever you want." So we skipped to the pool. Jeremy spotted a big, fuzzy bumblebee drinking from a beautiful purple hibiscus flower. He ran over to see it, beckoning me to follow.

"Look how fuzzy and pretty it looks," he whispered. "This is so cool!"

Suddenly he squealed with delight as a chameleon scurried over his toes. "Let's go catch it." He took off running. I could hardly keep up.

49

The chameleon was just a little too fast for us. Jeremy spotted the bee again, began buzzing, and held out his arms to flap his wings.

"Come on, follow me!" We buzzed and flapped our way over to the pier at the fishing pond. Several humongous frogs, croaking away in the bright Florida sun, greeted us. They floated on lily pads full of purple and white water lilies. As I took another deep breath, I looked around. It had been awhile since I had been in Florida. I forgot that everything is bigger than I'm used to. A fifty-foot tall rubber tree had a giant bright green philodendron wrapped around its trunk. I had a rubber tree houseplant at home, and a philodendron, for that matter. One of these leaves was the size of my entire plant.

"Listen! There talking about us!" exclaimed Jeremy.

"Who?"

"The frogs, silly!"

"What are they saying?" I asked.

"They're happy we're here. And that we're gonna have so much fun. And that Mommy will have fun too!" Jeremy looked away from me and stared at the water. His mood seemed to shift. He began to drift off somewhere and stood silent. His facial expression became solemn, as if he was in deep thought.

After a few minutes I asked, "Where'd you go, Sweetie?"

"Just thinkin'…" He continued staring at the water and remained silent.

The sun warmed my face as I gazed at the cloudless sky. I waited to see if he wanted to share his thoughts. After a few moments, he began, "How come God makes beautiful things grow in the spring, and in the fall, how come they have to die?" He sounded sad. He quietly repeated, "Why do they die?"

"Well," I replied, "wh…"

Delilah strolled up. I looked at Jeremy to see if he wanted to continue his conversation, but his face grew tense, and he looked away.

"Hi, you guys. What are you doing?" She asked cheerfully, in a tone I had never heard before.

"Hi, Mommy. We're talkin' to the frogs."

Delilah replied, "Talking to the frogs?" And then she did something I never expected. She let out a "C-r-o-a-k, c-r-o-a-k." So Jeremy and I joined her as we competed for who could croak the most authentically. Jeremy won hands down. I'd say Delilah came in for the silver. We all had a good laugh. That was refreshing.

We finished our conversations with the frogs and walked together arm in arm to the car, headed for Sea World. I had never felt so hopeful before with Delilah. She was the calmest and most relaxed I had ever seen. I actually had fun being around her. She had never let her guard down or allowed herself to be so spontaneous before. Maybe this trip was exactly what she needed. I felt remarkably hopeful and repeated a silent prayer for Divine Order to reign over the three of us for the day, for the whole trip for that matter.

We all sat in the front seat on the way to Sea World. Jeremy laid his head on his mom's shoulder, nuzzling up to her. "This is so much fun, Mommy. Thanks." The song "Wind Beneath My Wings" came on the radio and we sang our hearts out the entire way to Sea World. It was Jeremy's favorite song. Delilah responded positively to him more than I had ever seen. Jeremy ate it up. So did I. It felt great to see the two of them connecting like this.

"This looks awesome!" Jeremy screeched, running toward the open fishponds just outside of the ticket booths. They were filled with huge koi and goldfish. "Can we get one of those strollers over there, Mommy?" He pointed at one shaped like a dolphin, and jumped in. "In case I get tired, that is, they're so cool!" Delilah smiled as she approached Jeremy and paid the vendor.

We viewed many attractions. The most wonderful and spiritual experience, however, was not a staged event at all. After watching the Shamu show, we headed for lunch. The three of us walked by these open pools filled with seals. Jeremy stopped to get a closer look at them. When the seals saw us, several of them came directly toward Jeremy. One of them threw him a ball. He naturally tossed it back and they began to play catch. Several more came over and began to sing, splash, and play with him, causing quite a ruckus. The seals seemed to have a keen sense of what was going on with Jeremy on all levels — body, mind, and spirit. As crazy as this might sound, I felt it. And I wasn't the only one. People had begun to gather around us to watch the incredible connection that was happening. It was so quiet. The sound of Jeremy's laughter, and the seals splashing, were the only sounds heard.

51

When Jeremy clapped, the seals clapped back. It was phenomenal. It was like they were human. Seven seals formed a line and paraded in front of him. Each looked him directly in the eye and seemed to communicate, "We love you. You are very special."

In no time, a huge crowd gathered around the pools as other families joined in the experience. The seals continued to play only with Jeremy, despite the presence of many other children. They had singled him out to dance.

Most of the audience was pretty wet when they finished. Everyone applauded. Jeremy, bursting at the seams exclaimed, "What a blast! Did ya see that? They knew me!"

"I've never seen anything like it," Delilah confirmed, wearing a huge grin and widened eyes. "It was great." Jeremy grabbed her hand as we walked to the cafeteria. I was glad Delilah didn't pull back as I had often witnessed. I felt happy and hopeful as I watched them enjoying each other's presence.

In the middle of a bite of peanut butter and jelly, Jeremy asked, "Where do we go when we die, Mommy?"

Delilah looked at me, dumbfounded. Panic filled her big, brown eyes as if to say, "Oh my gosh, what do I tell him? Help..."

I smiled at her reassuringly and tried to encourage her, without words, to answer his question. Part of me wanted to answer for her, to rescue her, and give him some comfort. But he needed the comfort and sharing from her, not me. So I kept silent.

Delilah finished chewing a bite of her sandwich and sipped iced tea. A long, deep breath followed. "Well, Jeremy, I was taught that we go to heaven if we've been good and a place called hell if we've been bad... At least that's what I learned in church. Actually, I'm not so sure what happens or what I believe." Turning toward me she said, "I bet Robyn would have a good answer for us though, don't you think?"

"Yep, Mommy, I know she does."

I waited, certain Jeremy would have his own explanation. So I invited him to answer first, and he did with vim and vigor. "Remember that movie where the daddy asks is this heaven with the baseball players and stuff?"

"Yeah, Field of Dreams, with Kevin Kostner," I replied. "It's great."

"I liked it, too," added Delilah.

"I think that's what heaven's like." Taking a deep breath, he rattled off, "There's baseball games all the time whenever you wanna play, and you can race sports cars and not get hurt cuz God always protects you..." He placed his right index finger on his right cheek and continued, "Your guardian angels have lots of fun drivin' you around in your bestest sports car, and they play with you when you want 'em to." He spoke with such assurance, as though he remembered being there. "And you don't have to go to school if you don't wanna... oh yeah, you never have to sleep either... and it's like you know everybody, too."

I glanced at Delilah, wrinkling my eyebrows. She shrugged her shoulders in response, then asked, "What do you mean by that, Jeremy?"

"It's kinda hard to explain." Jeremy gazed out into the sunlight. "It's like you been there before, your real home." He looked directly at both of us and said, "We belong there." His eyes wandered toward the sunlight again, as he became silent, lost in his thoughts. I didn't want this moment to end.

Jeremy's innocence and purity reminded me of the story of the little boy who asked his parents if he could talk to his newborn baby brother alone. The parents allowed the boy into the baby's room and listened in on the baby monitor. The big brother asked his wise little brother something like, "Tell me what heaven's like cuz you just came from there, and I don't remember so good." Could it be possible that children who are terminally ill don't forget as easily as the rest of us either?

I watched and waited until Jeremy's awareness came back to the present reality before speaking, "I think I know what you mean, Sweetie. A lot of us feel a hole inside, an emptiness we just can't seem to fill while we're here in human form."

Jeremy zoned out in trance again when I said that, but Delilah listened intently. I continued, "Once in awhile we might feel a little of what you're describing, a wholeness and knowing that we had on the other side when we're in different form, back home with God. This patient at my last job, an elderly man, who was a great teacher to me, taught me about Jeremiah in the Bible."

Jeremy zipped back to the present and cut in, "Jeremiah? That sounds a lot like my name. Am I like this Jeremiah guy?"

"As a matter of fact, I think you are," I said. "Jeremiah was a young boy when God asked him to do great things, which Jeremiah didn't think he could do. God told him, "Before you were conceived I knew you; before you came to birth I consecrated you." In fact, it's Jeremiah 1:5. I memorized it. What it says to me, is that we come here from a place where God knows us really well. And we've agreed to do certain things once we get here. Whenever we're called back home by God, when we die, we return there."

Jeremy sat staring outside through the window. While watching him, Delilah added, "Maybe that's why some people describe dying as passing away. We pass away from here back to there...."

A grin formed on Jeremy's lips as he met his mother's eyes with his. Delilah continued gazing at him. For a brief moment I witnessed a deep connection between them, a capsule of time where Delilah remained in the present, looking into her son's eyes, listening, absorbing his wisdom and presence. He leaned toward her and whispered, "Yep, I know whatcha mean." He kissed Delilah on the cheek. "I love you, Mommy."

Then he asked matter of factly, with a smirk on his face, "Know how ya get to heaven? Ya fly. It takes a few days if you go nonstop." We laughed and continued eating lunch. After Jeremy finished eating, he sat back comfortably in his chair and stated, with much confidence, "I am like that Jeremiah guy."

"Yep," I answered, "You sure are. We all are."

"Could I be here for a very special reason too? To do a special thing only I can do?" He pointed at himself with both thumbs.

"Hmmm," Delilah mumbled, "I wonder..."

"I think it is true, Kiddo. I think it's true for all of us. You, your mom, and me."

"Can we go play and see some more stuff now, Mommy?"

"Whenever you're ready," she answered, clearing off our table. What a day this was turning out to be. Delilah seemed to be opening up just as I had hoped. I felt the cloud beginning to lift ever so slightly.

I breathed in a sigh of relief.

After spending a few more hours having fun at Sea World, we drove to the western show. Both Delilah and Jeremy fell asleep during the drive there.

As we pulled into the parking lot, the sound of gunfire awakened them. Upon entering the gate to the O.K. Corral, a man fell off the roof right in front of Jeremy. I had to grab Jeremy by the back of his shirt to hold him down. I bet if I hadn't, he would have grabbed the guy's gun and joined in the excitement. After the shootout, everyone headed into the restaurant. A cowgirl at the hostess stand saw Jeremy's "Give Kids the World" pin and led us to a ringside seat at a long table with several other families.

Our head cowhand introduced herself as Barb. Barb handed everyone at the table either a pirate or a soldier hat, and told us we had to wear them. Delilah did not acquiesce to Barb's request at first, but eventually warmed up when everyone else joined in the fun. The woman sitting next to Delilah coaxed Delilah into wearing her hat. The next show was, of course, a pretend sword fight between a pirate and a soldier. Jeremy's enthusiasm for the pirate was so contagious, he got our entire table, including Delilah and the opposing team, cheering for his guy.

Delilah had never appeared so contented. I watched as she joined in conversation with the woman sitting next to her. There was a moment when I looked at Delilah, and she looked at me, and she smiled. It made me think, was this really Jeremy's last wish? Or was it Jeremy's last wish for Delilah?

Barbecue chicken, ribs, baked beans, corn on the cob, baked potatoes, and salad were the grub served up for the occasion. Both Delilah and Jeremy ate more than I had ever seen them eat.

A cowgirl, dressed in turquoise leather, came into the audience to gather children for the next event. She saw Jeremy's "Give Kids the World" pin and asked him to lead it. She whispered in his ear. Immediately Delilah became agitated. She bit her lip while glaring at the woman. My chest tightened as I thought, *Oh no... Here we go again...* Without the blink of an eye, Jeremy walked on stage, and began parading the other kids around in a circle to engage them in the festivities. When they were finished, American Indians in full dress came out on stage and danced.

Even in the darkness of the room, I could see Delilah's unhappiness. Her tightly pursed lips and folded arms gave a clear message that she did not want Jeremy participating. Period. It surprised me that she allowed him to have fun in the first place, especially in public. Normally, the only time she'd ever allow him to play was at the clinic in the hospital. And that was only after the volunteers had begged and pampered her, so Jeremy could slip away. I felt greatly disappointed and saddened by the sudden return of the "usual" Delilah, but hung on to my hope. Things could change.

A woman came around and took each of our pictures with our silly hats on. Before the show ended, she made them into key chains and passed them out. To this day, I still carry Jeremy on mine, holding him preciously in my hand, with his pirate hat on.

After the show, we headed home, popped some microwave popcorn, and watched a Mickey Mouse video. When it was over, Jeremy and Delilah, who sat side by side on the couch, kissed goodnight. Delilah stood up and approached me. She put out her arms to hug me and I hugged her back. Jeremy leaped from the couch and joined us in a group hug, and we all went to bed. While lying in our room, Jeremy quietly said, "G'night, Robyn. I love you. I'm glad you came with. I'm havin' lots of fun."

"Me too, Jeremy. I love you, too. Good night."

As I was lying in bed saying my prayers, Jeremy asked, "Robyn...?"

"Yes, Sweetie?"

"Sayin' your prayers?"

"Yep. How'd you know?"

"Just did. Could ya teach me to pray...cuz...I just know one and I wanna know more."

"Would you like to sit on my bed for a little while?"

"Yeah, yeah, yeah," he whispered, sounding like Ernie from Sesame Street, as he jumped onto my bed.

"What prayer do you know?" I asked.

"The now I lay me down to sleep one."

"That's a good one..." Before I could finish my sentence, Jeremy interrupted.

"Not really. It doesn't seem real enough. I wanna real one. My real one. I want God to know just what's in my heart."

"Then you should tell God what that is."

"Whadya mean… is that what you do?"

"That's a big part of my prayers, having a heart to heart with God. I talk to God and tell God just what's going on within me. My deepest wishes and hopes and fears." Jeremy plopped down on my lap. "Sometimes, I even get mad at God."

"You get mad?"

"Yep!"

"Why?"

"Because sometimes I don't understand why things turn out the way they do, so I share how upset it makes me."

"Wow! What else do you say?"

"I say thank you a lot. And I ask that God's will for my life be done and for the people that I love. Do you know what I mean when I say God's will?"

"Whatever God wants?"

"Yep. Sometimes we don't understand what God has planned for us or why we have to go through certain things. We want things to be our way. But our way isn't always the best way for us, so I specifically ask God to take charge and do things the way God wants them done."

"That's neat. Kinda like Jeremiah, the guy we were talkin' about before."

"Yep, kinda like Jeremiah. Would you like to say a prayer together?"

"No, but can you pray so I can hear you. And then me. Deal?"

"Deal!" I prayed softly.

Then Jeremy took a turn. "Dear God. I'm really glad that I'm here to see Mickey Mouse and I'm already havin' lots of fun. Thank you for that. I hope you can help Mommy cuz I know somethin's wrong. Please help her. I pray for Robyn and Jim. And Toby and Winnie and Sammy, Robyn's cats cuz I love 'em too. And I pray that I have even more fun with Robyn and Mommy tomorrow, and I hope Mommy has fun again. Amen." Jeremy gave me a big hug and climbed into his bed. In a few seconds, he fell fast asleep.

PART THREE -- DAY TWO, EPCOT

The next morning, as we walked toward the deck, the smell of bacon made my mouth water. A breakfast buffet was served daily at the poolside. We heard laughter from the other families enjoying their tasty treats, from grits and eggs, to cereal, fresh fruit and muffins. Everyone appeared to bask in the camaraderie. Looking around, I was struck by the family-oriented atmosphere, which felt very loving, as parents and grandparents interacted with their dying, young, family members. Even Minnie and Pluto had joined in the fun, pouring orange juice refills and posing for pictures with the kids. Several children connected to ventilators sat in wheelchairs. Other children had no hair. Some looked quite bloated.

The sky quickly darkened and it began to rain. Pour actually. Everyone raced under the large yellow canopy, joining each other, complaining about the weather. Delilah chose a table isolated from the others and forbid Jeremy to move from the table, once we sat down.

How sad I felt for Jeremy, being forced to remain isolated amidst all the excitement. He did his best to contain himself.

The rain let up as quickly as it came, making it a sultry day. Steam rose from the sidewalk. Delilah asked if I would take Jeremy swimming so that she could rest. We had planned to go to the Epcot Center later in the afternoon. Normally, she wouldn't let Jeremy out of her sight.

Back at our villa, Jeremy got ready in a flash with his color coordinated water wings, swan float, brand new red dinosaur sunglasses, and striped swimming trunks. "Mr. Trendo," I called him.

I changed into my swimming suit as Delilah retired to her room for a nap.

Jeremy and I grabbed some towels and headed for the pool. We sang "This Old Man," until we got to the deck and sat our towels on a couple of lawn chairs. I watched as Jeremy approached the water. He began to tremble. He turned pale. He sat on the deck near the edge of the pool with his arms wrapped tightly around his legs, refusing to even dangle his big toe in the shallow end. A young girl swimming in the pool accidentally splashed him, and he ran to his lounge chair and clung to it, shaking. He climbed onto the chair and rolled himself into a fetal position. I ran over and handed him a towel. He wiped away his tears and tried to hide his face from me.

I wondered what was going on. I hoped this wasn't an indication of more abuse. I didn't want to make myself crazy thinking of that, so I tried to remain focused on helping him.

I sat down near his feet. "Hi, Little Buddy. Did you feel the water?"

"No," he said, his teeth chattering.

"Are you cold? Here, take my towel," I said as I tried to hand him mine, too.

"I'm not cold," he said, belligerently, like I should know better.

"Wanna go in with me? I'll stay in the shallow end, I promise," I said in a playful voice.

"I guess so," he whispered, sitting up, observing the pool with a critical eye. I picked him up. He locked his legs tightly around my hips. But as I took my first step into the water, he screamed, "No. Stop!"

I did. "What's wrong, Buddy?"

"I'm scared..."

"I can see that." I held him. I looked him in the eyes and asked, "Are you okay?"

He didn't answer and buried his face in my chest.

I gently pressed my lips against his forehead. "There now, there now, Sweetie, it'll be all right." I waited until Jeremy stopped shaking and asked, "Do you want to talk about what's scaring you?"

"No," he mumbled into my shoulder.

"Okay, but if you'd like to try to go in the water again, we can. I promise I won't let anything happen to you."

Jeremy wrapped his legs securely around me and said, "Let's go." I slowly stepped into the shallow water, while making playful sounds. He held on to me for dear life. It took him a while before he could relax and enjoy himself. He finally let go of me and began to do the dog paddle with his water wings on.

The further Jeremy swam away from me, the more he checked back with me by making eye contact, ensuring that I kept a close watch over him.

Two other little girls swam and played in the water, too. Jeremy swam over and introduced himself to them. I overheard the older sister introduce herself as, "Megan, age five, and my sister Michelle, who's three." Michelle, who looked quite ill, took to Jeremy immediately. And of course Jeremy was in his glory. Two new friends to play with.

I stayed in the water and watched the kids have paddle races in their swimming gear. Jeremy had jumped out to get his swan innertube because the girls already had theirs around their waists. Two of them took turns racing back and forth, while the third pretended to time them both with a stopwatch.

Delilah surprised everyone, when she joined us by jumping in the pool. She struck up a conversation with the girls' mom, who jumped in the pool with us and threw a beach ball to Jeremy. He started a game of volleyball. Jeremy stayed in his swan float while Delilah and I took turns pushing him around to hit the ball. We played volleyball for another hour before it was time to go.

As we walked back to our villa to get ready for Epcot, Delilah lagged slowly behind us. This had become a signal for me that Delilah wasn't handling things well. Her passive aggressiveness began to be her chosen coping style. At least she wasn't hitting Jeremy with a belt anymore. Something was up with her, though… again.

I turned around to look at her. The cold expression on her face indicated the veil of darkness that at times came over her was present again. I sensed her start to withdraw from us as we were getting out of the pool. The expression on her face said, "Don't come near me, leave me alone." I knew Jeremy had sensed it, too.

Therapeutically, this is the best time to confront someone on their feelings, when they're in them. So despite her cues, I questioned her. I didn't want to pass up an opportunity to break through her armor.

I waited until we changed back into our clothes. She and I stood in the kitchen, while Jeremy was still getting dressed in his bedroom. I asked, "Are you feeling all right, Delilah?"

"I'm fine," she said quietly, staring down at the floor. She turned her back away from me.

"It seems like there's something going on with you since we got out of the pool." She didn't respond. "If you change your mind and decide you'd like to talk, I'm here to listen," I said, hoping to leave the door open for her to talk in the future.

"Thanks. I'd rather not."

I hoped that whatever was troubling her wouldn't interfere with Jeremy's fun, or safety, for that matter. When Delilah got in these moods, these dark sides of herself, if Jeremy made a wrong move, or acted like a kid, she tended to hurt him one way or another. Sometimes she'd take it out on him physically, other times she'd withdraw from him emotionally. Jeremy always bore the brunt of Delilah's emotional baggage.

As we got in the car to drive to Epcot, she remained distant. Jeremy kept looking at me in the rearview mirror, like, "What's going on now?" I tried to reassure him, nonverbally, that we'd get through this one together. He seemed to understand as he gently touched my shoulder from the back seat.

On the ride in, Jeremy tried different ways to draw his mother out of her gloominess and help her lighten up. "Hey Mom, why did the radish like the banana?" he asked, wearing a great big grin on his face.

"I don't know, Jeremy, nor do I care," she snapped, having no patience for him. Or for anything.

"Because it had appeal!" Jeremy laughed. He tried to get his mom to join in, but she pulled away from him. Delilah retreated back to her cold, closed off self. She didn't even crack a smile. Another painful dance for me to watch. The rest of the ride felt strained and awkward.

We finally arrived at Epcot. I thought we'd never get there. Once we got in, we got the royal treatment. The guide gave us passes for the hospitality suite, where they gave us cookies, fresh fruit, and juice. We could go back there to rest if Jeremy felt tired. Another guide met with us and explained that Jeremy's "Give Kids the World" pin would get us in the back door of every attraction, so we wouldn't have to wait in the long lines.

"Awesome!" yelled Jeremy. He liked the idea of not waiting for anything. He wanted to get all of his living in quickly.

Jeremy's favorite exhibit there was "Journey Into Imagination." That's where Figment, the animated creature, takes the audience on a journey into one's mind and creativity.

After the Figment ride, we went up to the hands-on part of the show. Delilah loosened up again and joined in the fun. There's a room filled with different colored lights that make musical tones when you step on them. Delilah stepped out song after song for Jeremy and me to "name that tune." He did great, guessing their titles. We took turns trying to stump each other.

We had worked up quite an appetite. We walked to the Kraft Exhibit, "The Land," to have lunch. Our map said there was a large food court on the lower level of the exhibit. On the way there, I could feel Delilah's mood changing again. She was slipping away again from the present, to whatever darkness metamorphosed inside her. I wasn't the only one who could feel her caustic vibes, all you had to do was look at her and come close to her. You could feel them in the air.

She wouldn't talk. She wore a hateful expression and walked very slowly as if she didn't want to participate. I didn't like this emotional roller coaster ride I was on with her. And I didn't live with her like Jeremy did. It felt unbearable.

As the three of us stepped alone into the elevator, I asked, "Are you feeling okay, Delilah? What's going on?"

"Nothing's going on," she said haughtily, "I'm just fine."

"Can we go find a place to sit down so we can talk?"

"If you must," she huffed.

We grabbed an empty table in the food court. As gently as possible, I stated, "When I ask if you're okay, or if something's going on with you, you say no. But your body language is telling me that you aren't very happy or comfortable. It feels like something is wrong."

She said nothing and kept her arms tightly pulled in to her chest. So I tried again. "By sharing what's going on inside of us, it helps to free us from whatever's bothering us. By holding things in all the time, we tend to take them out in other ways that aren't so healthy." I made an analogy of a boiling, stoppered teakettle ready to explode because it had no place to let out its steam.

Still no response. By this time, Jeremy pleaded, "Come on, Mommy, what's wrong? Are you sick? Are you gonna be okay? Please let us help you." I could hear his sadness and frustration.

Finally she said, "Maybe if we have lunch, I'll feel better."

I didn't think lunch would cure whatever was bothering her, but it couldn't hurt.

As I looked at all the restaurants, my mouth watered. So many different types of food were being served. I wasn't sure where I wanted to eat. "What are you going to have, Delilah?" I asked.

"I'll just have a sandwich."

"I want a hot dog. They're in the line over there," Jeremy said as he pointed to the Vienna Hot Dog sign on the wall.

"I tell you what," I said, "Delilah, if you'd like to get in line to order your sandwich, I'll take Jeremy to the hot dog place and get my lunch over there, too." I didn't particularly want a hot dog, but since Jeremy wanted one, I didn't want him to have to wait in line all over again for my lunch. It was unfortunate that Jeremy's pin couldn't help us this time.

As we reconvened back at our table to sit down and eat, Delilah announced, "I'm going to the restroom." She got up and left without asking Jeremy if he needed to go.

As soon as she left, Jeremy climbed next to me and asked in a solemn voice, "Robyn, what's wrong with Mommy? Is she gonna be okay?"

"I'm not sure what's bothering her, Sweetie. I'll do my best to help her, though. She'll be all right. How are you doing with all of this?"

"I'm scared."

"What of?"

"She keeps acting funny."

"What scares you about it, Sweetie?"

"I'm afraid somethin's really wrong. I don't know how to make it stop. Maybe she doesn't feel good but she doesn't wanna tell anybody. I think she's scared. Things are gettin' worse. I don't want 'em to be like this. Sometimes I get scared of 'er. You know how she gets sometimes, you saw her. I get afraid, but I wanna help her."

I put my arm around him. I wanted to say so much but my hands were tied. I had to respect Delilah's wishes and not overstep her desire on how to handle their illness. "Yeah, I know what you mean, Jeremy. I'm really sorry that you're going through this. We'll get through it together. You're not alone in this anymore. I made a promise to you. Remember?"

"Yep! I remember." Jeremy put his arms around me and squeezed with all his might. I hugged him back, not wanting to let go. Surrounded by people enjoying themselves and being together, this whole thing felt unreal. Alone, isolated in the middle of this happy place, life felt too heavy.

"Jeremy, do you want to share with your mom how you feel?"

"Nope," he answered abruptly.

"That's fine, Little Buddy, you don't have to." I patted his knee.

I held out hope that maybe if Delilah heard from Jeremy how scared and hurt he was, while we were here for his last wish, she might open herself up and allow herself to feel how bad he felt. When she closed herself from her own feelings, she closed herself off from everyone else's as well. I hoped she could allow some of his love for her to shine on her heart and illuminate it.

I couldn't blame him for not wanting to tell her. She showed no evidence of wanting to hear the truth from anyone.

A long time had elapsed since Delilah left for the restroom. I didn't know where it was. Jeremy began eating his lunch. I decided to give it ten more minutes. If she didn't return by then, I'd go look for her.

My gut told me that's what she wanted me to do; go and find her and give her my attention. After nine minutes, which made a total of thirty that she was gone, Delilah came back to the table.

"Hi, Mommy!" Jeremy looked her in the eyes and asked, "Are you gonna be okay?"

"Eat your lunch," she barked.

My body stiffened. The trip to the restroom hadn't helped her one bit. So I asked, "Is there anything I can do to help, Delilah?"

"Not a thing, thank you."

"If you decide you'd like to talk, I'm here to listen."

"Right," she responded, staring at the floor. An uncomfortable silence went out from our table, while other families sat laughing and enjoying each other's company.

When we finished, Delilah, out of the blue, asked in a cheery voice, "Where would you like to go next, Jeremy?"

"On the boat ride into those gardens," he replied, pointing to the entrance. Jeremy looked at her with such innocence, as if to say, "See she does love me, she's nice again."

Here we go again. I felt like a pawn in a chess match.

Delilah started to warm up a bit. After the boat ride she asked if Jeremy wanted to pick something out at the gift shop. He raced there. She didn't even yell at him.

Jeremy had fun picking out a Mickey Mouse and a Figment doll to take home. When we left the shop, Jeremy asked if we could sit for a while. He wanted to put on a show for his mom using his new friends.

Delilah agreed. Jeremy beamed with radiance and gratitude as we watched his skit.

I began to know just how it felt to live with Delilah. Her mood swings and dark times regulated the mood for each and every moment, if you let it. I, as an adult, did my best to step back and detach from her... most of the time. It was difficult to do. Delilah was good at being manipulative.

Jeremy couldn't help himself. He rode out her every wave, hoping, praying his love would melt away her fears. She continuously rejected him. He always continued trying.

We left Epcot as darkness fell. I asked Delilah, "Shall we stop on the way home for dinner? Are you hungry?"

"Fine." She refused to look at me and stared out the window with her arms crossed tightly.

"Can we get pizza, Mommy? Please?"

"Fine," she answered.

We drove around the main strip near our villa and found a quaint little Italian restaurant a few blocks away.

We parked the car and stepped out into the darkness of the evening. The stars were just making themselves visible. Jeremy held the heavy glass door open for both of us. We stood at the hostess station and waited to be seated. It was a cute little family owned restaurant. White miniature carnations and bottles of Chianti added to the decor of the red checkered tablecloths. As the hostess escorted us to our booth, Jeremy engaged her in conversation.

"We just came from the Epcot Center. It was really cool. And we're gonna have my favorite pizza for supper."

"Epcot's a lot of fun. Did you enjoy it?" The hostess leaned over toward Delilah and I and whispered, "He has beautiful eyes."

Delilah ignored her. Jeremy answered, "Thank you. And I had a blast at Epcot."

I slid into the booth and Jeremy followed beside me. But before he could get comfortable, Delilah, standing outside the booth, yanked him out by his shirtsleeve and shoved him into the other side of the booth.

The hostess stood there, stunned. "Your waiter will be right with you. Enjoy your dinner." She raced away from the table.

"Why'd ya do that, Mommy? That hurt me."

"Sit next to me."

The waiter immediately came to the table. "Good evening. My name's Bob. I'll be your server this evening. How are you tonight little fella?" It seemed he had witnessed Delilah's tirade and was doing his best to rescue Jeremy.

"I'm fine. My name's Jeremy. I had fun at Epcot today. Have you ever been there?"

"As a matter of fact, I was there last weekend. It's great, isn't it?" replied Bob, winking at Jeremy.

"Yep, I liked Figment the best. He's awesome!"

"Did you go to the dinosaur exhibit by Exxon?"

"Yep, that was awesome too! I'm gonna order my favorite pizza. Is that okay, Mommy?"

Before Delilah could answer, the waiter asked, "And what kind might that be? No, let me guess... sausage?"

"Extra cheese and sausage," replied Jeremy with a grin. "Okay you guys?"

"Fine," stated Delilah abruptly slamming the menu on the table.

I chimed in, "Sounds good to me."

"How 'bout drinks guys?" asked Bob. "Let me guess. For the prince here, an ice cold glass of milk."

Jeremy burst out laughing. "The prince'll have milk, thanks."

Delilah and I ordered soft drinks. As Bob left the table, I could feel the tension coming from Delilah. Bob had done a good job at distracting Jeremy from the shoving incident. I made a choice not to bring it up, but I vigilantly watched her every move. He quickly returned with our drinks. As Bob left the table, Jeremy sat back and accidentally pulled the tablecloth, spilling his milk. Instinctively, Delilah's elbow raised toward Jeremy's head...

"Wait..." I screamed. Delilah froze.

She grabbed Jeremy by the arm, catapulting him toward the end of the seat.

"Come with me this instant. You're a mess."

My heart beat a mile a minute. My knees became weak. Oh my God, what was her agenda for the bathroom?

"Delilah, it was an accident. Calm down a minute before you take Jeremy anywhere."

She looked at me with daggers in her eyes and stood motionless. Jeremy appeared frightened.

"I didn't mean it, Mommy, I'm sorry."

"Let's go, Jeremy," she yelled, clutching his arm again, yanking him off the seat.

"I'll help," I stated, getting up to chaperone.

"He's my son. I'll handle it alone."

"Remember what I said, Delilah. Don't hurt him."

I wanted to go in after them, against her wishes, but something stopped me. I felt that for issues of trust, I needed to at least give her a chance to show me she wouldn't hurt him.

The bathroom was right behind our booth. If anything happened, I'd hear it and would be there in a second. I waited for what seemed like an eternity, when actually only four minutes had passed. Thank God, he came out in one piece. As Jeremy passed by to climb in his side of the booth, I couldn't help myself. The potential was there for another "whuppin" incident and I wouldn't feel comfortable until I checked him, especially after the last time I messed things up and didn't check. So I reached over and touched his back. Thank God, again, he didn't wince. I began breathing again.

"Why don't you check the rest of him?" Delilah asked with contempt. She shot me a dirty look and spoke in her eerie, calm, controlling voice, the one that sent shivers down my spine. Bad things tended to erupt when she was like this. What could she possibly be holding onto so tightly inside of herself that would cause her to be like an erupting volcano of rage toward her dying son?

We ate our pizza in silence. I, for one, had lost my appetite. Jeremy looked utterly exhausted. We took most of the pizza home. I paid for dinner and left Bob a juicy tip for coming to Jeremy's rescue, to my rescue. Angels comes in all shapes and sizes.

During Jeremy's prayers that night, I heard him whispering, "Please, God, please, you have to help Mommy. Please, I pray that you get through to her. I'm scared, and I don't know what to do. Please, help Robyn to help her. Pretty please, God. I love Mommy, but I don't think she knows how to let any love in her heart. Please, help me and Robyn help her. I love you. God bless Mommy, Robyn, Jim, Toby, Winnie, and Sammy. And God bless Mickey Mouse who we're gonna see tomorrow. And God bless me. Amen." And at the last minute, he added, "Oh yeah God, I'm having lots of fun, too. Thank you. Amen, again."

As I lay there in the bed next to Jeremy's, trying to stop myself from crying so Jeremy wouldn't hear me, I felt so helpless and hopeless. I could feel Jeremy's pain. How much he wanted for his mom to feel love and for everything to be okay.

I silently began to pray, to scream inside, "Why God, why is this happening to Jeremy? I don't understand. Make it stop. He's not safe. She's a bomb ready to explode. How much time does he have? I don't get it, AIDS and this, too? Where are you? You gotta help Jeremy. Make Delilah stop hurting him. Please, help me get through to her and through this."

I turned on my side. Jeremy climbed out of his bed into mine, and asked, "Can you hold me for a little while?"

"Sure, Sweetie, I'd love to."

I cradled him in my arms until we both fell asleep. I eventually placed him gently in his bed.

PART FOUR -- DAY THREE, DISNEY WORLD

Jeremy's most wished for day of the trip had arrived. Mickey Mouse awaited him. As I lay awake in bed, just after dawn, I prayed that Delilah would be able to put aside whatever she was going through from the night before, so she could enjoy herself with Jeremy like she did on the first day of our trip.

Both Jeremy and Delilah still slept, so I showered and got ready for Jeremy's special day. I went for a walk and ended up at the pool where the breakfast buffet had just been set up. I gathered an array of goodies for our breakfast. I brought back fresh squeezed orange juice, blueberry muffins, cantaloupe, strawberries, and other fruits, as well as cereal and milk. I entered an empty kitchen, loaded the goodies from my tray onto the table, and put the teakettle on.

Delilah came out of her bedroom, looking refreshed in her just pressed light blue cotton jumper. She looked right at me but said nothing and sat down at the kitchen table, as if I wasn't even there.

"Good morning, Delilah," I said, smiling, hoping she'd look at me. She shrugged her shoulders and tensed her back. So I repeated, in a more serious tone, "Good morning, Delilah."

Without turning, she mumbled, "Good morning."

I joined her at the table with my cup of tea and filled my plate with fruit and a muffin. I purposely didn't engage with her and opened the morning newspaper. I held it in a position where it blocked our sight of each other. I physically blocked her from my space. I leisurely began reading the front page. It worked.

After a few minutes, she asked, "Is something wrong?"

"Sure seems that way to me."

"What is it?" she asked, as if I was the one with the problem.

"Seems like something's up with you again this morning. You're withdrawing again."

She inhaled deeply and let out a sigh.

"I don't know how else to help you, Delilah."

She fumbled around in her seat, pulling her arms in toward herself, retreating. Her left knee nervously started to bounce up and down.

"Please, tell me how to help you. Every attempt I make to support you and try to help you deal with your mental anguish, you push me away. I'm running out of ideas, and we're running out of time." She shifted her body further from me.

"You asked me if something's wrong. Do you want to talk about it?" I waited for her answer, but got none. I continued, "I don't want things to turn out like they did yesterday. You chose not to share what was happening with you. You snapped when Jeremy spilled his milk. I wasn't sure you were going to control yourself. This scares me, Delilah, you can't continue to handle things this way. It's not working for anyone." I walked toward the window and sat on the couch so that I could see her. She lowered her eyes.

"Please, say something. I'd like to talk about this."

She placed her hand under her chin, remaining silent.

"I know this is hard for you. Please, give it a try. For your sake, your son's sake, and your new baby's sake, you've got to try and open up."

She moved onto the couch, next to me, and began picking at her skirt. "You're right, I can't open up. I don't know how. I'm scared. I've never trusted anyone in my entire life, and you're asking me to tell you my secrets. I'd like to... I just can't."

"What are you scared of?"

"That I'll completely lose it."

"Lose what?"

"Lose control... my mind. I'm scared of what'll come out."

"What's inside can be scary. But can it possibly be more scary than losing control and hurting your son, who is terminally ill?" Her head hung low. "By not sharing what's on the inside, it's forcing you to lose control on the outside."

Shame escaped from deep within her. I felt her self-condemnation.

"I know that you love Jeremy. He loves you very much, too, but he bears the brunt of your anger and rage. You lose it and take whatever's going on with you out on him. He doesn't deserve that, and you deserve to feel better than you do. But if you don't start to make different choices about your behavior, something'll have to give. I'm here to help you. Tell me what I can do."

Blinking away her tears, she answered, "I do love my son. I know I hurt him. This big dark thing comes over me. It takes over. And the next thing I know, I'm hitting him."

"What do you think the big dark thing is?"

"I don't know. I just know it scares me when it takes over. And lately, it's taking over a lot more than ever."

"You mean it's been there before?"

"Oh yeah..."

After over an hour of intensive one-on-one, in which Delilah was completely absorbed, she verbalized the "thing" as her negative feelings; fear about her situation, and rage and hatred toward Jeremy's father and her own stepmother. She still couldn't bring herself to say "AIDS." She elaborated on how she knows she takes her anger and stress out on Jeremy and shocked me when she asked me, "How do I not hit him?"

I felt thrilled by her openness and candidness, but didn't want to overwhelm her with too many suggestions. This was the first time she had ever asked for help.

"If you feel the urge to lash out, hit something, not someone. Pound on the couch, a pillow, beat anything but Jeremy. You could call me, Hannah, Carolyn, even a hotline, and scream as much as you need to until you get out what's bothering you. Separate yourself from Jeremy, give yourself time to pull it together."

Our discussion ended quickly when Jeremy walked in. "Hi you guys! Ya ready to go meet Mickey?"

"How about going later this afternoon," Delilah said, "and playing here this morning after breakfast? We've never explored the other fun things here like the video games..."

"Video games, yippee!" Jeremy jumped with delight, slapping his mom a high five. We all sat at the table and giggled our way through breakfast. I hoped to have more time alone with her later, so we could finish up our talk.

Delilah made a suggestion that we first play on the playground before playing the video games, so we could take pictures of each other.

"Smile," exclaimed Delilah in a silly voice, "say cheeseburger!" Jeremy hammed it up for her, smiling his biggest grin.

"Delilah, how 'bout I take a picture of you and Jeremy with my camera?" I asked.

"Sure." Delilah asked Jeremy to pose with her. He hung on the monkey bars while she pretended to tickle him.

"Can I take one of you and Jeremy?" she asked.

"That'd be great, thanks." After that picture, I asked an older girl, who had been swinging on the swings, to take a picture of all three of us. Delilah stood between Jeremy and me, and we all held hands. Then we pushed each other on the swings and sat at the pool to take a little break. I hoped she'd keep her fun loving side out the rest of the day. For that matter, the rest of her life.

"Anyone want a drink? My treat." Delilah grabbed change from her pocket.

"I do, Mommy...how 'bout a nice Hawaiian punch?" I ran over and gently punched both Delilah and Jeremy on their shoulders. We all laughed.

"Can I go play video games now, Mommy?"

She turned toward me and asked, "Would you mind if I take a nap? I'm really tired. Could you take him please?"

"Sure. Are you okay?"

"I'm just tired."

"See ya later, Mommy. Have a nice rest so we can have fun meeting Mickey!" After playing several games of Pacman and pinball, Jeremy and I returned to our villa for lunch. We heated up the leftover pizza and both fell asleep while watching Bambi. Delilah woke us both up at 3:00 to get ready for Disney World. It didn't take us long to get there. Upon arriving, we didn't go to the hospitality suite as we could have, Jeremy was too excited. He didn't want to waste any time. We got a map and rode the trolley toward the Kiddie Park.

Spontaneity was the call for the day. When Jeremy saw Space Mountain, he had to ride it.

"Come on, Mommy, let's all ride."

"No thanks, Jeremy, you and Robyn go. I don't like roller-coasters." Good thing, because when we got up to the front, the sign warned pregnant women not to ride.

Jeremy and I rode together and had a contest who could scream the loudest during the ride. Jeremy won. After the ride, as we met up with Delilah, Jeremy announced, "I have to use the bathroom. Mommy, can I please go in the men's by myself? I'll be super careful."

"No," she snapped, "Come in the women's with us. This is a big place." So we all filed into the huge women's rest room. Jeremy and Delilah went into the room on the left and I stayed in the room on the right, near the sinks.

While in the stall, the sound of a child's blood curdling scream filled my ears, penetrating throughout my entire body, sending shivers down my spine.

Then it registered. *Oh my God, it's Jeremy.*

I burst out of the stall, barely put together. Jeremy came ripping around the corner with blood dripping off his face.

"Mommy hurt me," he managed to get out between sobs and gasps of breath.

He was shaking, heaving to catch his breath. He had the wind knocked out of him. Delilah came around the corner behind him, shaking her index finger at him, "Jeremy, don't listen to me one more time and see what you get." She had a look in her eyes I had never seen before. Deep, deep hatred. Venom.

It happened so fast. I felt like rubber.

Oh God, help me.

I didn't have my damn gloves. So I grabbed some paper towels and handed them to Jeremy. He placed them on his face. I knelt down and held him. I felt like vomiting.

I looked at Delilah and said, "You will not touch, hurt, or threaten him. We will discuss this after Jeremy's cleaned up."

I led Jeremy to the sink and stood between them. Delilah began helping him.

Should I call the police? Do I call their child welfare people? Dear God, what should I do. Please God, help me do the right thing.

The blood gushed out of Jeremy's nose. He had to lie down on the bathroom floor with his head back for awhile to get it to stop. He gagged from the blood that dripped down his throat. A distinct welt of Delilah's handprint covered the entire right side of his face. I wadded up a bunch of paper towels, ran them under the cold water and handed them to Jeremy to hold on it. People moved away from us.

When he was cleaned up, we silently walked out of the restroom right into Goofy, who stood at the door. He seemed to be waiting for us. Jeremy pulled himself together, took a deep breath, and grabbed Goofy's hand. Goofy picked him up, hugged him, and twirled him around.

I took Delilah aside. "What happened in there? What did you do?" I cried out as my voice cracked with emotion.

"He wouldn't listen to me," she stated, trying to stare me down, with her hand placed on her hip.

"Tell me exactly what happened."

"When we went to the other side of the restroom, I found two empty stalls next to each other. I told him to go in the stall next to mine. He disobeyed me and went into another one. So I followed him in and locked the door. I slapped him. He fell down and bumped his head."

Before she finished her sentence, Jeremy came over, grabbed my hand tightly, cowering behind me. I felt him tremble. When she finished her sentence, I turned toward him and knelt down.

"I'm really sorry that this happened, Buddy. Do you want to talk about it?"

"Yeah," he answered, glaring at Delilah with his eyes squinted.

"It's all right," I responded, "go on."

"I wanted to go in the boy's bathroom by myself, but she wouldn't let me. So when I went into my own toilet in the girl's bathroom and tried to close the door, she busted in after me and hit me so hard I got knocked down. I whacked my head and tummy on the toilet really hard. I'm really scared, Robyn, she hurt me real bad." Then he motioned for me to bend down toward him. When I did, he whispered into my ear, "Ya gotta help Mommy, Robyn, ya just gotta."

"I will, Buddy," I whispered softly in his ear, "I will."

He kind of fell into me and surrendered as I held him in my arms, and he sobbed and trembled. When his body stopped heaving, and he was ready to get up, I tried to get up with him. My legs felt like rubber. I found it hard to stand and walk.

"Let's get something to drink," I announced. I needed time to think, to sort out what had just happened. I still didn't know, professionally, what I was supposed to do. If we were home, I would have called the police and made a hotline report.

So I stayed close to Jeremy to help him feel as safe as possible. I stood between them, using my body as a shield to protect him *from his own mother*. Delilah stood in line for our drinks. I found a bench to sit on in a quiet, somewhat secluded spot, although I didn't want it too secluded. People stood in line at another attraction about 50 feet away.

"Jeremy, can you come here for a minute, please?"

I walked him over to a flower garden at the right of the bench. "Would you please drink your pop here? I need to talk to your mom privately for a few minutes."

"Are you gonna be right there, Robyn?" He pointed to the bench.

"Yes, Sweetie, I'll be right there."

"Good. I'll be okay." He took a sip of his pop, placed it on the concrete ledge that circled the garden, and began skipping around the flowerbed. I watched as he stopped and bent down to smell a pink rose. A little girl approached him. I overheard him say, "Hi, I'm Jeremy. What's your name?"

I sat next to Delilah, trying hard to regain my composure at least enough to talk to her in a sufficiently low voice, so Jeremy couldn't hear.

How could she do this?

As I turned to face her, she stared blankly at me. It was as though she had an empty shell inside. I tried to remain as professional as I possibly could, although my voice shook. No training in the world could have prepared me for this. I spoke quickly, purging the words out from my body.

"You need help desperately. Your abusive behavior is very serious. You cannot continue to act like this and hurt your son.

Something is very wrong here and it is with your behavior and actions, not his. If you don't change immediately and stop hitting and hurting Jeremy, you will lose him. Do you understand? He will be taken from your custody. Our agency has been instructed to assist you in every way possible to help you remain together. Your actions make it impossible for me to support keeping you together. I do not trust that Jeremy is safe with you. Either you accept our help and start making changes, or this opportunity will be taken away. Stop hurting him, now!"

I didn't wait for her response. I got up and approached Jeremy. I kneeled down and looked into his eyes. "Hi."

"Hi," he replied.

"You okay, Little Buddy?"

"Yeah. I made a new friend. But she had to go. She's coming back in a little while to go on the spaceship ride."

"This ride right here?" I asked, pointing behind us.

"Yep."

"That's nice. Need more cold towels or anything?"

"I'm okay. Robyn?"

"What Little Buddy?"

"I'm scared. Something's really wrong. Mommy doesn't act like this. Please, you have to help her. She needs your help. Promise me you'll help her." He started to cry and reached for me. I held him tightly. My tears were for his compassion and love for her.

As I held him, I prayed. *He's only six years old. Why God, Why? I don't understand. Where are you in all of this? No adult should have to go through such pain, never mind a kid dying from AIDS. Please, help us.*

Jeremy stepped back from our hug and looked over toward his mom. She had her back turned from us as she sipped her drink. I looked back at him and asked, "What would you like to do now, Sweetie? If you feel like leaving, we can. Or we can stay if you want. You be the boss."

"Oh no, we can't go yet. We haven't seen Mickey. And we have to go on more kiddie rides, and my friend is coming back to go on the spaceship thing. Look, there she is! Can we go on the spaceship now? Please?"

77

"Sure, Sweetie, whatever you want to do. We'll make the rest of this day extra special, deal?"

"Yeah, yeah, yeah," he answered doing his impersonation of Ernie, from Sesame Street, "let's go."

He grabbed my hand and skipped toward the entrance. He stopped on a dime, turned around, looked at his mom and asked, "Could you ask her to come with?"

A small line of people had formed at the entrance. Jeremy's friend saw him and waved. When Delilah and I approached Jeremy, he looked her straight in the eyes, grabbed my hand tightly and said with confidence, "Mommy, you hurt me bad. Don't ever do that again. You shouldn't act that way, Mommy. You have to let Robyn help you."

Looking him back in the eyes, Delilah answered softly, "I'm sorry, Jeremy. I don't know what comes over me." She lowered her head to hide her tears. The line began to move and we boarded the spaceship.

Jeremy sat next to his friend, and I sat between he and Delilah. I had a little time to think. In my fury, I told Delilah she would lose Jeremy if she continued to behave violently. In reality, I had no way of knowing what might happen. You would think that I'd be able to say, with confidence, he'd be removed from her custody, but I couldn't. The state could keep Jeremy safe by placing him in protective custody, but I didn't have a lot of assurance in their doing so. So far, there was still no "founded" evidence on record against Delilah. And to top it off, the state had just been on one of those prime time newsmagazine shows where it was scrutinized publicly for its inadequacies. Neither Shauna, his caseworker from the state, nor I had the power to remove him directly. Only a police officer or a member of the Child Protection Team from the state could physically remove him.

If our team did want to have him removed, Shauna would have to bring the case to court with evidence as to why she thought Jeremy needed to be placed in protective custody. Then it would depend upon which judge the case was assigned and what his/her philosophy and views were on keeping families together, or on removing a child. But unfortunately, to play by the rules, his case would only go to court when there were "founded" incidences of abuse and/or neglect. His "falling" out of a second story window was unfounded - no witnesses. His school made a child abuse hotline report when he had the big welt under his eye. That was handled by putting a rush on our agency's involvement with them; another unfounded incident. And I messed up and didn't call the time I made a visit and Jeremy couldn't sit down because Delilah beat him with a belt when he urinated. And now she beats him up at Disney World, out of the jurisdiction of our state. Delilah knew just how to work the system and the people in it, to not get caught.

Here I am, literally "the agency," trying my hardest to help Delilah stop hurting Jeremy and this happens. Now what were they going to do? I couldn't guarantee that they would do anything to keep him safe and protected. And the only way he would be safe was if he was removed from her custody. She could be lethal. She was not making any attempts to change her way of coping other than by lashing out and hurting him.

Jeremy tapped my leg. The spaceship had landed. Back to reality. The black cloud I felt surrounding Jeremy's situation was becoming unbearably thick and heavy. I felt so alone, like it was me against the world. I had promised Jeremy that I'd keep him safe, and I would continue to hold myself accountable. I wasn't sure how my vow would unfold at this point, but I knew it absolutely had to. Jeremy had to be safe and protected for whatever time he had left. The Bible says that if you only have the faith of a mustard seed, you can move mountains. I clung to my faith and prayed out of desperation for a mustard seed.

All of Jeremy's wishes for being at Disney World came true later in the day. He met Mickey and rode the kiddie rides. I had to wonder on some level, if maybe things were supposed to happen this way. I got to experience first hand just how out of control Delilah really was.

We left the park and went to Red Lobster for a late dinner. Delilah was on her best behavior. She poured on the pleasantries, trying to mask her guilt. Jeremy repeated a couple of times, "You hurt me, Mommy, real bad today. Please, don't ever do that again." Whenever he would get me by myself, he begged me to help her.

To passersby, we appeared to be having a normal dinner together. How insane. I felt like a ping-pong ball, being slammed here and slammed there, with no end in sight.

We returned to our villa for the night and immediately went to bed. Jeremy didn't say his prayers. He was so exhausted. He fell asleep as soon as his head hit his pillow. After I heard silence from Delilah's room, I went into the living room and called Jim. I couldn't stop sobbing. Jim was wonderfully supportive. I was so scared for Jeremy. I did not trust Delilah in the least bit. Jim and I agreed that I needed to call my supervisor first thing in the morning. He gave me her home phone number.

I barely slept, tossing and turning, ruminating over the day's events. It wasn't even near the end of our trip. We had three long days left. How in the world would I ever get through this? And what about poor Jeremy? My first instinct was to go home, but we couldn't. For one thing, Jeremy would never have another chance to fulfill his wish. And more important was the fact that Jeremy would continue to be in Delilah's custody, even after we returned home. At least staying in Florida would give her a few more days to cool off. If we returned home early, Delilah might have been further angered, thus increasing his risk for abuse.

I decided that I could handle the rest of the trip. I had to. I felt that I had no other choice or anywhere else I could turn.

PART FIVE -- DAY FOUR, BUSCH GARDENS

I woke early the next morning, feeling like I hadn't slept at all. I took a long hot shower, hoping it would help lift the heaviness around and within me. I got dressed and entered a quiet living room. The clock read 6:03. As I peered out the front window, the sunlight created a beautiful rainbow on the grass out of the morning dew. The mom in the next villa was out in her jogging suit picking up her morning newspaper.

In the peacefulness of the moment, I was suddenly filled with an all-encompassing sadness for Jeremy and a rage toward Delilah. I couldn't stand it. I had to get out of there. I felt like I would jump out of my skin. I went for a walk.

The warmth of the morning air brushed my face as I walked hard and fast, hoping my feelings would dissipate. Instead, they intensified. I stopped and looked all around me. I was in the midst of a community, built out of love, specifically to bring happiness to dying children and their families, and this had to happen. I tried to step back from my feelings for the moment, for my own mental health. I breathed in the peacefulness of the dawn. The sound of birds chirping and the sweet scent of beautiful flowering gardenias and jasmine filled me. As far as my eyes could see, beauty enveloped me, inviting me to partake of it with all of my senses. It really did look and feel like paradise. The enormity of the villas, the whole purpose of the community was to "Give Kids the World."

Then my mind wandered back to Jeremy. I continued walking toward the pond. My heart was overcome with loss. All along I had said that the only way to prevent Jeremy from being abused by

81

Delilah was to be with him 24 hours a day. Now that I was, it still didn't make a difference. I still couldn't protect him.

I found a secluded spot near the pond and sat down. I began pounding on the sandy grass as hard as I could, talking out loud, saying what I really wanted to say to Delilah, "How can you do this? He's your son for God's sake. He has AIDS. You can't hurt him anymore…" My body shook with anguish as I pounded harder on the ground. I redirected my anger to God and sobbed, "How could you let this happen during his last wish, God? Where are you in all of this? I keep wondering where you are and why you're letting us down…"

I cried until I had no more tears to shed. Slowly, I became aware of my surroundings again. I took several deep breaths. The silence of the morning was astounding. I stood up and walked to the edge of the water. I collected a handful of pebbles from the sand and started skipping them across the pond. I watched, as the ripples of water grew larger and larger until they disappeared. In the stillness of the moment, I felt as though the Universe was holding me, comforting me, trying to refuel me and give me enough strength to go back and deal with the reality I had to face. Jeremy's reality.

I spotted two young boys carrying fishing poles, who had walked around to the other end of the pond. They definitely were brothers. I watched as the older one set up their fishing gear. The younger one waved to me. I waved back.

I walked to the playground and sat on a swing, thinking about these two boys. How lucky they were to have each other. Their innocence, their freedom, and of course, I became angered again when I thought, *why can't Jeremy have that?*

I whispered a prayer for strength, wisdom, and the energy to finish out the trip. I prayed for Jeremy's protection, and I sat and thought up a plan for the day. The first night of the trip, Delilah, Jeremy, and I talked about going to Busch Gardens in Tampa and possibly spending the night at my mom's on Clearwater Beach. We had also thrown around other options like MGM Studios and the water park. I had asked Mom, before the trip, if we could stay with her a night. She said she'd be delighted to see us.

That was it, I made my decision. We'd spend our last two days visiting Mom. God knows I needed her support to make it through the rest of the trip.

We'd spend the day at Busch Gardens, sleep at Mom's, and play at the beach the next day. I was sure Jeremy would love it and frankly, I didn't care what Delilah wanted at that point. I was going to do my best to ensure that Jeremy was safe and that his last few days were the most fun yet.

I walked back to the pond. The boys were still fishing on the other side of the water. They waved again. I waved back. A mother duck watched ever so carefully as her four fluffy babies plopped into the water. Several turtles leisurely swam the breaststroke in the bright morning sun.

When I felt ready, I walked back to our villa. I opened the door to find Delilah ironing. The minute I saw her, my heart raced again and my angry feelings came back hot and heavy.

"Good morning," she said in a friendly manner, as though nothing had happened. She didn't look up from her ironing.

I didn't want to answer her, but I forced myself to. "Hi," I breathed almost inaudibly. I couldn't look at her.

"Did you sleep well?" she asked.

"No." I walked away and went in to look in on Jeremy. At least he slept soundly. The clock read 7:51. I walked back into the living room.

I sat down in the overstuffed living room chair and picked up a magazine. I couldn't concentrate. I put it down. What I really felt like doing was going over and shaking Delilah by the throat and screaming, "What are you doing? Don't you get it?" So I asked myself if I should go heart to heart with her one more time. I had nothing to lose. I looked right at her and announced, "We have to talk." I had to look away. I was too uncomfortable making eye contact with her.

She stopped ironing, but remained standing in the same place.

"Look, Delilah, I'm really having a lot of difficulty with all of this. You say you want my help, you say you want to keep your son and you want to work things out differently and then you go and hit him so hard, your hand is imprinted on his face. I don't believe you anymore. I don't believe you want to change or that you want to handle things any differently. If you did, you'd stop hurting him. Your actions speak very loudly." I surprised myself when I stopped and heard the quiet in the room. I realized I'd been screaming at her.

83

"Well," she responded, "I'm trying...."

"Trying isn't going to cut it. This is your son's life we're talking about. Either you hit him or you don't. It's that simple. There is no trying not to hit him. You make a choice each time, to hit him or not. You have to control yourself. That's all there is to it. If you don't, you will lose your son. Did you hear me? I said you will lose Jeremy."

I didn't even stop to see how she was reacting to me. I was so furious with her, at that moment I didn't care about her response. I wasn't responding as her social worker, I screamed at her from my gut, from one human being to another.

In the silence of the room, the last words I pronounced echoed in my mind in slow motion... `you will lose your son'. They hit me hard. Then I looked at her. Her mouth hung open, her eyes forlorn. My heart sank.

My emotions shifted. I felt flutters in my chest, and my anger melted. I had to blink hard to fight my tears. "Look, Delilah, I care about you very much. I don't like the actions you are choosing. I know you're hurting too, but you have to accept help. Now. You can't do this alone without things getting worse and I can't sit back and wait, hoping you'll change. We don't have time. Your behavior is too out of control, and your son is too ill!" And with that, I stormed out, slamming the door behind me.

I got in the car and took off to find a pay phone. I needed Jim, and I had to call my supervisor.

I spotted a pay phone a few blocks down the road in front of a small hotel. It was attached to the front of the building, a few feet from the entrance. I pulled over. I dug through my purse trying to find my calling card, but I had blurred vision from my tears.

Finally. There it is. Jim...Help me...

I frantically dialed all the damn numbers. When I heard Jim's voice, I broke down again.

"Did something else happen?" he asked softly.

"No. I can't do this. It's too hard, it's too much for me."

Just then, a car pulled up to the hotel entrance. I squeezed myself between the phone and its glass enclosure, retreating from the outside world.

Jim stayed silent for a while and let me cry. "Everything's gonna work out, Robyn. We'll get through this one together. Somehow, we'll see Jeremy through 'til the end."

"I couldn't sleep last night, I'm so afraid for him, Jim. I don't know what else to do to get through to her. I want to whisk Jeremy up and run as far away from her as I possibly can. How can I protect him if he still lives with her?"

"You'll have to make the system work for him. I'm sure you have enough evidence to take into court and get him removed from her. Maybe that's why this happened."

"That thought had crossed my mind."

"And you know what Sally always says, 'God can do anything. God is all-powerful, and what we live with here is just an illusion. Look beyond the veil and see and know that God will do the work and prevail.'" Sally is our wonderful minister, who taught us to meditate, "Praying is talking to God, meditating is listening."

"You're right." We were both quiet. "Thanks, I needed some inspiration. I came to the right place. I better call Connie and tell her what happened and see what she wants me to do."

After promising Jim I would call him back, we said our good-byes. I called Connie.

Thankfully, she was home. When I began telling her what had happened, I couldn't help it, I started to cry again. I felt so raw. She responded by saying, "I wouldn't have imagined she'd do this on the trip. Did something happen that may have triggered her striking him?" I picked up an accusing tone in her voice.

What's she getting at here? I started to pace back and forth as far as the phone cord would allow.

"No, Connie, nothing happened. Delilah said it was because he didn't listen to her. My goodness, Connie, she left a welt of her handprint on his face. I managed to get a picture of him standing next to Goofy shortly after it happened, in case we needed some evidence. I didn't know what to do. I thought of calling the police, but decided not to. So we finished out the day, and I got your number from Jim late last night, but it was too late to call you."

"You did the right thing. Try to keep them separated as much as possible. Do you think you'll be able to finish the rest of the trip?"

"I'll do it."

"Good. If you need anything, call me. Otherwise, when you get back, we'll schedule a meeting with the caseworker and our liaison, and decide what we need to do. Hang in there."

I called Jim back. I told him what Connie had said. I felt better. At least Connie knew about it now. It wasn't all on my shoulders any more. I thanked Jim for his help and hung up.

When I got in the car, I started to pray. "Heavenly Father, Mother God, I pray for Divine Order to reign over this situation. Please continue to protect Jeremy with legions of your guardian angels and continue to show me the way to help them. Please, help me get through the rest of this trip. Thank you. Amen."

I drove back to the villa. Jeremy was sitting at the table eating a bowl of Cheerios with banana slices in it. "Hi, Robyn! Where'd ya go?"

"I had to make a couple of phone calls. How are you doing this morning?"

"Fine. What are we gonna do today?"

"Well, how'd you like to spend the day at Busch Gardens in Tampa and sleep over at my mom's? Remember I told…."

And before I could finish my thought, he broke in, "Yeah, yeah, yeah!" He answered with his familiar "Ernie" impersonation. "Can we swim at the beach and in her pool? Please, Mommy, can we go?"

Delilah looked at me. I turned away from her. Thank goodness, she said, "Yes."

"YIPPEE!" shouted Jeremy as he danced all around the kitchen singing, "We're going to Nanny's house. We're going to Nanny's house, hip hip hooray!"

I had talked about my mom when we were planning the Make - A - Wish trip and referred to her as Nanny. That's what my niece called her. Jeremy remembered.

I immediately called Mom. I told her we'd be there around dinnertime. She sounded excited that we were coming, I hadn't seen her in almost a year. She added that she heard something wrong in my voice, though.

We packed an overnight bag and headed for Busch Gardens. It didn't take as long to get there as I thought it would. Delilah acted especially nice and accommodating during the ride there. She asked,

"There's lots of animals at Busch Gardens, Jeremy, should we get more film for our camera?"

She turned to me and said, "Didn't you say you wanted to bring back something for Jim? I bet you'll find a nice shirt or something there...."

Busch Gardens is very different from the Disney scene, less crowded and much earthier. It's famous for its natural animal settings. The people are contained, and the animals are free to roam within an extremely large area. They have a train that drives around the perimeter of the park, so you can see all of the animals. As we rode the train, Jeremy stared at all of the animals with his mouth gaping. When we exited and started walking around, Jeremy suddenly became a little scientist, reading all of the signs, fascinated by the animals. He studied their movements and talked about their interrelatedness with each other and their environment.

The white tiger cub mesmerized him as it romped with its mother under a waterfall while chasing a huge blue ball. Jeremy could have watched them for hours. Twice we wandered back to the mom and cub. For some reason, Jeremy didn't want to leave them.

We made it in time to see the zookeepers giving the elephants a bath. Bubbles floated past us in the air. Jeremy wanted an elephant ride, but the line was too long and he looked like he was ready to collapse. We walked to the next concession stand to get him a drink and take a little rest, although he didn't want to stop.

Next, we rode the train to the kiddie rides. Jeremy rode every ride there. The airplanes, bumper cars, and remote control boats were his favorites. The three of us went on the Congo River Rapids ride together and got soaked.

Jeremy and I rode the flume ride three times in a row while Delilah waited patiently for us to finish. On most other occasions, she would have insisted that Jeremy control himself and only go on once, if she let him go on at all. We took turns to see who could scream the loudest, while splashing each other as our log crashed down into the water. I momentarily lost my voice. Jeremy won.

Strange looking black and white screeching monkeys inhabited a large cage as we exited the flume ride. Jeremy had a blast screeching back to them. When one of the monkeys picked at the other, Jeremy picked at me. As the baby monkey cuddled up with its mommy, Jeremy cuddled with me. We stood for a long while, while he enjoyed imitating them. Delilah sat at a picnic table just behind us, smiling. For once, Jeremy acted like a normal kid, and neither he nor I were fearful of her response. I think she knew I had had enough.

The park closed at dusk. On our way out, I called my mom and told her we'd be there in about an hour. As we drove to her condo, Jeremy and Delilah fell asleep. I felt exhausted too, but greatly relieved.

Mom knew exactly how to be with small children — she wasn't afraid of acting like a kid herself. As we walked in the door, she swept Jeremy off of his feet, tickling him until she heard belly laughter. She greeted Delilah politely and with respect.

"You and Jeremy can have my room, it's bigger and has its own bath. I put fresh linens on the bed."

Mom always let me sleep in the spare bedroom when I visited. I have fond memories of that room. My mom nursed my dad in that room up until the day he died. He had prostate cancer that had metastasized to his bones, which is extremely painful. I remember having to be careful when I sat on his bed. That never stopped Dad from inviting me to do so, so we could snuggle each time I visited.

Once we settled in, we went to Bob Evans for dinner. Jeremy sat next to Mom, who recited just about every nursery rhyme and riddle that Mother Goose had ever written. She had Jeremy laughing so hard, other tables joined in. His giggles were contagious.

As Mom began reciting, "Tweedle deedle dumpling, my son…" Jeremy piped in saying "Jeremy." Then Delilah added the next sentence, "Went to bed with one wet herring." We cracked up. Jeremy shared Mom's coffee and catfish, even drinking from her cup. I was so relieved to be with her.

Delilah scolded Jeremy for asking Mom so many questions during dinner. Mom gracefully replied, "Oh Delilah, don't worry about Jeremy. He's fine. I'll keep an eye on him. Sit back and enjoy yourself with Robyn, I'm sure you must be exhausted from the long day." Delilah appeared to be responding well to Mom's suggestions and requests. She liked the attention so much; in fact, she seemed to be eating it up. Mom had such a big heart when it came to the underdog and to children. I knew she would do whatever she could to not only help Jeremy and Delilah, but me as well.

On the way home, Mom and Jeremy sat in the back seat and tickled each other the entire time. As we passed Clearwater's public beach, about a block before my parent's condo, Mom yelled, "Stop the car, please Robyn."

I immediately pulled over and turned around to see what was going on. "What's wrong?" "Nothing. I just want to get out. I'm taking Jeremy for a walk on the beach in the moonlight. Take your shoes off if you want to Jeremy, I'm taking mine off and rolling up my pants. Let's go wade in the Gulf."

"Yahoo!" Jeremy squealed as they jumped out of the car.

Thank you, Mom, I thought to myself. *What a treat for both of them.* Jeremy needed to have fun, and feel safe and loved. I knew he'd feel all of those things with Mom. Once we were inside the condo, I made tea for Delilah and I. We sat on the balcony looking at the moon's reflection on the Gulf of Mexico. We sipped our tea in silence, relaxing.

"Your mom's pretty neat," Delilah said with a wishful sigh.

"Thanks. She is."

"I'm glad we're here."

"You are?" I asked, raising an eyebrow. "Why is that?"

"It's really nice here. I get to see where you used to live and meet part of your family. It makes me feel like you think I'm important and that you still care." I could tell by her tone of voice, that this was another test.

"What do you mean by that?"

"Well, sometimes I get the feeling that I'm not important and no one cares about me. It seemed like you cared, but sometimes I'm not so sure."

"When are you unsure about it?"

"When you tell me that I'm disciplining my son wrong, that I'm hurting him."

"I can understand how you might feel that way. A parent's way of disciplining their child is very personal. But when it turns toward what the law defines as abuse, it makes it a public issue. I'm sure it's uncomfortable for you to hear me talk about this, but it doesn't mean that I don't care about you."

Delilah stood up and walked over to the railing, keeping her back to me.

"The truth is, I care deeply for you and for Jeremy. I wouldn't be involved with you if I didn't. It tears me up to watch what you're going through. If you'd only start opening up and handling things differently, you'd have someone to be with you through this whole thing. I want to help you."

Again, nothing but silence. She fidgeted with her sandal.

"Things will become more difficult as the disease progresses. This could be a very special time for you and Jeremy to share with each other. You could become closer than ever. But it won't happen if you continue to make choices that isolate and hurt Jeremy."

I stood up and joined her at the railing. The sky was lit by what looked like a million twinkling lights. The sound of the waves soothed my soul. It was perfectly tranquil. A red light from a late night fishing boat could be seen in the distance.

Delilah remained quiet, although her expression changed. Her face became softer, more relaxed.

Just then, Jeremy and Mom burst in the door singing "E-i-e-i-o. And on his farm…"

"Hi, guys," I yelled, "we're out here."

I turned to Delilah and said, "If there's anything else you'd like to talk about, we can…."

Jeremy answered by yelling, "Do we have to come out there? Nanny promised she'd show me pictures of you when you were little." He came running out to the balcony to tease me. "She said you were really cute."

"Oh yes, Jeremy," I teased back, feeling somewhat embarrassed, "a heart throb." Delilah laughed. Jeremy ran back into Mom's room, jumped onto the bed, and watched anxiously as Mom pulled our old family photo albums down from the closet. Delilah joined him on the bed as I stood, watching from the doorway. I felt pretty vulnerable, unsure if I wanted to join with them. Part of me felt kind of angry with Mom for not asking me if it'd be okay. I walked out, onto the balcony, for a breath of fresh air. I could hear them laughing and carrying on all the way outside. Jeremy's laughter melted through my defensiveness and made me want to join in their fun. When I walked into the bedroom, Jeremy and Delilah were lying on their stomachs looking at my old drawing from sixth grade art class; a cocker spaniel puppy, with a bow around its neck, sitting in a wrapped Christmas box. I could see Mom's pride as she carefully pulled out each item to share. Delilah and Jeremy ate it up. I joined them on the bed as we strolled down memory lane until late into the evening.

I looked at my watch around 10:00 p.m. and stood up to stretch. "I'm gonna hit the sack," I said yawning. "This has been great, but I'm exhausted."

"I really enjoyed myself, too. Thanks for including me in the fun. Good night." Delilah reached her hand toward mine.

"How 'bout a hug?" I asked.

"I'd like that." Jeremy came rushing in from the kitchen, saw us hugging, and winked at me as he slid past and jumped onto the bed. Jeremy and Mom joined in our hug and we all said good night. Delilah closed their bedroom door.

I got my pajamas on and stepped out onto the balcony. Mom went into the kitchen and made tea. She brought us both out a cup.

"What's going on, Little One? You look like you've been through hell." She sat down and stroked my forehead.

"I have, Mom, I have."

"Tell me what happened."

As I explained the trauma we'd all been through, Mom held me and continued to smooth my hair like she always did when I was a kid, whispering "There now, there now, it's all right." As I gasped for breath between sobs, she whispered, "He's safe while he's here. Not to worry. Shhh...Everything's going to work out."

I was home, safe in her arms.

"I have an idea," she said.

"What?"

"If you don't have any plans for tomorrow, you and Jeremy could go to the kiddie pool next door at the Holiday Inn. Since our pool is being fixed, we have permission to use theirs. I'll stay here with Delilah, so you can have a bit of a break. Anyway, Delilah has been very pleasant around me. Maybe she would like to spend some time alone without Jeremy."

"Are you sure you wanna do that, Mom?"

"I'm sure. But what do you think? Would Delilah go for it?"

"Go for it, are you kidding?"

"I can handle her. That way, you and Jeremy can have a little fun."

"Sounds great, thanks. I really appreciate you letting me bring Jeremy and Delilah here."

"Just doing my part, that's all."

"Good night, Mom. Sure you don't want to sleep in Daddy's room? I can sleep on the couch."

"No, Sweetie, I'll be fine on the couch. Good night. I love you."

"Love you, too."

I fell asleep as soon as my head hit the comfort of my dad's pillow.

PART SIX -- DAY FIVE, CRABBY BILL'S

The sun shined brightly through the closed mini-blinds of my room as I climbed out of bed the next morning. I put Mom's robe on and walked into the living room. Mom and Delilah were already dressed and out on the balcony drinking tea. They were enjoying each other's company, talking and laughing.

"May I join you?" I asked, not wanting to intrude.

"Of course," answered Mom, "Good morning, Angel."

"Good Morning." I kissed her on the cheek.

"Good morning, Robyn," said Delilah cheerfully. She sat next to Mom. She looked especially radiant and beautiful. She wore an immaculate, freshly pressed light purple, Victorian looking cotton jumper, which had a lace petticoat underneath. Her face appeared more relaxed than ever. She had styled her hair into a French braid, which accentuated the top of her head, almost like a crown. She looked vibrant.

"Good morning," I responded. "Don't you look beautiful this morning! How'd ya sleep?"

"Very well, thanks, how about you?" She was blushing.

"Like a log," I responded, yawning, "thanks."

Mom rubbed my back then went into the kitchen to make a fresh pot of tea. Another magnificent sunny morning, not a cloud in the sky. The air smelled fresh and salty as a northerly breeze blew a touch of cool morning air. Sailboats filled the Gulf. Just then, three dolphins peeked their heads out of the water, swimming in unison. Delilah and I stood at the railing and took turns watching them with Mom's binoculars. "What a great way to start the day! I've never seen anything like it," said Delilah.

93

Jeremy came out and joined us. "You should've seen, Jeremy, there were three dolphins swimming by a couple of minutes ago. Look over in that direction." Delilah pointed toward the public beach.

Mom came back out with the tea, gave Jeremy a big squeeze, and invited him to help her cook breakfast. Delilah and I shared the morning paper, sipping tea in the warmth of the sun.

In no time, Jeremy and Mom brought out the goodies; cinnamon French toast, bacon, and fresh squeezed orange juice.

"What are we gonna do today, Nanny?" asked Jeremy, while he shoveled in a bite of French toast, dripping with butter and syrup.

"Why don't you and Robyn go play in the kiddie pool next door? Your mom and I will spend the day here, relaxing together, if she wants to, that is." Mom looked over at Delilah who had been absorbing her every word.

"I'd like that." Delilah answered, smiling.

Thank you, Mom!

"Look!" Jeremy stood up so fast, he knocked his chair over. The dolphins had turned around and were swimming back toward us. Delilah picked up the chair and smiled, then joined him at the railing and adjusted the binoculars for him. No elbows flying this time.

"How about if we go to Crabby Bill's for a late lunch before you guys have to take off for Orlando?" asked Mom.

"Sounds like a great idea!" I said.

Mom walked over to Delilah and said, "It's Robyn's favorite restaurant. They have their own fleet of fishing boats and serve the freshest seafood in town. Do you like fish, Delilah?"

"I like shrimp."

"Great," replied Mom, "they have quite an assortment to choose from. And it's fun, too. You sit at large picnic tables, which you share with other people."

"Hey, Mom, remember the time we ordered blue crabs?" I said laughing.

"How could I forget. Robyn was hammering away at one, and a piece of it flew off and hit a man at the other end of our table. It's a great way to meet people."

"Sounds fine," said Delilah.

"Can we go to the pool now, Robyn. Is it okay, Mommy? Please?" Jeremy began anxiously jumping up and down.

94

"When Robyn's ready to take you," answered Delilah.

"Let's go get our suits on," I answered. "Race ya!" Jeremy and I took off toward our bedrooms.

While we changed into our bathing suits, Mom packed a thermos of cranraspberry juice, blew up the raft and beach ball, and brought out my niece's old sand toys. We were ready! We needed to be back around 1:00 to get ready for Crabby Bill's before it got too crowded. Jeremy gave Delilah a kiss, then Mom. Off we went.

We walked to the Holiday Inn, next door to Mom's condo. After securing two chairs by the kiddie pool, we threw our stuff down, grabbed the bucket and shovel, and went for a walk on the beach. We walked toward the Sand Key Bridge, a favorite fishing spot. It's the only way out to the Gulf of Mexico from Tampa Bay, so there are always a lot of boats and people fishing above from the bridge and below from the beach.

As we walked on the hot white sand, Jeremy commented. "I smell coconuts and something else in the air. What is it? It smells yummy."

"It's the smell of the salt water from the Gulf mixed with suntan lotion."

"I'll always remember it. I like it. This is fun!" He ran underneath my legs and dove into the sand.

"Sure is, Jeremy." At that very moment, an elderly man just ahead of us reeled in a sea turtle on his fishing pole.

"Look, Robyn," Jeremy pointed, "a turtle! Can we go see?" He ran toward the man holding the pole. "Wow! I've never seen anyone catch a turtle before. They're my favorite. Teenage Mutant Ninja Turtles, Raphael, Donatello, Leonardo, Michaelangelo," he said laughing as he gently punched my shoulder.

He asked the man, "How'd he get here?"

"He lives in the Gulf. Lots of creatures live there."

"Like what else?"

"There are so many different kinds of fish. Sharks, dolphins, blow fish...."

"Blow fish?" Jeremy asked, "What's that?"

"It's a really neat fish that knows how to protect himself, so he won't get hurt. He blows himself up like a big ball with really sharp spikes, which makes him hard to handle, or eat if you were another fish looking for dinner."

"So he's safe?"

"That's right, young man. You're not from around here, are you?"

"Nope. I'd sure like to be! I love it here. My friend Nanny lives here. We're just visiting her. Can I pet your turtle?" The man had placed the eight-inch turtle in his large, white fishing bucket. His other bucket was full of live shrimp for bait.

"Certainly," the man replied, pulling the turtle out and handing it to Jeremy. "But it's not my turtle. I'm going to release him after my grandkids get here. The poor little guy'll be held captive 'til then. Unlawful to keep a sea turtle you know."

"Glad it is," sighed Jeremy. "Turtles are the best. They always have a home, just like snails."

Jeremy pet the turtle for a while. "I'm getting too hot, Robyn. Could we go back to the pool now?"

"Sure, Sweetie. It is hot. Let's go."

"Thanks, Mister, this was fun." Jeremy handed the turtle back to the man.

"My pleasure. You enjoy yourselves now, bye bye."

"Bye."

"Race ya...." Jeremy yelled, taking off, "Full speed ahead." I could hardly catch up with him. He suddenly stopped cold, turned around and held his arms out so I would run smack into him. I did.

"Whoa!" I yelled. "What are ya doing?"

"I just wanted to stop for a minute and tell you something." His smiling face turned very serious.

"Okay." *Uh oh....* My heart skipped a beat.

"Can we sit right here?" His tone quickly became solemn.

"Sure."

"Could ya hold me?" he asked, looking into my eyes.

"Come here."

We plunked down in the cooler, wet sand. I placed him on my lap. "You okay?"

He didn't answer. After a few minutes, he looked directly into my eyes and said, "I still wish you were my mommy." He snuggled in against my chest and closed his eyes. I felt his warm tears trickle down my chest as he silently wept. I wrapped my arms further around him, enclosing him closer to my heart. I comforted him until he was ready to get up. Hand in hand we slowly walked to the pool, collecting seashells along the way. To this day, I still have them.

Before we even found our chairs again, Jeremy jumped into the kiddie pool. "Can ya throw me the beach ball, please?"

I threw it to him. He tossed it to another boy and they became instant friends. I plopped down on the lounge chair, took a sip of ice cold juice and closed my eyes. *Ahhh....*

I became lost in the warmth of the sun and the smell of fresh air. For the first time since I could remember, I could finally relax. It tickled me to see Jeremy enjoying himself, playing with the other kids in the pool, not a care in the world. I rested my eyes for a few minutes but my attention quickly returned to the external world when Jeremy poured cold water over my feet. He slid onto my chair, facing me. "Hi. Could ya take me in the big pool?"

"I'd be honored." I carried him into the shallow end, which was just up to his neck. After pushing him on the raft awhile, I overheard someone say it was 1:00.

Darn!

Neither of us wanted to leave. We gathered our things and forced ourselves to head home.

Just before we arrived, Jeremy stopped, grabbed my hand, looked up at me and said, "I had a super fun time. Thank you. I love you."

"You are so very welcome. I love you. And I had lots of fun, too. Thank you." I knelt down and we hugged.

As I opened the lobby door with my key, Jeremy burst inside, running. He exclaimed, "Hurry up. I wanna tell Mommy and Nanny all about our adventures."

"Yes, sir," I answered, saluting him.

Just as I pulled Mom's door open, Jeremy took a deep breath and began shouting down the hallway to Delilah and Mom. He found them on the balcony and continued his detailed review of our time together.

"It sounds like you had fun, Jeremy. We also had a nice time. Let's get you changed and get ready for Crabby Bill's," said Delilah. They walked hand in hand to the bedroom.

"How'd it go, Mom?" I whispered.

"It went well. I enjoyed talking with her. She told me quite a bit about her life, like how she was abused as a child and how she just found out she never knew her real mom."

"She really trusts you."

"She also said that you've helped her a lot in a very short time. She appreciates your honesty. She knows what to expect. You don't pull any punches. I could tell, even though she trusts you probably more than she's trusted anyone, she's still very frightened."

"Did she say anything about Jeremy?"

"She said she's stopped using a belt on him since one of the times you pleaded with her. She admitted that her ways of disciplining children are very strict. I told her that I never spanked you and shared other ways I used to discipline. She seemed to be taking it all in."

"Thanks, Mom. I appreciate everything." We hugged.

"I told Delilah she could call me if she ever needed to talk. She said she would. Then she kind of asked, that since her real mom isn't around, maybe I could be her substitute mom."

"What did you say?"

"I told her that would be fine. I was a substitute mom for a lot of kids when you guys were growing up."

"Yeah, but you have a lot on your plate right now with your own health." My mom had terrible cortisone induced osteoporosis and was constantly breaking bones.

"Before we panic, let's see if she even takes me up on it. I can handle it. If I can help in even the smallest way so that she doesn't hurt Jeremy, I'll do it. Jeremy's an Angel."

"He's so wise and compassionate. He's always thinking of ways to get through to her. An incredibly old soul inside a six-year-old's body. I'm thankful I know him."

"It shows. And thanks for sharing him with me, too. Now go and shower if we're going to make it to Crabby Bill's before the line gets too long." She slapped me on my bottom and sent me on my way.

"Thanks for the break, Mom, and thanks for being there for Delilah, too."

We piled into the car and drove to Crabby Bill's, enjoying the beautiful intercoastal waterway along the way. Jeremy wanted to know everything. He pointed out the window, "What are those birds? And why are those trees growing in the water? How come those houses are up in the air like that?"

"Those are homes built on stilts, in case a hurricane comes," answered Mom.

"Cool, same kinda stilts like a clown uses in a parade?" asked Jeremy.

"Absolutely. My you're an inquisitive young man," said Mom as she tickled his tummy.

"And what about the trees?" Jeremy looked at them with purity and innocence. This was all so new to him.

"They're called mangroves. They grow in the shallower parts of the water and become home to pelicans and other birds that build their nests in them. Right down the road past the next light is a bird sanctuary, where thousands of birds have built their homes.

The beauty of nature that surrounded us mesmerized Jeremy. Mom was entranced by Jeremy's beauty.

We arrived at the restaurant before the early dinner rush and enjoyed a heavenly meal as usual. Jeremy ate a cheeseburger and fries. Delilah, Mom, and I shared Cajun shrimp, fried shrimp, and grilled grouper. I had to have my dozen oysters on the half shell. Jeremy thought they were, "Gross and disgusting!"

After dinner we walked behind the restaurant to a shopping plaza built on a pier overlooking the intercoastal waterway. To our delight, we strolled into an ice cream social and a live band, which played big band music. Mom bought us each an ice cream cone. She began dancing something that resembled the Charleston to a Glen Miller song. He and Benny Goodman were her favorites. Jeremy quickly joined her.

I sat down on the wooden bench next to Delilah. "They look like they're having a good time," she said. Tears had formed in her eyes.

"They sure do," I commented. "Would you like to go for a walk?"

She took off at a fast pace.

I caught up with her and grabbed her hand. We continued walking.

"Would you like to talk?" I asked.

"I don't know what to say."

"That's okay. Take your time." We walked on in silence and continued holding hands.

She began shaking and stopped walking. Tears fell from her eyes. I squeezed her hand to give her some encouragement. She began, "You guys have so much love for one another. Your mom took us in even with this stupid virus and opened her home and her heart to us. And you, you love Jeremy so much and even me, despite what I've done and how I've acted. I know you really want to help us."

Suddenly, she yanked her hand from mine. Her expression quickly changed, her voice got louder. She spewed words at me as if in accusation, "You have your mom, and Jim, and other friends. I don't have anybody." And before I could respond, Delilah took off, fleeing from me.

I caught up with her. "Please don't run away this time, Delilah. Let's try and stay with this feeling. I'll be right here with you, I'm not going anywhere." I thought this might be a good opportunity for her to experience her anger instead of dumping it on Jeremy or running from it. Then we could get to the next layer of feelings underneath the anger.

She stopped, but abruptly turned her back from me, saying nothing. I couldn't stand the idea of her putting up her wall again; she was doing so well around Mom. I broke the silence. "Sometimes it's really hard to open up to our feelings. It's easier to run or to lash out than to face our pain."

Her back remained rigid. She showed no sign of letting her guard down. "I had to work hard on myself before I could be in the kind of relationships I have now. I had to face my own demons and pain from my past. At one time or another, most of us have hit some kind of bottom in our lives — maybe we grew up with alcoholism or drugs, or abuse, or never feeling loved — None of us have it perfect. And we heal by acknowledging what's inside and slowly letting it out. We give our feelings a voice. If we don't, they start to eat us up."

Again, she said nothing, sitting there motionless.

So I waited. I was losing my patience and growing tired of not getting through to her during these crucial times when she was so close to feelings that were right under the surface. I decided to confront her one more time, to try and break through her wall. "We share our pain. You run away from yours and then you explode and don't know why."

She slowly turned around. Her body faced me but her eyes remained fixed to the ground. "I'm still here for you, Delilah. I'm listening. Please, tell me your truths. Take a risk. Open up. If you don't start making different choices about how you're going to handle your anger and stress, you could lose your son. It's up to you."

She looked up at me, seething, and blurted, "What do you mean I don't have a choice about my behavior. I don't purposely take things out on him. It just happens."

"Nothing 'just happens', Delilah. You have control over whether you'll maintain custody of your children. Stop reacting out of your pain and taking it out on Jeremy. Stop reacting on the outside and become aware on the inside of what is causing you to lash out. Facing our pain is the first step in changing ourselves. It makes us grow. I'll stand by you. I'll help you anyway I can, but you're the one who has to get started. I can't make you."

Delilah folded her arms tightly, grinding her teeth and clenching her fists.

I spoke from my heart; "It's up to you, Delilah. I hope you take me up on my offer." I gave her a minute to respond, but she didn't. I had nothing more to say. I turned and ran back toward the pier, my tears falling to the ground. Delilah had clad herself again in her full coat of armor. Nothing could stop her fury in the time Jeremy had left. Jeremy needed to remain safe. This disease was not going to get any better.

As I approached the dance area, I dried my eyes, and joined Jeremy and Mom. Mom had bought Jeremy a squirt gun. They were taking turns squirting each other, having a great time.

Delilah arrived within a matter of minutes, with a smile painted on her face as though nothing had happened. I could feel her begin to distance herself. This time she even included Mom in her distance.

The ride back to Clearwater Beach felt uncomfortable. Delilah didn't talk. Her body remained tense and rigid. Mom kept looking at me like, "What the heck happened now?" So did Jeremy. Mom did her best to keep Jeremy focused on the scenery.

We had to get to Orlando before it got too dark. As we were saying our good byes, Mom gave Jeremy a zippered bag full of Clearwater Beach sand and seashells, as a remembrance. Jeremy jumped into her arms for a big, long hug. I was afraid Mom might break a bone, but she didn't seem to care. She was soaking up every last ounce of Jeremy she could get. She gently placed him back on his feet.

Delilah approached Mom. "Thanks for letting us stay here. I really enjoyed our talks." Mom leaned over and hugged Delilah. Delilah hugged her back.

Mom reminded her, "Remember my offer and call if you need a shoulder to lean on." She handed Delilah a piece of paper with her phone number on it. I hugged Mom, and we were on our way.

Both Jeremy and Delilah fell asleep and slept the entire way back to Give Kids the World. When we arrived at our villa, we packed. We had to be at the airport by late the following morning to return the car and catch our flight.

Jeremy was utterly worn out and fell asleep on the couch by 8:30. Before Delilah retired for the night, she said, "I appreciate your talk earlier. You've given me a lot to think about."

"I hope so." She smiled and said good night.

PART SEVEN -- DAY SIX, HOME SWEET HOME

Delilah remained cool and aloof all morning. She only spoke when absolutely necessary. We got to the airport without incident, for which I was thankful.

Delilah sat in the window seat on the plane, and Jeremy sat in between us. The plane took off. As I sat watching Jeremy put his headphones on, beginning to enjoy himself by listening to his Walkman, images of our trip flooded and insulted all my senses. Remembering Epcot, the pizza joint, and worst of all, Disney World made me feel sick to my stomach. Each one had left its indelible mark on my soul... and worst of all, on Jeremy's.

My mood felt heavy and sad. The emotional roller coaster ride, which I had stepped onto with Delilah, had finally changed course; I had changed. I had lost my hope. My hope that Delilah would open up and alter her behavior — her ways of coping. My hope that I could keep Jeremy safe so he could live out his last days with his own mother, before AIDS would rob us all of his presence.

I feared, yet felt strongly, that once we got home, Delilah would revert back to her same old ways of coping and pull away again. But this time, she could take Jeremy with her. I had no authority to stop her. At this point, because of the choices the state had made, they had no authority either.

I feared for Jeremy's safety — for his life — as never before.

By the time Jim picked me up from their apartment, it was dark outside. The emotional turmoil of the Make – A – Wish trip had begun to settle in my body. I felt like the life force had been drained from me. I was never so exhausted in my life.

CHAPTER SIX -- FIGHTING WITHIN THE SYSTEM

Thank goodness, I had the weekend to try and recuperate. I needed some time to myself before I returned to work on Monday. I sat, most of the weekend with the lights off and the curtains closed, curled upon the couch with my cat, Sam, in my lap. My whole being had shut down. I needed quiet. I had nothing left inside to give, even to myself. I needed to heal. I could tell Jim was worried about me. He kept checking in with me, bringing me tea, and asking if I was ready to talk. It took me until Sunday to take him up on his offer.

"I'm sorry that I've been so neglectful of your needs since I came home, but I've never felt more frightened for Jeremy. Even the few times Delilah acted more normal on the trip and allowed me to go inside of her world, that's just the beginning of what she needs to do every day. And she couldn't even do it through her child's last wish!" And before Jim could get a word in edge wise, I continued.

"Nothing I do is getting through to her fast enough to keep Jeremy safe. It's like I'm in a race against time between Jeremy's AIDS, Delilah's explosiveness, and an inept child welfare system. And no one else in the world seems to care. How can we possibly win?" Jim held me and comforted me as I cried some more.

Without training in psychopathology, it's difficult to know just how disturbed someone with borderline personality disorder can become. My job didn't require me to work from this perspective and the majority of state workers don't come from this mental health background, either.

Seeing Delilah swing into action in Florida made it absolutely clear that Jeremy was the outlet for Delilah's borderline rage and impulsiveness. Now that she and I had entered into a somewhat intimate relationship, I ate, drank, and breathed her tumultuous way of being, trying to spare my Little Buddy. I hated it. I didn't hate her, but I hated her behavior.

I dreaded returning to work on Monday, but dragged myself to the office. Carolyn took one look at me and said, "You look like hell," and poured hot coffee into my mug. "Tell me what happened."

"The trip from hell is more like it." I filled Carolyn in on all the details. Afterward, I mentioned that Connie agreed to call Shauna and have her attend our Wednesday staff meeting to discuss where to go from here.

Carolyn then shared the news, "While you were in Florida, we found out that Shauna isn't Delilah's worker anymore, a woman named Debra is. I talked to her the other day. She seems better, not easily manipulated like Shauna. What do you think they should do about Jeremy?"

"Honestly, Carolyn, I don't trust Delilah. She claims that she tries to not hurt him, and then she stores it all up until the next time. I don't think she's capable of making any other choice right now. On some level she wants to, but she's either unable or unwilling to do what it takes."

"Think our parenting group would help?"

"Nothing'll help fast enough to keep Jeremy safe. He needs to be placed in protective custody so she doesn't have the opportunity to beat him any more. My God, Carolyn, he has AIDS. What do they want us to do? Wait around until she kills him? Is it worth the gamble to keep them together, just because she's his mother? He could die tomorrow for all we know."

"You're right, Babe, you're right. Calm down." She patted my arm and told me to take a sip of coffee.

"I'm sorry, Carolyn, I don't mean to go off on you. I'm so frustrated. I don't think anyone's hearing how volatile Delilah really is. They're sure not acting like it."

"Until now we didn't have any eyewitnesses against her; at least any who were willing to tell the truth about her abusiveness. This is the first big incident we can prove."

"That's true," I said sitting back in my chair.

"Maybe that's why it happened while you were there."

105

"You aren't the first person to say that. Jim told me that, too."

I tried to keep myself busy with our other cases the rest of the day and the next.

By the time Wednesday rolled around, I was so apprehensive about the meeting. I couldn't carry a cup of coffee without spilling some of it. I hadn't heard from Delilah and chose not to call her until I knew how the state wanted to handle things. Debra, Delilah's new caseworker, and our HIV program liaison, Julie, from the state came to our staff meeting. I shared the details of the trip. I was proud of myself. I held it together and didn't cry.

In response to Jeremy's story, I was shocked when I heard the discussion turn in a direction which made me very unhappy: that maybe seeing all of the dying children and their parents had set Delilah off and we should give her the benefit of the doubt. "Jeremy and Delilah should continue to remain together." Both workers agreed. And because I had such a "good working relationship" with Delilah, they wanted me to not only convince her to attend the parenting group Connie ran as part of another program, but to get her to continue to see me for weekly counseling sessions. They thought I'd have more leverage if I told her the state required her participation.

I was told to keep a close eye on Delilah and Jeremy, and update both workers with any more incidents, since we had no other "founded" reports of abuse.

I couldn't believe it. I almost lost control myself, but managed to swallow my emotions and acquiesce to their decision. After all, they were the child welfare experts, not I. I had already made one grave mistake; by not pulling Jeremy's pants down to see his welts, I'd lost a chance to get "founded" evidence against her. I didn't want to blow it again.

To say I was thoroughly disgusted with the outcome would be a gross understatement. They made me responsible again for making it work. I couldn't. For God's sake, when I was with them 24 hours a day, I still couldn't stop her from losing control. Neither state worker had seen her rage first hand, nor experienced her mood swings or darkness. In fact, they had never even met her.

I called Delilah the next morning to inform her of the state's decision. She agreed to comply, but would not commit to a time for our session, claiming to have a lot of appointments that week. She remained unapproachable during the call.

Carolyn picked Delilah up the following Tuesday and brought her to the office for her first parenting group. Delilah spent the majority of group time in the restroom. She told Connie the baby was pressing against her bladder and Connie accepted her explanation.

I didn't buy it. I called Delilah Tuesday evening from home.

"Hi, Delilah. It's Robyn."

"Oh. Hi."

"How are you feeling?"

"Fine, thank you," she said.

"That's good. I was in court all day with another family. How'd the group go?"

"It was all right."

"Did you get anything out of it?"

"Well...."

I gave her time to finish, but she left it at that.

"What didn't you like about it?" I asked.

"I didn't fit in. Some of the other mothers seemed like they were on drugs. A couple were teenagers."

"How'd you handle it?"

"Honestly?"

"That's the only way." We both laughed. This seemed to break the ice a bit.

"I went to the bathroom. A lot. The baby's pressing on my bladder, but I guess I stayed in there a little too long."

"Is there another way you could handle it? If you hang in there, you might benefit from the instruction. Connie offers good ideas about disciplining children and coping with stress."

"I suppose I could try again."

"Good. Then I'll see you next week." She agreed, and we said good bye.

The following week, Delilah attended another group and again spent much of the time in the restroom. But she attended. That's all the state required.

She cancelled our next session. "Another rescheduled doctor appointment," she said.

Delilah's baby was due any day now. Toward the end of May, with Julie's help, a homemaker service was hired for Delilah and Jeremy, for eight hours daily, until Delilah gave birth. They'd have someone stay overnight with Jeremy once Delilah went in for the baby's birth. Once she returned home, they'd resume eight hours per day to give her extra help.

Once in place, Delilah wouldn't let the homemaker do anything to help her. If the woman managed to assist in some way, Delilah criticized her to shreds. The worker refused to return to Delilah's after the first few days. The new worker assigned sat quietly doing absolutely nothing all day, which evidently was acceptable to Delilah. Delilah continued to let her come.

During our next counseling session, Delilah shared feelings about her dad's death. She said that she always felt great hostility from her stepfamily and that the physical abuse started after her dad died. This had finally made sense to her after she found out on her birth certificate that her dad's wife wasn't her real mother.

Delilah elaborated on the physical abuses she suffered from her stepmom and stepbrothers. She stated that she coped by locking herself and Jeremy in her bedroom, which continued to be her current pattern for coping — completely isolating from the rest of the world. She said that the last straw was when her stepmother hit her over the head with a glass jar during an argument. This was the impetus for her and Jeremy to move into the homeless shelter the past January.

Delilah also shared her resentment toward the state for making her move back "home" with her family when Jeremy was in the full body cast.

As soon as the session was over and we walked out of my office into the real world, Delilah zipped up her coat of armor and reverted right back to her closed off, rageful self.

She missed the next two parenting groups and counseling sessions, saying she didn't feel well so close to her due date.

My gut said she was pulling away. I did feel a minuscule amount of relief — at least during the homemaker's shift, Jeremy wasn't alone with Delilah. I continued to keep in contact by phone, although Delilah remained distant. I never did connect with her for a home visit before the baby was born; she dodged my every move.

In mid June, a month after our Make-A-Wish trip, Delilah gave birth to a baby boy, Simon. Hannah called me at the office the following day. She had gotten a call from the homemaker who said that Jeremy needed to talk. Jeremy told Hannah his medicine was empty. Delilah had not refilled his prescriptions in preparation for her hospitalization.

Hannah got one of Jeremy's doctors to write the prescriptions and arranged for the pharmacist to fill it and give it to us without payment. Delilah had not left Jeremy's medical card at home either. Another oversight?

I called Jeremy so I could make arrangements to take him to the hospital to pick up his medicine. I thought he'd like to visit Delilah and Simon too.

"Hi Jeremy. It's…"

"Hi Robyn, did ya hear? I have a beautiful new brother. He has super big brown eyes and lots of black curly hair. Just like me." I could feel him beaming even through the phone.

"Congratulations, Little Buddy. You sound so happy! How's it going?"

"Good. I have to get my medicine though. I ran out. Mommy's not here to fill it."

"I'm proud of you for calling Hannah to tell her you were out of medicine. That was a very good thing to do. How 'bout if I pick you up in a little while and take you to the hospital to get it. Then we can go visit your mom and Simon, if you want."

"Yeah, yeah, yeah. I want to bring Mommy a present and make her a card, too. I found a planter in the closet that looks like a baby bootie. Can you bring me something to put in it?"

"Sure, Sweetie. I have flowers in my back yard, different colors, pink and…"

"Pink's perfect! Mommy likes pink! Hurry up and get here, I have lotsa work to do."

I left the office and raced home. I dug pink and white begonias out of my garden and grabbed crayons and construction paper for Delilah's card. I drove across town to get Jeremy.

He must have heard me coming up the stairs. The door burst open before I had a chance to knock. Jeremy charged at me, jumping into my arms. "Those are so pretty! Mommy's gonna love 'em, thanks. My new baby brother will too, cuz look at the pot I have for 'em." He pointed to the planter on the kitchen table and without taking another breath continued excitedly, "I found it in Mommy's closet. It's from when I was born. I want my brother to like it, too. Do you think they'll both like it, Robyn?"

"I sure do, Little Buddy. You're very thoughtful."

"Quick, put me down! I have work to do!"

He sat at the kitchen table, picked out a piece of red construction paper and carefully folded it in half. He began drawing pink and white begonias on the cover. He had written the verse on a piece of scrap paper before I got there.

Roses are Red
Violets are Blue
Can't Wait Till You Both Get Home
I Love and Miss You

I planted the flowers in the bootie. In no time, we were on our way to Jeremy's hospital. He couldn't sit still the entire ride. He sang, "Rockabye Baby" over and over.

When we got to the pharmacy, Hannah met us with a glass of juice so Jeremy could take both medicines immediately, his white AZT pill to treat his AIDS and his pink liquid antibiotic. Even from the first day I met him, I never heard a complaint out of him as he swallowed his medications.

Hannah took me aside. "I took Jeremy to see Delilah and Simon yesterday. While we were in the gift shop, Jeremy spotted his 'daddy.'"

I interrupted, "Who?"

"Simon's biological father. The guy looks Jeremy right in the eyes and completely ignores him. That didn't stop our Jeremy — he put his arms out to hug him and the guy brushed him off. All he said was 'hello'. When we got up to Delilah's room, she treated us pretty coldly, too. I hope she acts warmer today."

"Me, too." Our conversation ended when Jeremy came back from the water fountain. Jeremy and I hugged Hannah good bye and headed for my car.

On the way to Delilah's hospital, Jeremy announced, "I'm super hungry. I only ate breakfast today cuz I wasn't hungry at lunch." I looked at my watch. It read 3:00.

Would you like to stop for a Happy Meal or get something at the hospital?"

"I want to get there super quick to give her my present." So we drove straight there. Jeremy was so excited, I had flutters in my chest for him. Things quickly changed, though. As we entered Delilah's room, my heart became heavy. You could cut the tension with a knife. Delilah sat in bed, arms crossed tightly, glaring into space. Jeremy and I said, "Hi."

She mumbled, "Hi."

Jeremy sat himself down on the edge of her bed and attempted to hug her with one arm and swing the present out from behind his back. She completely ignored his hug, pushed him away, and began picking at his hair, yelling, "Who fixed your hair? And why are you wearing that outfit, you have nicer things to wear to the hospital."

Before he could answer, she went into a tirade about how the homemaker was a complete failure in caring for him.

Jeremy sadly placed the plant and card on her bedside table, staring at the floor. I watched as his eyes wandered over to the window. A beautiful fruit, wine and cheese basket sat on the table. Jeremy noticed it, walked over toward the basket and asked, "Mommy, can I have a pear? I'm hungry."

She responded curtly, "No. That's for me. It was a gift from the staff at your hospital."

Jeremy slouched his shoulders and hung his head low. He hedged toward me, while staring at the floor. He sat motionless on the edge of my chair. Uncomfortable silence filled the room. I waited to see what her next move would be. She sat staring out of the window, saying nothing.

I thought of running down to the cafeteria to grab him a bite to eat, but I didn't think this was the right time. Delilah wasn't in a good frame of mind to leave Jeremy alone with her. So I mentioned, "Jeremy hasn't had lunch," hoping she'd have second thoughts about the pear. Instead, she went off in another rage about the homemaker and how she couldn't even feed her kid lunch.

What did I expect? Oh yeah, and what about his medicine? Or how about letting him eat your precious fruit?

Biting my tongue, I went to the nurses' station and had the nurse order Jeremy a food tray. He would have a grilled cheese sandwich within a short time.

When I returned to the room, Jeremy, still on the edge of the chair, stared out the window. Delilah broke the silence to ask me, "Would you give the bottle of White Zinfandel to Connie? I bet she would like it."

This was a little passive aggressive gesture done to spite me.

"Sure," I said. I wondered why she was so hateful at the moment. I felt like telling her what she could do with it.

The grilled cheese arrived. Jeremy quickly gobbled it down.

The nurse wheeled Simon into the room in his bassinet. Jeremy grabbed my hand and led me over to Simon. "Isn't he beautiful, Robyn? He looks just like me."

"He sure is, Sweetie, and he certainly does look like you." I answered. Simon's huge, dark eyes greeted Jeremy with a calm and knowing look.

"Can I hold him, Mommy?"

Delilah agreed he could. Jeremy sat on Delilah's bed and held and cuddled Simon like a big brother with a lot of prior experience. He gently cradled Simon's head. After some time passed, I glanced at my watch. It read 4:30. "We better get going, Jeremy. I need to get you home and stop at the office before I head home."

"Bye, Mommy. Bye baby brother. I love you." Jeremy gently kissed Simon's forehead.

"Thanks for coming to see me," Delilah added as we gathered ourselves to leave. "You can take the pear with you, Jeremy, if you're still hungry."

"Thanks!" He sunk his teeth into it as soon as he pulled it out of the basket. As we walked hand in hand out of the hospital toward my car, Jeremy stopped cold in front of a beautiful bed of early blooming Missouri Primrose. He turned toward me, squeezed my hand, looked up into my eyes and asked, "Can you be my mommy, and can Jim be my daddy? And could I come and live with you? Please? I'll be real good, I promise."

I swooped him up into my arms, whirled him around in a circle, and said, "I love you, Jeremy. And I'll continue to do everything in my power to keep you safe. But right now, you still have to stay with your mommy and your new baby brother. And I'll keep on working with your whole family to help make things better. Okay, Sweetie? Everything will work out. I promised you, remember? And I don't break my promises."

"Is that the only way it can be?" he asked, with a forlorn look on his face, never letting go of my hand.

"That's the only way."

"But you won't leave me, ever, will you?"

"No, Jeremy, I will never leave you. I will always be here for you, no matter what."

"Good, cuz I love you, Robyn."

"I love you, too, Jeremy. You're my best buddy in the whole world, you know that?"

"Yeah, I do. And you're my best buddy in the whole world, too."

The whole drive home, Jeremy chattered away about plans he had for Simon, "I'm gonna teach him how to play Nintendo, and how to play catch, and oh yeah, about all my dinosaurs."

"That sounds wonderful, Sweetie."

"Ya know, Robyn, I'm havin' lots of fun with Cheryl, the lady staying with me. She takes me to the park after school and lets me play with the kids there. She even lets me play with the kids in our building. They're my new friends. I wish Mommy would let me and Simon do that."

I do, too.

I walked Jeremy up to his apartment and met Cheryl. She greeted Jeremy with a big hug.

Delilah came down with a mysterious infection and high fever. The doctors couldn't figure out what caused it -- so characteristic of HIV. She missed Jeremy's seventh birthday, less than two weeks after Simon's. I had only known Jeremy for four months now, but felt like I had known him forever.

Cheryl threw Jeremy a small birthday party and invited the kids from the building. She baked him a cake and got party favors for the kids. Jeremy had a wonderful time — he even got presents from his new friends. It was probably the first real kid birthday party of his life.

When Delilah was finally discharged from the hospital after two weeks, she entered her apartment. Cheryl greeted her. Jeremy was no where in sight. When Cheryl told her he was downstairs playing with his friends, Delilah fired Cheryl on the spot and raced downstairs to get Jeremy. She questioned him to find out what else had been going on. After hearing about his birthday party, she grounded Jeremy for a month; no toys, no Nintendo.

Both state workers, Julie and Debra, got to experience for themselves Delilah's convoluted ways of dealing with things. Their intention, to help reduce Delilah's stress, backfired on them; the homemaker's presence made Delilah so angry, it increased the risk for abuse. After much deliberation, Delilah's decision stood firm. The state did not rehire a homemaker.

Delilah began to fail my appointments and continued to miss parenting group. When I went to her apartment for scheduled visits on two occasions, no one answered. When I finally got a hold of her by phone, she claimed she had to reschedule doctor appointments again. Soon after, she stopped calling me and changed her phone number to an unpublished one.

The following week, I got Delilah's new number from Hannah and called. She sounded surprised to hear from me, "I had a fight with Simon's dad and didn't want him to be able to call. I was going to give you my new number, but haven't had a chance to call."

Right.

"By law, you have to keep the state informed of your whereabouts," I said. "Since our agency is contracted with the state, we need to know, too." She hadn't informed Debra either.

Before the call ended, Delilah agreed to let Carolyn and I schedule a home visit for the following day. We had some baby gifts for Simon, which had been donated by the state, and I had gotten Simon a gift, also. The following afternoon, Carolyn and I entered Delilah's apartment carrying beautifully wrapped presents. As we both sat on the couch, while Delilah changed Simon's diaper, Jeremy ran toward us from the bathroom. Delilah quickly demanded, "Sit right there and watch television."

"But Mommy, I wanna sit next to Robyn and Carolyn. I haven't seen..."

"You'd better obey or I'll punch you so hard you'll fly through that brick wall. Now do it!"

Jeremy looked at me and looked away. He slowly, "obeyed" his mother, dragged himself over to the T.V., and sat, heartsick, on the floor.

"Are these the gifts for Simon?"

Carolyn answered, "Here you go," and handed them to her.

As I watched Delilah open the handmade baby quilt and two layette sets, I sat absolutely stunned by her threat. I needed to figure out how to handle it. I felt strongly that this was a blatant attempt, on Delilah's part, to test my reaction. If I didn't react the way she needed me to, I was sure she would beat Jeremy to show me who was in control.

So I didn't react at all and ended the visit quickly. When Carolyn and I reached the office, I left a message for Debra, Delilah's caseworker, and told Connie, my supervisor, what Delilah had done. Connie's response was that Delilah must have been mad about something, and that she was sure we'd be able to work it out. I never heard a response from Debra.

Delilah gradually slipped further away from me over the next few weeks, taking her children with her. She missed every appointment she had with me. I reported everything to Debra, Julie, and Connie, as required.

Again, Connie's response was that Delilah must have been, "mad at me," because she was keeping her doctor's appointments and only missing my appointments.

Over a month later, Connie decided to telephone Delilah. She wanted to see if Delilah would meet with both of us to discuss what was happening "between us," Delilah and I that is. I didn't like the sound of that. Delilah agreed to meet.

When the day arrived, I rode with Connie in her car to Delilah's apartment. Connie continued to call the shots once we got upstairs. "Why don't you wait in the living room with Jeremy while Delilah and I talk." Simon was asleep in his carrier, in the kitchen, so Jeremy and I made the best of it playing in the living room. I was infuriated with Connie. I felt like she was treating me like I was a child, and she was letting Delilah be in control. I bit my tongue and played with Jeremy as instructed.

We sat on the couch and played catch with his beach ball. Jeremy got bored, so we put on a puppet show with Kermit the frog and Jeremy's collection of dinosaurs.

Connie and Delilah finally came out of the kitchen. Connie spoke first. "Delilah's agreed to work with you again. You can get together next week. I'll tell you the details on the ride back." We all said our good byes. They both looked like they wanted me to jump for joy.

Connie shared the plan: Delilah agreed to resume counseling with me. I was to pick the three of them up every Thursday at 9:00 a.m., drop Jeremy off for summercamp at the hospital, and then meet with Delilah and Simon once a week for the entire summer.

Connie then scolded me for playing catch with Jeremy in the living room during their talk. She said I should've found something quieter to do and that those were the kinds of things, which made Delilah angry. Frankly, at this point, everything Jeremy did seemed to make Delilah angry.

Connie also suggested that Delilah was jealous of the time and attention I gave to Jeremy and intimated that Delilah and I had had a "lovers' spat." By dropping Jeremy off and spending "quality time alone" with Delilah, Connie thought it would "help mend our relationship."

It made me ill to think of what happened between Delilah and I as a lovers' spat! When was someone going to realize the seriousness of Jeremy's situation?

I did as instructed, and telephoned Delilah the following Wednesday to confirm our appointment. I called five different times throughout the day. The phone was busy each time.

Off the hook maybe?

I decided to call early Thursday morning, before driving all the way out to their apartment to pick them up. No one answered the phone, but I went anyway, since Connie had just made the arrangements with her on Tuesday.

I knocked on their door. The neighbor Annie answered.

"Oh, hi, Robyn."

"Good morning, Annie."

"They're not here. I heard them leaving before seven this morning. Did she know you were coming?"

I didn't want to break any confidences, so I just said, "Must have been a mix up."

"I'll tell her you stopped by when I see her later."

At first I thought maybe something happened. But the longer I sat with it, my gut said she blew me off on purpose. I called Delilah several more times that day and finally reached her that evening from my home. Jeremy answered.

"Hello." Jeremy sounded despondent.

"Hi, Jeremy, it's Robyn. Are you all right?"

He dropped the phone. Delilah got on. My heart began to race.

"Delilah, it's Robyn. Is everything okay?"

"Fine." She answered with hostility in her voice.

"Is Jeremy feeling okay?"

"I didn't touch him, if that's what you mean."

I'm not even gonna bite.

After much prompting, Delilah admitted she and Simon had taken Jeremy to daycamp via public transportation, "forgetting" our appointment.

"It's not like you to forget anything, Delilah. I thought you wanted to try and work with me again. If you've changed your mind, you need to tell me so I can let the state know your decision."

"No," she quickly stated, "that won't be necessary."

"Shall we go ahead and schedule our next visit, then?"

"Sure."

We agreed that I'd pick them up the following Thursday, and kept the same plan of dropping Jeremy off at the hospital for daycamp and spending time together.

I hung up, feeling very uncomfortable. When Delilah acted this cool, she tended to be abusive toward Jeremy.

Normally, I would have made a verbal contract with her, to promise to not hit Jeremy and call if she felt the urge to hurt him. This time however, I was sure my concern would have angered her more, possibly causing her to really lambaste him. So I said nothing more to her and prayed hard for Jeremy's protection.

The following week, I found a message on my desk. "Delilah called to cancel her appointment." That's all it said. When I finally reached her by phone, she said she had to take Simon to the doctor, he didn't feel well. We rescheduled again, for the following Thursday.

I found out from Hannah that Simon had a cold for several days, and of course, Delilah chose to take him to the clinic the day of our appointment. It was the same clinic where Jeremy had daycamp.

The pieces fit together more and more for me. Delilah was growing further and further out of control. She did not want me in the picture.

The following Thursday, when I pulled up in my car, I realized I hadn't seen Jeremy in almost three weeks. He must have been waiting for me. As I parallel parked, Jeremy flew down his front stairs. My heart sank. In such a short time, his appearance had changed drastically. His body looked like it would give way. I jumped out of the car, picked him up and whirled him around in a circle. He gave me a big hug and squeeze, and whispered, "I missed you," as he snuggled his head onto my chest and closed his big, brown eyes.

The Universe seemed to stop as we stood holding each other. His heart beat fast against my chest. For this one moment, we could both let go. We were both safe.

When Jeremy loosened his grip on me, I gave him the once over. I could smell the starch from his blue oxford shirt and perfectly pressed blue jeans. His black winged tipped shoes gleamed in the sunlight. Delilah had faultlessly arranged every lock of his curly brown hair in place on his head.

Seeing Jeremy again, touching him, smelling him, filled me with a sense of urgency and desperation as never before. His body had deteriorated to just skin and bones, and his cough sounded wetter and deeper than I had ever heard. I felt Jeremy slipping away from me, not just from AIDS, but because of Delilah's grip as well. She'd soon try to completely keep him from me. The idea of losing him terrified me. Time had run out.

Delilah came down the stairs carrying Simon in his infant seat. I greeted her warmly. She sat in the back seat with Jeremy and Simon and kept conversation to a minimum. I tried to engage her by talking about Simon and about how she was adjusting to being a newborn's mom again, but she responded with one-word answers. She asked if during our "session," I could take her to look at a couple of apartments. Since Simon was born, they needed more room. I agreed to take her apartment hunting. She remained unapproachable during the rest of the afternoon.

The following Wednesday evening, Delilah called me at home to cancel for the following day. Jeremy wasn't feeling well. He needed to go to the clinic for special breathing treatments. I offered to drive them to the clinic and help with Simon while she tended to Jeremy. She refused, but did reschedule our appointment for the following week.

Two days later, Delilah called me again at home. The attorney called her regarding Jeremy's school situation. He needed to see us the next day to help him prepare for a hearing to have Jeremy reinstated back in school in the fall.

I spent the following morning rearranging my schedule so I could bring Delilah, Jeremy, and Simon to the attorney's office that same afternoon. I had to drive to Cabrini Green to cancel with one of my families in person; they didn't have a phone. I also rescheduled a meeting with a caseworker from another case.

When I pulled in front of Delilah's apartment, I felt exhausted from all the running around I had done in order to accommodate the attorney's appointment. I honked my horn and waited. Jeremy came running down to greet me, with exuberance as usual. Delilah, on the other hand, barely uttered a word the entire ride. In front of the attorney, however, she behaved as though we were extremely close. She supported everything I said to the attorney and played up what a devastating impact this whole school issue had had on her... and Jeremy.

Jeremy stayed out in the waiting room during the meeting. When we finished our discussion, the attorney escorted Delilah, Simon and me into the waiting room. Jeremy had been playing with a small set of Legos, which he had built into an elaborate helicopter. The attorney was so impressed; he gave Jeremy the Legos. Delilah returned to her frosty mode as soon as we left his office. She did schedule our weekly Thursday session, however.

But when I went to pick them up for the Thursday visit, no one answered again. I telephoned Delilah that night. She had never sounded so down and withdrawn. After much pulling and coaxing, she managed to tell me she had missed her doctor's appointment that week. She had made a decision to refuse her pentamidine breathing treatments and AZT.

119

Through much exploration, Delilah admitted her strong belief that taking these medications would bring on her symptoms and not prevent them. "If something's not broken, don't fix it," she recited. After a long talk, she did promise me that if she got sick, she'd start again. She had the disease over seven years, and except for the brief infection after Simon's birth, she hadn't experienced any symptoms. I assessed her for her potential to commit suicide. She had no plan, and still felt hopeful over Simon's birth.

Another two weeks passed. Delilah missed both of her weekly appointments with me. My telephone calls to her went unanswered. She was up to something; I felt it in my bones. Near the end of August, I met again with Debra and Julie and voiced my grave concern that Delilah was slipping further away, dragging Jeremy with her. Julie agreed to inform Debra's supervisor of the situation. She told me to still reach out to Delilah and try to get her to return to the weekly parenting group and individual treatment. If she refused, I was to threaten her with a court order from the state, forcing her to comply.

Delilah never did make it to another appointment with me ever again. She continued dodging my calls. I finally gave up and stopped calling her and chasing her.

I couldn't force someone to take my help if they didn't want my help. But what would that mean for Jeremy? So I began to pray and pray for Jeremy's safety. Everyday, all day.

Hannah still saw Jeremy and Delilah at least monthly for Jeremy's clinic visits. The state remained adamant; they didn't have enough founded evidence against Delilah to have Jeremy removed from Delilah's custody.

Julie and Debra made a decision to find another agency for Delilah to work with. Maybe Delilah and I, "just couldn't work together any more."

It made me sick. *Didn't they get it? She knew I was on to her. She had no intention of working with anyone. Someone had better do something!*

I was so distressed about Jeremy's safety; I was making myself crazy. I felt so totally hopeless, at Delilah's mercy.

I started a prayer circle for him. I had everyone I knew praying for his protection.

After a few more weeks of not seeing him, I confided in Carolyn that I was ready to take Jeremy's case to the newspapers in order to get the state to make a move. The state always seemed to work more expediently with the media breathing down their neck.

I just didn't get it. Here, the state hired our program to prevent further incidences of abuse, I'm in there doing the best I can to prevent things from getting worse, and they tell me we don't have enough evidence to remove Jeremy. If we hadn't been in there, he might be dead. And now that she wouldn't let us back in, didn't they know what she could do?

Each week I'd remind Julie and Connie that I hadn't been able to connect with Delilah. What was their plan? And each week, I'd get; we're trying to hook her up with such and such agency. And each week, they were always unsuccessful for one reason or another, but they kept trying.

At the end of September, Delilah herself did something no one ever thought she would do; she missed one of Jeremy's clinic visits, for his monthly treatment protocols. When one of the nurses called to see if everything was all right, Delilah informed them Jeremy would not be returning to the clinic — she was withdrawing Jeremy from all medical treatment.

This was medical neglect and reason for the hospital to make a child abuse hotline report.

However, during the call, the nurse talked Delilah into meeting with the two physicians who headed the clinic. Delilah could share her concerns and needs with them. The nurse begged her to bring Jeremy in for his treatments anyway. Delilah said she'd wait until she met with the physicians first, leaving everyone hanging and hoping until the meeting. After the call, she again changed her phone number to an unpublished one.

Delilah did meet with the doctors and rescheduled Jeremy's clinic appointment. Hannah called to fill me in on the details. A hotline report had not been filed by the hospital because Delilah eventually complied with their requests. I suggested they make a report anyway to at least document what had taken place. Thank goodness, Hannah did.

But Delilah had us again. Another unfounded report.

What did Jeremy have to go through to live out the rest of his life? Another game, another power play on her part, another cry for please pay attention to me and show me you care? I was fed up of playing by her rules and by the system's rules.

After meeting again, the state finally decided to go "against all odds" and file a petition for custody anyway, without any founded reports against her. Debra was sure it would not work — no judge would remove a kid without these reports. I was sure no judge in his or her right mind would keep a kid with a parent like this.

Once Debra, Jeremy's caseworker from the state, finally decided to file a petition for temporary custody of Jeremy, she called me to say she needed my help. She came to our office the next morning to have me fill out some paperwork. "I need your help filling out a preliminary report for the state's attorney."

Debra pulled some forms from her briefcase. "I need dates and details of incidences of abuse which you've personally witnessed. Try and remember everything. I'll help you write it all down. You're responsible for building the case against Delilah. You'll have to make the evidence against her crystal clear if you want to get Jeremy away from her."

It was all on me again. Suddenly, my butterflies left and I felt sick to my stomach. I was incredibly excited at the prospect of Jeremy finally being safe; but that meant I'd be taking Jeremy away from her. How awful that made me feel. Without my testimony it would not be done.

"I'm not the only witness, am I?" I asked.

"No. Hannah will be subpoenaed, too, but your testimony weighs heavily since you're her social worker."

So Debra and Carolyn helped jog my memory as I sat and wrote dates and incidences of abuse which I had personally witnessed. When the report was finished, I asked, "What happens now?"

"I'll set up a time for us to meet at the state's attorneys office. They prosecute the child abuse and neglect cases. I need you and Carolyn to go with me. We'll meet with an assistant state's attorney, they'll read my report, probably ask you a lot of questions, and then make a decision as to whether or not we have a strong enough case to take into court, since there is no founded evidence on file."

"No problem. Then what?"

"If they think we have enough evidence to remove Jeremy from Delilah's custody, they'll file the report with Juvenile Court and set a date for the initial custody hearing. It's up to the assigned judge though, whether he or she feels there is enough evidence to remove Jeremy from Delilah and place him in protective custody."

All this uncertainty made my stomach churn. The way the child welfare laws were written, the system tried to keep families together. It's called, "Family Preservation." Although the decision in each individual case is up to the law and the discretion of the judge, too often the newspaper headlines report something like, "State Underfire Again; Another Child Dies at Hands of Abusive Parent." I felt frightened, yet hopeful.

Could it be over soon?

My mind overflowed with questions. How soon would the court date be set? Once Delilah was served notice to appear in court, cognizant of the fact that we were trying to obtain custody of Jeremy, how could we ensure Jeremy's safety while she still had him? And what if the judge decided against Jeremy being placed in protective custody? What would Delilah do then? I started to make myself absolutely crazy, worrying about this whole new set of problems.

I finally had to surrender, to let it go. I remembered what Sally said, "God is most powerful." And I kept repeating an affirmation that Jim had put on the fridge for me; ALL DETAILS TAKE CARE OF THEMSELVES. IT IS SAFE TO LET GO.

But I couldn't. I tried and failed completely. My mind wouldn't stop racing, wouldn't stop coming up with more and more questions... If Jeremy is removed the day of the hearing, where will he go? To a cold institutional shelter run by the state?

I calmed myself and pictured in my mind a wonderful loving foster home that would take him in. Then other thoughts began intruding and my heart rate soared again... If there isn't a real home available, Jeremy will be all alone in a shelter with other abused and neglected kids who have no place to go. How many of those kids would be dying of AIDS?

My whole world came crashing in all around me. I quickly picked up the phone and called Hannah for support. Hannah gave comfort when she said, "I know the perfect home for him, Robyn." But the comfort left when she added, "There's a glitch; the foster parents already have a foster child with full blown AIDS and have room for only one more. There's another HIV positive boy who might be placed in protective custody before Jeremy. The court date's already been set for this other boy."

Hannah went on to describe the foster home; Jeremy knew the foster child already living there. They both had the same clinic day at the hospital. Lindsey, the foster mom, was a registered nurse who quit her full-time job to become a foster mom for kids with AIDS. Lindsey's husband, Wayne, was a clinical psychologist working in the field of developmental disabilities. They lived in a huge, beautiful old house near Lake Michigan with a swing set in their backyard, along with eight cats and a friendly golden retriever. Their own daughter was away at college.

Jeremy would have his own bedroom. He'd still be within the geographic limits of attending his same school, and the school bus would pick him up right in front of his new house. Sounded perfect. Hannah and I agreed to pray for everything to work out for Jeremy, and the other boy, too. We talked at length about our concern for Jeremy's safety once Delilah was served her papers, but before the actual court date. Delilah could easily flee with Jeremy, or even worse. The only plan Hannah and I could come up with was to somehow have Jeremy hospitalized until the hearing. But right then, he wasn't sick enough to warrant hospitalization. So we schemed to figure out a way to keep him safe — maybe Jeremy's doctors would agree to come up with a reason for hospitalizing him for something, anything. Hannah agreed to ask them. At work the following morning, Debra telephoned me. "Be ready Friday, at 3:00. We'll bring the report to the state's attorney then."

That night, as I went to bed, I prayed harder than I ever had in my whole life. I found myself pleading and begging God to save Jeremy. When I turned to Sally, our minister, she kept affirming for me that God's Divine Will would be done. As I declared Divine Order every step of the way, and continued to see Jeremy through, as God's instrument, it would be so.

But worry overcame me. How would all the details work out? I couldn't fathom how all of the players involved would be able to ensure Jeremy's safety. I repeated my affirmation, ALL DETAILS TAKE CARE OF THEMSELVES. IT IS SAFE TO LET GO, many times a day. It was my salvation. It was a phrase I needed to believe, in order to maintain my sanity. Obsessing over the unknown wouldn't help in the weeks ahead.

I knew deep down God would absolutely come through somehow. It was we humans, including myself at times, I wasn't so sure about.

CHAPTER SEVEN -- THE DREAMS

I walked with Debra through the double glass doors of the state's attorneys office, only to find that the offices were empty. We heard a lot of talking and commotion toward the end of the hallway, so we followed the voices down the bleak concrete walls until the hallway dead-ended into two open rooms. We peeked into one of the open doorways and found that the assistant state's attorneys were having a party. They filled both rooms. An attractive woman noticed us, came toward us, and asked if we needed any help. I remember her distinctively. She had dark brown, fine, straight hair that rested upon her shoulders. She wore a black and white wool herringbone skirt and jacket with a white blouse, which had a beautiful antique-looking lace collar.

When I turned for a second, Debra vanished and left me standing alone with the woman. I introduced myself and whom I worked for, and told her I had to talk to someone about a little boy with AIDS, who was in danger from his abusive mom. I wanted to brief them, so they'd be ready for action.

The woman escorted me to the doorway adjoining the rooms and yelled loudly to get everyone's attention. She asked them to please quiet down and listen. I heard myself take a deep breath in the quiet of the room. I told Jeremy's story. His whole story, from the full body cast, the welt on his eye, the "whuppin," Disney World, and the medical neglect incident. You could hear a pin drop in the room.

The woman with the herringbone suit took a special interest, asking more specific details and very astute questions like, "Do you think he'll be safe with his mother until the actual day of the hearing?" And, "Who is this woman, the character from <u>Fatal Attraction</u>?"

"Yes," I responded triumphantly, "Yes, she is." *Yes! Someone is finally hearing me.*

The woman said she thought we had an excellent chance of saving Jeremy. Debra joined me from wherever she had disappeared to. The attorney gave us the information we needed to file the petition and get the ball rolling.

I woke up. Words don't do justice to the relief I felt as I sat up in bed. Before I had gone to bed the night before, I prayed hard for God to show me, in a dream, anything I needed to know to help Jeremy. I stated all of my concerns for Jeremy, including the foster home situation, Jeremy's safety, and each and every other fear I held. I ended my prayer by asking for God's Divine Order to reign over Jeremy's life and affairs, and then I visualized Jeremy in a Pepto-Bismol pink bubble and released him to the Universe for God to handle. Pepto-Bismol pink is the color symbolizing love.

My dream gave me hope and encouragement that all would be in Divine Order. I got out of bed, showered, made Jim and myself breakfast, and actually got to work early. I had been feeling so depressed since the Make - A - Wish trip; the kind of depression that makes you want to stay in bed forever.

I raced to the office to tell Carolyn my dream. She remarked, "Well girl, let's keep praying and hope that God takes care of it just like that...."

At 2:30, Carolyn and I went to Juvenile Court. After showing our ID badges to the security guard, we sat down near the state's attorneys offices. We quietly prayed together again, asking that Divine Order reign over Jeremy's life and affairs. Then we asked for the White Light of Christ to surround everyone who would be involved with Jeremy, including Jeremy and Delilah. We patiently waited for Debra.

At about 3:15, Debra joined us with the report in hand. She briefed us on what would take place, and we walked in the offices together. The receptionist told us she'd send out the next available assistant attorney as soon as possible.

Since there was no waiting room, we stood, watching, waiting for someone to take us in. Their offices weren't what I had expected.

I'd thought they'd be nicer. Many doorways lined both sides of the long, bare, white concrete hallway. Behind each doorway was a small, cluttered, bleak office furnished minimally with a couple of desks, chairs, and a table. Each time the receptionist hung up her phone, it immediately rang again. Her desk was filled to capacity with stacks of paperwork and manila file folders, spilling over to piles on the floor.

I felt so anxious that my shirt pulsated with every beat of my heart. It stuck to my perspiration soaked underarms. And then... a woman came out of one of the offices and approached us. Her straight, dark brown, fine hair hung to her shoulders. She wore a black and white wool herringbone skirt and jacket. She even had on the white blouse with the antique, lace collar, which I had admired. She introduced herself as Sheila, an assistant state's attorney. She beckoned for us to follow her to her office where another assistant attorney waited. I grabbed Carolyn by the hand and whispered, "Oh my, Carolyn, it's her. She's the one in my dream."

Carolyn smugly replied, "I know Babe, I recognized her from your description. With God on our side, all things are possible." With that, we stepped in and closed the door.

Sheila and the other assistant attorney, Brian, read the report and asked if we had anything else to add. Debra spoke. "Jeremy has AIDS." The words sent goosebumps down my spine.

This information was not allowed to be in the written record because of the AIDS Confidentiality Act.

Sheila responded, "The judge needs to be told in chambers of this fact at the time of the hearing."

Back in 1990, Juvenile Court was pretty new at dealing with HIV infected children. There hadn't been that many HIV cases in court, prior to that time. Jeremy having AIDS was of vital importance to the case, but to protect his confidentiality, it had to be omitted from all documentation.

When Sheila said, "At the time of the hearing," I interrupted, bursting at the seams, "You mean you think we have a case?"

"Absolutely," she replied. "An excellent one."

My sight blurred from tears. Sheila continued, "That doesn't mean it's going to be an easy one to prove, however. We haven't accumulated the evidence against her the way we normally do — by founded hotline reports, but by hiring your agency to work with this mother and child, we've probably prevented worse things from happening to this poor kid. Let's hope that after hearing your story, the judge will feel the same way and remove him immediately. Depending upon which judge it's assigned to, that is."

My heart sank. "What does that mean?" I asked.

"Some judges are more inclined toward family preservation than others. Let's hope we get one who will rally for this boy," said Sheila. "I can hear in your voice how much concern you have for him, Robyn. When you testify, that will come across in his favor."

"Good," I said, dabbing my eyes with a tissue.

Sheila told us that depending upon which docket opened up first, she or Brian would be our prosecuting attorney. She was assigned to courtroom G where one judge presided. Brian was assigned to courtroom H with a different judge. They had to schedule the hearing with whatever docket had the next available court date.

As Sheila walked us out of the office, she asked me if I thought Jeremy would be safe with Delilah, once she was served notice of the impending court date.

"No, and that scares me. I don't trust her at all. I'm not sure what she'll do once she finds out we're taking her to court."

"Well," Sheila stated, "unfortunately our hands are pretty much tied unless she hurts him and a hotline report is made. If that happens, the police can pick him up and take him out of there, but it will be after the fact. Otherwise, a hospital is the only other place that he'd be safe. If she tried to hurt him while he was in there, the staff would be legally bound to intervene."

"We're working with the hospital to see if they can help. Someone from the hospital is supposed to get back with me as soon as she gets an answer," I replied.

"You guys are really on the ball. I'll let Debra know as soon as we get a court date and she can pass on the good news. Thanks for coming in. You guys have done tremendous work for this boy and his mom."

As Carolyn and I walked back to the office, we uttered prayers of thanksgiving. I had never had such a clear-cut, prophetic dream before. "God truly is on our side," as Carolyn had so eloquently stated. And this was only the beginning.

Early the following week, I received a phone call from Hannah. The doctors wouldn't go along with our scheme and make something up to hospitalize Jeremy.

"They don't think she'll hurt him," Hannah reported. "They don't know her like you and I do."

So we both promised to surround Jeremy in prayer and put this one in God's hands, too.

That same day, Debra called. Our court date was in less than two weeks. Delilah would receive notice in a few days. She'd have almost a week to escalate herself into whom knows what. It had been more than a month since I had seen Jeremy.

Hannah telephoned me at home that evening. The foster home situation took an astonishing turn: The other boy's court date had been rescheduled... for the day after Jeremy's.

Thank you, thank you, and thank you again, Universe.

Waiting for the court date felt like the longest two weeks of my life. I really missed Jeremy. I tried to focus on other things both at work and at home, but was unable to get him out of my mind. So many things were still up in the air. I didn't like not having control.

So again, before falling asleep that particular night, I prayed hard, "Please, Dear God, please — surround Jeremy with legions of guardian angels for protection. Please keep him safe and well until this is all over. I pray for Divine Order over the hearing and over the foster home situation. May your will be done. Thank you. Amen."

Just before awakening in the morning, I was given another dream. No sound though, only a vision. I found myself in an apartment with my sister, Sandy. We were snooping around. I saw Jeremy's dinosaurs on a table, so I assumed it must have been Delilah's apartment. No one was home. Sandy and I searched for evidence of abuse. While we were in the bedroom, we heard a door open. Delilah and Jeremy came home. We hid in the bedroom. So far, we were safe. No one had seen or heard us.

The door to the bedroom suddenly opened and a Caucasian woman entered the room. I felt like I had swallowed my heart. She had beautiful, long, thick, auburn hair and wore a white robe with a rope belt that resembled a priest's robe. Her eyes turned to the wall on the side of the bed where we hid. She seemed to know exactly how to find us. Her eyes became very expressive, and without words, she conveyed to us that she was there to help. She exuded peace, comfort, and safety. She motioned for us to stand and come out of hiding. She telepathically communicated that much more went on within the confines of those walls than the eyes could see. In fact, she let us know that Delilah continued to beat Jeremy. She gestured that something had to be done quickly to protect him.

Suddenly, I found myself in what seemed to be Jeremy's bedroom. I sat alone on his bed, waiting, expectantly for... I wasn't quite sure... then Jeremy walked directly into the room and came right to me, looking deeply into my eyes. We connected soul to soul. Then right before me, Jeremy transformed into a cherub. Beautiful curly locks of hair surrounded his piercing blue eyes, and almost translucent powdery skin. He wore a white shirt with gray pants. From behind him stepped six identical figures. All seven of them formed a circle around me. Almost blinding, bright white light filled the entire room. There are no words to describe their presence. The closest I can come is to say I never felt so much love, comfort, and peace in my life. Their strength, wisdom, compassion, and dedication enveloped me. It became clear to me; they had a much higher purpose in this situation than was humanly possible to imagine.

The woman with the auburn hair and my sister entered into Jeremy's bedroom to secretly lead us out, so that Delilah would not see us. The cherubs disappeared as soon as the others came in the room. Sandy and I got out safely. I awakened.

What the heck was that all about? So I got up and pulled two books off of my bookshelf; The Mystical, Magical, Marvelous World of Dreams and The Metaphysical Bible Dictionary, from the Unity Church.

I looked up the colors white and gray in the dream book. White — purity, perfection and holiness. One of the definitions for gray fit nicely — a balance between black and white or darkness and light. *Hmmm, interesting. That seems to be exactly what Delilah struggles with....*

When I read the definition for cherubim from the Metaphysical Bible Dictionary, it brought to mind the discussion we had at Sea World about Jeremiah. I remember Jeremy questioning out loud if he had been brought here to do a special thing that only he could accomplish. The definition said, "God's word is materialized when we conform our ideas and mind to God's ideas and mind, and set them into action."

It made me step back and ask myself *could it be possible that Jeremy's spiritual self knows exactly what he's getting into here on his short, incredibly painful human journey? Maybe his higher purpose is to teach Delilah unconditional love and acceptance, to show her the way out of the darkness and ignorance she struggles so hard with.*

And maybe through his story he will teach it to others, as he has taught it to me.

To me, Jeremy was purity, perfection, and holiness. Maybe my lesson was to trust more and know that with my hard work and invoking God's will directly with every action I took surrounding Jeremy, I was being shown God's works made manifest for all to see... for me to see.

It began to sink in for me that Jeremy was protected... on many levels. Levels I probably couldn't even imagine, never mind understand. If his soul had agreed to come here to help his mom, but the time had run out for her to get the lesson, God would <u>have</u> to protect Jeremy through till the end.

There had to be a spiritual purpose for Jeremy's suffering. When I let my humanness, instead of my spirit rule my mind, I failed to understand. If my frame of reference is that we are human beings sharing our spiritual experience, I relate to my physical body as who I am.

When I shift my reference to we are spiritual beings sharing our human experience, my whole view of life takes on a different feel and meaning. Our humanness, in this respect, is something we do; our spirituality is who we are. When I allowed my spirituality to take the lead, I surrendered and trusted the greater purpose for everything. I began to see how important it was for me to come from this spiritual perspective when dealing with this whole Jeremy experience.

Both of my dreams reassured me that right in the middle of all this destruction and darkness, God and the Universe were hard at work. Light would be triumphant in the end. If only I could keep stepping back and not let my humanness keep getting in the way....

As I walked into my office that morning, I became ever so aware that Delilah would have been served her papers by now.

Jeremy could be in grave danger. I hadn't seen him in over six weeks. I personally could do nothing more to help, except keep praying. Trusting in the Universe to take care of all the details unfortunately didn't stop me from feeling frightened, anxious, and worried, though. I guess I couldn't help being human. My whole being ached from holding my tension so tightly.

I poured myself a cup of coffee and sat at my desk, deep in thought. When the phone rang, I jumped. I took a deep breath and answered it. "Robyn, it's Myra. You gotta help me." Myra was another of my HIV mom's. "One o' my boys needs the doctor right now, he been pukin' all night, and fallin' over and stuff. You know I was supposed ta bring 'em all in ta get tested, but I didn't do it. Not, yet. God, I hope he don't have this awful thing, too..." Her voice trailed off.

I grabbed my appointment book. *Good, nothing 'til this afternoon.* "I'll pick you up in twenty minutes. Hang in there, Myra."

I drove Myra and her three boys to the HIV clinic at the hospital, Jeremy's hospital. Donny, the boy vomiting, had flu-like symptoms. Myra was supposed to get all three boys tested for HIV since both she and their dad were infected, but kept putting off their appointment. Since Donny hadn't been feeling well, she decided to get them tested that morning, hoping his vomiting wasn't a symptom of something deadly.

I felt heaviness in the pit of my stomach as the five of us walked into the clinic. As I turned toward the nurses' station, something hit me hard on the back of my leg, almost knocking me down. I quickly turned around. Jeremy grabbed my legs and held me very tightly. An IV pole dragged beside him.

I knelt down and held him tightly. I didn't want to let go. I thanked God he was safe. He was thinner than ever before... dressed to the hilt. *Oh my God, Delilah's here, too.* My heart began to race. I became aware that someone was staring at the back of my head. I turned around. Delilah sat on the couch with Simon, staring at me with vengeance and hatred in her eyes. I smiled at her, politely said "Hello," and looked away. She did not respond.

I leaned down and whispered,"How are you, Buddy?"

"Okay," he said quietly, gazing at the floor with sad eyes.

"I'm here with another family. I have to go help them now. Maybe we can visit later if you think it would be all right."

"I think so. I miss you."

"I miss you, too. See ya in a little bit."

"I love you, Robyn."

"Love you, too, Buddy" I whispered.

I needed to gain a little distance. *Did she get the papers yet? Is he really okay?* He looked the worst I'd ever seen, and she looked at me with the most hateful expression she could muster. She had to know. *Dear Lord, help me handle this.*

At least for the moment, I knew Jeremy was all right, another of my fears to cross off the list.

I stepped into the examining room where Myra and her sons sat waiting. The phlebotomist entered the room to draw each boy's blood for their HIV test. As the first boy took a turn, I held his hand and assisted Myra in keeping him calm and still during the procedure. Two of them were very anxious and feisty. As the last boy was getting tested, I managed to look down at my watch. An hour and a half had flown by.

Since Darin, the oldest boy, sat calmly while having his blood drawn, I asked Myra to excuse me, and I walked toward the waiting room. I glanced into another examining room down the hall from Myra's and saw Delilah and Simon inside. Now was my chance.

I rushed into the waiting area and spotted Jeremy sitting on the floor flying a space shuttle toy filled with astronauts. As I approached him, I saw Myra out of the corner of my eye. She winked at me. Her three sons had finished up in the examining room and joined the other kids playing on the floor.

I sat down on the floor next to Jeremy. His eyes darted around the room to find Delilah. "She and Simon are in the examining room. It's okay. We can talk."

"Good," he said as he tried to stand to hug me. His tangled IV prevented that, so he climbed onto my lap. He looked in my eyes and asked, "Mommy said you're taking her to court so a judge can take me away from her. She said that I won't ever see her again. Is that true?"

I felt so flabbergasted by his statement; it took me a moment to gain my composure enough to speak. She had made it sound like I was the one at fault for having him taken away from her, not her behavior. And telling him that he would never see her again, that wasn't true. What did I expect? On the other hand, a part of me still felt terrible for her and somewhat guilty, because indeed I would be responsible for testifying to have Jeremy removed from her, along with Hannah.

I finally was able to answer, "Yes, Sweetie, I am taking your mommy to court."

"Why?"

"Because I want you to be safe. I want to make it so you're not afraid anymore and so that you're happy."

"Ya mean so she won't be able to hit me anymore?" he whispered as he looked around the room to see if anyone else could hear him.

"No, Sweetie, she won't be able to hit you anymore. I'm gonna tell the judge what she does, and he'll help you. He'll make sure your mommy gets help, too. You will be able to continue seeing her, hopefully not without someone watching you, though."

"You saw how she does, Robyn. I get really afraid, I don't know how to make her stop. And I try my best to help her, too, but nothin' seems to work anymore. You tried, too, Robyn."

"I know you've done your best, Sweetie. And I know how scary it is to be around her a lot of the time. That's why I want the judge to make you safe. I get scared, too. I'm so sorry you've had to go through this. How does it make you feel that I want to tell the judge how your mommy treats you?"

"Maybe I wanna tell him, too. Maybe you can be there with me. Can you?"

"Absolutely. High five." And we did. "You are very brave, Jeremy. I'm very proud of you, and I'm very thankful that I know you and you are a part of my life and Jim's life."

"And Toby, Winnie, and Sammy's life too?"

"Yes. All of us. If you get scared or if anything happens between now and when we go to court, please, call me at home."

"I will, but Mommy said I got nothin' to worry about cuz she's not gonna touch me since the court date's comin' up."

I had no idea what that meant.

135

"You still have my number pinned inside your book bag, just in case?"

"Yep."

"Good job, Little Buddy," I said as we slapped another high five. "I have to get back to those other boys. If you need anything, you call me. See ya. I love you." We hugged and Jeremy didn't want to let go of his grip on me. I felt the same way.

"Love you, too."

I walked away, relieved, but feeling furious at Delilah. I sat down on a couch on the other side of the waiting room, somewhat away from the crowd, to collect myself. I closed my eyes and took several deep breaths. I told myself, *Let it go, let it go.* As I opened my eyes, I saw a woman sitting a few feet from me working on a beautiful needlepoint tapestry. I watched her hands create the intricate blue floral pattern. I went into a trance, staring at her moving fingers.

I came out of it when I saw her glance at me. She had wonderful smiling eyes and long, straight, thick auburn hair. "Hi," she said. Are you okay?"

"I will be, thanks." I responded, trying to place her face. Then it hit me, my dream. She was the woman in the white robe that helped us escape unseen. *Who is she?* Then a thought popped in my head. *Could it be Lindsey, the foster mom?* So I asked, "Are you Lindsey Ross?"

"Yes, I am," she responded awkwardly, "and who might you be that you know my name?"

"I'm pleased to meet you. I'm Robyn, Jeremy Miller's social worker. Hannah told me all about you."

"Hannah told me about you, too… but… how did you know I was the one Hannah spoke of?"

"Uh…Hannah's very descriptive…" I blurted out, feeling somewhat embarrassed.

"Oh." She looked at me and lifted one eyebrow.

"If you have a few minutes, I'd like to talk with you if you don't mind," I said.

"Sure," she answered.

I began to share some of my concerns for Jeremy with her. My hope was to win her over so that she would want to help him. I thought that if somehow, she learned what an incredible child he was and what he had been through, maybe she would want to reserve the last placement she and her husband had open, for Jeremy.

I prefaced my conversation with "I'd like to share a few things with you in hopes of giving you a better understanding of what Jeremy has been through." She agreed, saying it might assist her in making a better decision if she was given a choice of children. She also said if she ended up with Jeremy, it would help her to understand him and help her to make his adjustment a little easier.

"I'll hold the information with the utmost confidence, but I'd like to share it with my husband, if that's all right." I liked her already.

I told her my concern for Jeremy. I explained how explosive Delilah could be. I told her about the Florida trip and how frightened I was for Jeremy's safety.

I gave examples of Jeremy's capacity for love and fun. By the end of the conversation, Lindsey and I were both convinced that Jeremy would soon be placed with her family and looked forward to spending more time together. "I know that you're going to be the best foster mom for him."

As I left the clinic with Myra and her kids, Hannah passed us in the hallway. I stopped to talk with her.

"Jeremy's so skinny," I stated sadly.

"Yes, but at least he's here. It's been over a month since we've seen him in clinic. Besides his weight loss, he actually looks pretty good."

"He said Delilah told him about court and said she wouldn't touch him again because of that. What the heck does that mean? She won't hit him or literally touch him?"

"You can never tell with her. Did you get a chance to talk about going to court with him?"

"Yeah, he handled it well."

"He's quite a child," replied Hannah.

"He sure is," I said. "If we only knew how to keep him safe until the court date, I'd feel much better."

"Me, too," said Hannah.

The following evening, Hannah called me at home. Jeremy had just been hospitalized through the emergency room. His temperature was over 104 degrees. Delilah hadn't been able to get it

137

down, so she brought him in. Hannah was sure that he'd respond to treatment and that we had nothing to worry about... this time.

Hannah and I both realized that our prayers had been answered: Jeremy would now be safe and protected from Delilah's possible rageful outbursts prior to the hearing later in the week.

Jeremy and God worked this one out perfectly.

CHAPTER EIGHT-- JUVENILE COURT

The long awaited day finally arrived. Carolyn, Connie and I arrived at Juvenile Court at 8:27 a.m. The fresh, crisp air of Indian summer filled my lungs, as I inhaled deeply. There wasn't a cloud in the sky. Temperature was in the upper 60's.

My heart raced with nervous excitement. I worked hard the night before on letting things go. I repeated the affirmation, "God is most powerful. Let go and let God," about a million times before I fell asleep.

Waving our staff ID cards to the armed sheriffs allowed us to bypass the metal detectors and enter the lobby of the huge concrete building. As Connie approached the information desk to find out which courtroom we'd been assigned, Carolyn and I said a prayer for Divine Order to reign over everyone and everything involved with Jeremy's case. We were ready. In fact, I couldn't wait to tell Jeremy's story. It had weighed me down too long. It gave me relief to think the judge would soon carry the responsibility for Jeremy's fate.

"Courtroom H, ladies. After you," said Connie, smiling. I remembered Brian would be the prosecuting attorney for that courtroom and judge. I also remembered that judge was supposed to be the, "Hard core, pro-family judge." *Oh well,* I thought, *God will work everything out. Let it go.*

As we entered the waiting area, Debra anxiously paced the floor, anticipating our arrival. "Good morning. Everything's set on this end. Hopefully, they'll call Jeremy's case early." Her voice shook. I had never seen her so nervous.

The waiting area, which was outside of the actual enclosed courtroom, was filled with dark brown wooden benches. A walkway down the center of the benches led into the courtroom.

Within minutes, Hannah arrived, accompanied by another woman. Hannah introduced her as Sharon, a supervisor at the foster care agency responsible for placing HIV children in foster care.

Good, I thought, *the more people on Jeremy's side, the better.*

Hannah handed me a copy of the report she had prepared for the judge. It documented several incidents, which my report had not: In June of 1990, Jeremy playfully ran 10 feet from Delilah and Hannah while walking down the street. This angered Delilah and in retaliation, Delilah took a swing at Jeremy. He dodged it and pleaded tearfully, "Please don't hit me, Mommy." Another incident occurred in July of 1990, when Jeremy had accidentally dropped Delilah's keys behind the washer in the laundromat. Delilah reported to Hannah that she had planned to sell all of Jeremy's toys and ground him for months. A few days later during a clinic visit, the report stated that Delilah remained visibly angry with Jeremy and refused to allow him to play with the other children in the clinic. Hannah's report also described the medical neglect incident in detail.

Hannah concluded the report by saying she remained very concerned about Delilah's angry and punitive reactions toward Jeremy's normal childhood behavior. She also stated how extremely concerned she remained regarding his safety.

After I finished reading the report, I hugged Hannah, and thanked her for her help. We all sat in the waiting area on the hard wooden benches. I sat between Hannah and Carolyn. Hannah told me that Sharon, the foster care supervisor who had accompanied her, was Timmy's social worker. Timmy, after being diagnosed with full-blown AIDS, had been living with Lindsey and Wayne for over a year now. Lindsey and Wayne were the foster parents we hoped to place Jeremy with.

Sharon heard Hannah and I talking. She leaned over Hannah, patted me on the arm, and assured me that if the judge placed Jeremy in protective custody at the hearing, he'd definitely go home with Lindsey and Wayne. The other boy's hearing was the following day.

Another answered prayer, thank you.

Several times I had to get up and walk around. I felt numb from sitting so long on the hard bench, waiting and waiting for the sheriff to call even one case to be heard in front of the judge. The waiting area quickly became stuffy, filled to capacity. People leaned against the walls, waiting, slouching, shifting restlessly, and listening for the sheriff to call their name. Children ran around fidgeting. Some appeared frightened and withdrawn. We had been sitting for over an hour when the sheriff finally stood. "All cases are postponed, the judge will not be coming in today."

Connie immediately stood and approached the sheriff to ask why. "Judge is on vacation, Ma'am."

Now why hadn't they known that before? *They can't get away with this. Jeremy's case has to be heard today.*

The rest of us furiously approached the sheriff to ask what we needed to do to have an emergency case heard. She instructed us to speak to the state's attorney to find out.

Great. He had just left. Connie asked another attorney who was still hanging around. "I'm not sure, but if you wait here for just a minute, I'll find out for you," she said with confidence.

I had no idea my heart could actually beat that fast without coming out of my chest. She came back quickly, "Go to courtroom D and speak to the attorneys there. If they think you have an emergency, they'll allow your case to be heard by their judge. Good luck!"

We marched into the jam-packed waiting area for courtroom D. Connie approached a group of well-dressed adults standing together, assuming they were the prosecuting attorneys for that courtroom. She assumed correctly. One woman asked a lot of questions. She introduced herself as Lisa. After hearing my story and Hannah's, she said she'd squeeze us in on her docket. One hitch though — the judge hadn't shown up yet. No reason as to why he was so late.

After waiting another 45 minutes, the sheriff on this docket made an announcement. "We have just been informed the judge is sick. He will not be hearing any cases today...."

This is a joke, right?

A comedy of errors was more like it. Well, maybe not. Suddenly it clicked. *Center yourself. You prayed hard for Divine Order. Remember that God is in charge. Surrender!*

141

Before I even got a word out of my mouth, Lisa said, "This is ridiculous. I'm not going to let this go. I'll find you another courtroom. Be right back." She stormed off.

She came back, guiding us to courtroom C, for yet another judge to hear our case. "I'll even escort you over if you'd like. I can talk to whoever's there and give them the scoop." We gratefully accepted and appreciated her gesture.

After arriving at courtroom C, I sensed something strange going on. I couldn't quite put my finger on it... yet. The other courtrooms were jam packed with people, while this one barely had a soul in it. "Lisa, why is this courtroom so empty?"

"The judge must have a small number of cases to hear today, or something. Seems kinda unusual."

Lisa entered a small room with two other well-dressed women, and closed the door. In a few moments, she came out and asked us all to join them. All three women, who were prosecutors from the state's attorneys office, needed to hear everything from Hannah and I. After finding out that Jeremy had AIDS, they seemed even more concerned about our allegations. One asked a question that caught me off guard.

"Where's the mother? Isn't she coming today?"

In all my concern and excitement, it hadn't dawned on me that Delilah wasn't present.

Where is she? Why isn't she here?

Hannah shared that Delilah had mentioned she might not be in court because of Jeremy's hospitalization. She felt it was more important to be with him.

"Does this mean the judge won't hear our case?" I asked.

Lisa explained, "Her absence in court will be perceived as apathy. If she truly cared for her son, she'd be here fighting for him. It's actually better for your case — there's no one to dispute your arguments in front of the judge."

Whew!

They instructed us to sit down and relax for a bit. We'd be called within the hour. This judge had not yet arrived either. Within a few minutes the sheriff announced, "Miller, Jeremy Miller."

Oh my God, this is it.

My heart felt like it was coming out of my chest. I got an instant headache. Both knees trembled. I felt like I could throw up. Hannah was the secondary witness, and I was the primary one. According to Debra, my testimony supposedly weighed more heavily than Hannah's did, since I was the one working most closely with both Delilah and Jeremy. I quickly said a prayer for Divine Order over the entire courtroom and everyone involved in Jeremy's case, and I asked that the White Light of Christ surround everyone also.

Carolyn and I exchanged glances and crossed our fingers. The bailiff told me to stand to the right of the judge, Hannah, to my left. The bailiff then swore us both in. The three state's attorneys stood to my right. The public defender, representing Delilah, stood on Hannah's left. To her left was a Guardian Ad Litem, the attorney for Jeremy.

The judge had soft white hair, wire rim glasses, and rosy cheeks. His eyes, a beautiful crystal blue, were piercing with clarity. *Just like Jeremy's in my last dream.* His eyes seemed to look through each one of us. I remember thinking that about Jeremy when I first met him.

Lisa, our prosecuting attorney, began. "Your Honor," and before she could get another word out, he spoke.

"Excuse me, if I may," he said gently. "The state's attorney has so kindly informed me in chambers of the details surrounding this boy's case. Is the mother present?"

"No, Your Honor, she is not," answered one of the women.

"All right then. I have read both of your reports. Ms. Accetturo, you look like an honest, conscientious woman. Ms. Hanley, you do, too. In the absence of the mother, I can only believe that what the two of you have written in your reports is true. Ms. Accetturo, do you swear that everything you have disclosed here is true?"

"Yes, sir." I answered wholeheartedly.

"And you, Ms. Hanley, do you solemnly swear that all you have disclosed is true?"

"Yes, your Honor."

"I hereby order custody of Jeremy Miller to the state of Illinois, office of Public Guardian. Thank you ladies for your time and hard work. Have a good day."

143

Hannah and I grabbed and hugged each other. I looked back at the judge, tears streaming down my cheeks, and whispered, "Thank you, Sir, thank you." I walked arm in arm with Carolyn and Hannah out of the courtroom.

Carolyn whispered, smiling mischievously, "Kinda reminded me of Santa Claus..." When we got to the waiting area, the attorneys reconvened with all six of us in the little room. Lisa stated excitedly, "Congratulations! That was easy, huh ladies?"

"Wow!" was all I could manage to get out.

"I have never seen that judge before. Must have been a fill in from another court," said another attorney.

"Now what happens?" I asked.

Lisa answered. "There will be many other hearings. The mother will have 18 months to be able to show the court she can stop abusing Jeremy and earn his custody back. If she can't prove it to the judge in that amount of time, there will be a permanency hearing, and Jeremy will be placed under permanent custody of the state, and up for adoption. Her visits with him need to be supervised from now on."

"Where will he go now?" asked Connie.

Sharon answered, "He'll be placed in one of our foster home's. I'll handle all of the details."

Yeessss!

Hannah addressed Debra. "Who's going to tell Jeremy what has taken place today? And when will Delilah be told?"

Debra responded, "As far as Delilah goes, I'll tell her. I'll try to reach her after I leave here. And Jeremy... well... Robyn's the closest to him..." She looked over at me. "You know him the best. He'd probably take the news better from you... Would you do it? Please?" She asked, looking directly into my eyes.

My immediate reaction was, *No way. That's your job, Debra.* So I said, "Let me think about it for a minute...." As I held an internal conversation with myself, I reasoned with myself. *Debra's right. I am closest to him. But does that make me the one responsible for giving him the news? Although I would probably be the one who could handle his reaction, no matter what it might be, and let him know that he's safe and protected from his mom's rage. I guess Debra is right. Oh my.* "Sure, I'll do it. I'll go see him tomorrow in the hospital."

Lisa took me aside. "Please, let Jeremy know I'll be coming to see him tomorrow, also." She handed me her card to give to him. As his newly assigned attorney, she needed to speak with him directly.

When I went home that night, Jim and I celebrated the good news with dinner out, and a prayer of thanksgiving. God had handled everything perfectly, down to the last detail.

An Angel as the judge... Thank you, thank you.

CHAPTER NINE -- TELLING THE TRUTH

First thing on my agenda, the next morning, was to go to the hospital and break the news to Jeremy. I managed to swallow a few bites of bagel while I continued to practice over and over again what I wanted to say to him. I had rehearsed several times before falling asleep the night before. I also gathered several symbolic gifts for him.

The state had given me handmade quilts, the size of crib blankets, for our HIV children. Various groups throughout Illinois had created them specifically for children and infants with HIV. I picked out the most brilliant, bright red, patchwork quilt for Jeremy. The artists were a group of second graders from a school in Southern Illinois.

A different child drew each square of the quilt, in crayon. Magnificent drawings of stick people, animals, trees, and other drawings filled a checkerboard pattern. Some of the artists autographed their square. It was quite an impressive sight.

I selected a special stuffed animal from my own collection – a sheep, belonging to my niece since her birth. She gave it to me when she "outgrew" it on her 14th birthday. I wanted Jeremy to have it as a gesture of my love for him, and Jim's love, too. Sheep are harmless and innocent, just like Jeremy, and Christ always watches over his flock.

I wrapped the lamb like a baby inside the quilt and headed to the hospital. On my way, I said a silent prayer. I passed by some freshly planted mums in the hospital's fall garden. I couldn't help myself. I glanced to see if anyone was looking. I bent down and picked a bouquet of yellow mums for Jeremy. After placing them in the sheep's paws, I rewrapped it and entered the hospital lobby. I got on the elevator and let out several sighs. I prayed all the way up to the seventh floor.

Trepidation filled me as I stepped out of the elevator. I hoped Delilah wouldn't be there. I wasn't prepared mentally to meet her face to face. I needed all of my energy, to remain centered, to be with my Little Buddy. I walked to the nurses' station, introduced myself to the nurse that was there, and informed her of the nature of my visit. Hannah had already written in the chart what had taken place the previous day in court.

The nurse informed me that Delilah had stayed there all night. She had just left a few moments before I had arrived. I breathed a sigh of relief.

I paged the charge nurse and explained that Delilah's visits with Jeremy needed to be supervised from now on. The nurse checked Jeremy's chart. Hannah had already made a note of the court's demand. The nurse said she would alert all of her staff.

It was now or never. I had to walk into Jeremy's room and tell him the truth; that he had just been removed from his mother's custody, in order to protect him from her violent outbursts. As much as I wanted for it to happen, it would break my heart to tell him.

I said another quick prayer, took a deep breath, and entered his private room. He looked up from his game with his shining face and exclaimed, "Hi, Robyn. Look at my awesome football game. I'm winning, 21 to 6." He reached over his IV to show me. His left arm, taped securely to a metal board, was connected to three IV bags. "That's great, Sweetie!" I tickled him as he lifted the blinking screen to my eyes. "How are ya, Buddy?"

"I'm okay. Mommy just left. She said I couldn't see her anymore. The judge said so. Is that true, Robyn?"

"No, Sweetie, it's not true even one bit. You'll be able to see your mommy as long as someone is there with you. We met with the judge yesterday. He said that for now, you're gonna live with Timmy and his foster mom and dad, in their house. The judge…"

Jeremy interrupted, anxiously bouncing up and down on his bed. "You mean, Timmy, from the clinic?"

"Yep, your friend, Timmy, from the clinic."

"Yippee!" he shouted at the top of his lungs. And with that, he started to punch me hard, in my shoulder. "Timmy from the clinic, ha, ha, ha, ha, ha," he sang punching me even harder. I grabbed one of his pillows and put it against my arm. He struck it more forcefully with every blow. Tears streamed down his face. I remained silent, holding the pillow.

Within a matter of minutes, he collapsed into my arms, sobbing. I held him, stroking his hair and forehead. "It's all right, Sweetie, there now."

When he stopped sobbing, his little body still heaved and he gulped for air every few seconds. I placed my hand under his chin, bent down to look in his eyes and asked, "What kind of feelings go with those tears?"

"I don't know…"

"Let's try to name them together, okay?"

"Okay… Are you sayin' that she can't hit me anymore?"

"That's right, Sweetie, she can't hit you anymore."

"You know how she gets, Robyn."

"Yes, I do Jeremy. I was with you when it happened in Florida…"

"Yeah, she was really mean. You're the only one who really knows, Robyn."

"Yes, I do. That's why I fought so hard to have the judge hear about you. We needed to make sure you are safe and protected."

"I remember the day you promised me at the zoo. Are you positive that I'll still get to see her?"

"Yes, I am absolutely positive you'll still be able to visit her. The judge will make sure of that. This is all being done so that your mommy can have time to learn how to not hit you."

Jeremy sat motionless, staring into space. "I'm happy. But I'm sad, too. How come?"

"Well, let's try and figure this out. Whaddya think's makin' you feel happy?"

Jeremy remained silent at first, deep in thought. "Mommy can't hit me anymore. And I get to stay with Timmy, and he has kitty cats."

"That sure sounds happy to me. It's okay for you to feel that way, ya know."

Jeremy picked up his football game, turned the power switch to off, and set it back down on his bed. He looked back up at me.

"It's okay?"

"Most certainly. I'm happy, too, that your mom can't hit you anymore."

"Me, too..." Jeremy's voice trailed off, and he stared out toward the window. Two big smokestacks with steam pouring from them filled the view.

"Whaddya think's makin' you feel sad, Buddy?"

"Mommy's hurting inside." He caressed the bed with his left hand and punched the pillow with his right. I had to fight back my tears. "I want her to stop hitting me, but she keeps on doing it."

"Yeah, I know," I answered in a quiet voice. Jeremy turned his head away from me and stared out his window again.

"That's why I had to do something. You've been working so hard to help her. You always show her your love. No matter what has happened, your deepest feelings of love and concern always shine through. I'm so sorry that you've had to go through this, Little Buddy." I reached over, carefully picked Jeremy up, sat down on the bed and placed him on my lap. He put his head on my shoulder and started sobbing again. "It'll be all right. Shhh, there now, you're safe now," I whispered, holding him securely in my arms.

When Jeremy was ready, he finally pulled himself upright. He looked at me and gently wiped the tears from my cheeks with the back of his free hand. He stopped for a moment and whispered, "I love you, Robyn. Please don't ever leave me."

"I love you, too, Jeremy, and I will never leave you. We're Buddies forever!"

"We are Buddies forever!" As he leaned in to squeeze me, he spotted the gifts I had brought him. "What's that?" He pointed over to the quilt.

"Presents."

"For me?"

"Of course!" I handed them to him. He tenderly unwrapped the quilt. "Wow, I've never gotten flowers before. And yellow, my favorite! I'm gonna name the lamb Stephen... he's so soft." He rubbed the lamb against his face and cuddled it. "All for me..." He laid Stephen down on his pillow and rubbed noses with him.

"They're all for you to take to Timmy's. A class of second graders made the quilt for you because you're so special."

"Look at the trees. And all the people! And all those pretty hearts. How'd they know what I like?" His eyes twinkled with delight.

"They just knew. I thought you'd like this one. Stephen used to belong to my niece, Christina. He was her favorite stuffed animal when she was a little girl. Lean in close, I have to tell ya a secret."

"I'm good at keepin' secrets."

"I know you are. If you ever feel scared or alone, pick up Stephen and imagine that Jim and I are right there with you giving you a big hug. Always and forever, we love you, Jeremy."

"Stephen can be my buddy just like you call me your 'Little Buddy'."

"Yep, just like that."

"Can you get me some water to put my flowers in? Please?"

As I filled a glass with water, I heard a knock on his door. I turned and saw Lisa standing at the doorway. "Can I come in?" I introduced her as I pulled her card out from my pocket to give to Jeremy.

"My own attorney, how cool. But why do I need one?"

"I'm gonna give the two of you some privacy, Buddy. I'll be right down the hall if you need anything, okay?"

"Okay… love you, Robyn. You'll come back, right?"

"For sure. I love you, too, Jeremy."

As I stepped out of his room, I felt buoyant. The enormous pressure that had tensed my shoulders eased with every breath. At least so far, Jeremy handled the news tremendously well.

I walked down the hallway to the waiting area. I no sooner stopped in when Bart, the social worker who worked with the infectious disease team, approached me. He had known Jeremy longer than I had. I thought he'd be thrilled with the court's ruling. My heart skipped a beat when I saw the look on his face.

"Delilah told me what happened. She was here all night with him," he stated, putting his emphasis on "all night."

"I heard. She told him she'd never see him again," I said, hoping to encourage Bart's empathy for Jeremy. After all, Bart would continue to work with Jeremy during his inpatient stay and then outpatient when Jeremy returned to the clinic.

Instead, he glared at me and the words that came pouring out of his mouth stunned me so much that, in all honesty, I barely heard even one of them. Bottom line though, he didn't agree that Jeremy should be removed from Delilah. My heart raced as I felt my face turn red.

"I did what was best for Jeremy." I stormed off and punched the down elevator button.

I rushed to the cafeteria and got a cup of soothing herbal tea. Between sips of hot tea, I managed to gulp down my tears. I needed to let Bart's insensitivity go. It took me a while before I could.

I finished my tea, boarded the elevator, went back upstairs, and peeked in Jeremy's room. Lisa saw me and motioned for me to come in. "Hi, guys," I said.

"Hi, Robyn. Look, look! Lisa let me wear her watch. It's so cool."

"Wow, let me see your arm young man."

"He's impressive," Lisa stated.

"He sure is," I boasted proudly, winking at Jeremy. He winked back.

"I must be going now, Jeremy. You have my card. Please, call me anytime," she said in a reassuring voice.

"Super!"

Lisa reached her hand out to shake Jeremy's. He shook her hand and then snuck in a kiss on the back of it. She pulled him toward herself and gave him a big hug.

"Bye," Jeremy said, with sadness in his voice.

"Bye. Nice meeting you, Jeremy. See you later, Robyn, thanks."

"Your welcome. Bye."

"Robyn, can you ask the nurse to wheel the Pacman game in here please, and can you play it with me? Please? I'll beat you!" Jeremy quickly became upbeat again.

"That's a challenge I cannot pass up. Be right back."

As I stepped out, the nurse came around the corner toward me. "I heard that," she laughed, entering the doorway. "He is quite a challenge, isn't he? How about if I get the game after I change your IV needle. All right, Jeremy?"

"If you say so," he answered, rolling his eyes.

The nurse cautiously changed Jeremy's needle to another position. His arm had become quite puffy where the old one lay. I walked out with the nurse after she finished.

"How's he doing?" I asked.

"He still has a very high fever. We can't seem to knock it down. The doctor just ordered a stronger antibiotic to see if it will help. It should be here shortly. They haven't found the source of the infection yet, and he has a terrible case of thrush."

"Do they think he'll be okay, though?"

"Time will tell."

That was for sure. Jeremy beat me at every game we played that morning, be it Pacman, Nintendo, or the video football game his mom had gotten him at the airport in Florida.

After a couple of hours, I needed to get going. "Sweetie, I have to go now." I placed Jeremy on my lap. "I want you to know that I will always be there for you, no matter what happens. You can always count on me. Same goes for Jim, too."

"Same goes for me." We embraced for a long time. When we were both ready to let go, we giggled as we reached for the same tissue to dry our tears.

"Let me write my phone number on a piece of paper in case you want to call. I'll call later to say good night."

The next day, while sitting at my desk writing a report, I got a call from Hannah. She said that Jeremy's fever mysteriously broke shortly after I had left, even before they administered the new medication. He was being discharged that afternoon. Hannah asked if I could be there to make Jeremy's transition to his foster home easier on him. I put my report away, raced to my car, and took off for the hospital.

Lindsey and Timmy were in Jeremy's hospital room, helping him get dressed. He had only one change of clothing that his mother had brought to the hospital, his jacket, and the gifts I had given him. He was explaining to Timmy, who Stephen his new lamb was, when he saw me.

"Hi! I get to go home today with Timmy, Stephen, and his mommy!"

"Wow, Sweetie, you sound so excited!"

"Yep!"

"Me, too!" shouted Timmy as they started to wrestle on the bed.

"All right boys, that's enough," laughed Lindsey. "We'll have time for that once we get home. For now, we have to get ready. Who wants to go to McDonald's for lunch?"

"We do!" the boys screeched in unison. Their laughter was infectious. Lindsey and I joined in.

"Looks like you're going to have your hands full. May I help you down to your car?" I asked.

"That would be great, thanks."

The elevator ride was a hoot, both boys trying to one up the other by pressing the elevator button, or jumping out of the door first. They took turns playing follow the leader all the way to the car.

As Lindsey helped them fasten their seat belts, I wrote my home and work phone numbers down for her. "Please feel free to call me, anytime. Jeremy knows he can, too. And thanks for doing this for Jeremy. I am grateful." I reached toward Lindsey to give her a hug. She hugged me back.

I stuck my head in the car to say good bye. Jeremy was so busy playing with Timmy, he couldn't be bothered. "Bye, Robyn," he said without looking up. "See ya. Love you."

"Bye Sweetie, I love you, too. Talk to you soon." I blew him a kiss.

As I started to walk toward my car, Jeremy yelled, "Can I have a hug? A big hug?"

"I never thought you'd ask." We made silly grunting noises, too.

Looked like a good beginning to me.

CHAPTER TEN -- THE ADJUSTMENT PROCESS

I called Jeremy every evening during his first few days with Lindsey, Wayne, and Timmy. Just wanted to check in, let him know I didn't forget about him. His excitement continued holding fast. Our second call, I got a full report. "One of the kitties, Suzie, really loves me. I mean really a whole bunch."

"How can you tell?" I asked, thrilled to feel his happiness.

"Cuz she sleeps on *my* bed every night, not Timmy's, or Lindsey's, or Wayne's, *only mine*. And when I come off the school bus, she waits for me at the back door."

"Wow! What a friend. What does she look like?"

"Well, she got black all over and a little white. But mostly black. She got two white paws and a white nose. She's super cute, and she loves me. Guess what else?"

"Umm... I give up, what else?"

"You should see all the toys in my room. I have my own crayons, and puzzles, and scissors, and there's Legos in my room and paper. And Stephen sleeps on my bed, too. And Lindsey lets me eat macaroni and cheese, and she let's me put chocolate in her coffee!"

"Chocolate in her coffee?"

"Yeah! It tastes great. You should try it sometime. And she even lets me eat bologna and cheese sandwiches for supper if I want. She's super nice. I really like it here."

"I'm really glad for you, Sweetie. That makes me happy. You sound happy."

"Yep. And the bus drops me off right in front of my new house. When are ya comin' to see me?"

"I have to meet your principal at school and sign some forms so I can pick you up from school once a week, and we can talk and stuff."

"Then hurry up and do it, please. I miss you already."

"I miss you, too. I'll try and get there before Friday so I can see ya next week. Okay?"

"Okay. I gotta go. Lindsey's here with medicine for Timmy and me. We're gonna watch a Teenage Mutant Ninja Turtles movie. I love you. Bye."

"Love you, too. Bye."

I began to call less frequently. I wanted to give Jeremy space and time to adjust. I did speak to Lindsey a couple of times. She said the boys were getting along fine, "like brothers." Jeremy seemed to be doing adequately in school, too. I reaffirmed my commitment to her and her husband — they could call anytime, day or night, if they needed my help with anything.

Debra said I could continue to see Jeremy for counseling during this transitional period. She wanted me to remain a "stable presence," in his life. Sharon made accommodations for me to do my weekly sessions with Jeremy at her office, since mine was across town.

I met with Jeremy's principal to sign the proper documentation, so I could pick him up every Thursday from school. She introduced me to his teacher. I gave the principal my work and home phone numbers and told her, "I'd do anything for Jeremy. If I can be of any assistance, please don't hesitate to call."

When the first Thursday rolled around, I felt excited, but slightly anxious. Jeremy had become such an important part of my life, my personal life, and now I had to play the role of his "therapist," something I had never really done formally with him. You can learn a lot about a child through play therapy to help them to act out what's happening mentally, emotionally, and even physically. So I gave it my best shot.

As I stepped into Jeremy's second grade classroom, I greeted the teacher. My eyes searched the room for my Buddy. He was bent down, rummaging through his desk for something. When he looked up and spotted me, he came running over, giving me a big hug. The other kids watched us, with wondering eyes. Jeremy quietly told a few, "She's my friend."

His teacher made him line up with the rest of his class and wait until the bell rang, before we could leave.

As we stepped outside into the bright, warm Indian Summer afternoon, Jeremy yelled, "You brought my favorite car, thanks!" He ran toward it and I followed. I threw him the keys, and he unlocked both doors. Our red Nissan was sportier than our other car. I made sure I always drove it when I had Jeremy.

As I pulled onto Lake Shore Drive, Jeremy inquired, "Where we goin'?"

"To Sharon's office."

"How come?"

"So we can have some private time to talk."

"That'd be good. D'ya know how to get there?"

"Not really, but we'll pretend."

"Can we pretend I'm drivin', too?"

"Sure."

The whole way there, Jeremy concentrated on his driving, remaining quiet, serious. He imitated my every move. We managed to get lost at least twice, but eventually got to the agency. Sharon wasn't there, but they were expecting us. The secretary led us to a closet full of toys and showed us the office we'd be using. I let Jeremy pick out whatever he wanted from the closet. He chose a ferris wheel with four "Little people" which fit in it, a frog game, and a ball.

We entered the office and closed the door behind us. He plopped down on the floor, laid down on his tummy, set up the ferris wheel, and gave me instructions. "You be the boy, and I'll be the mommy."

"Sure." I plopped down beside him.

"This is the daddy and the friend." He placed the two of them on the ferris wheel and stood my doll in the corner. "You're in time out," he said sternly.

"What did I do?" I asked in a childlike voice.

"You're not listening."

"Okay, Mommy," I answered.

The mommy continued, "I want you to know that when you don't listen or you do something wrong, I won't hit you. You'll have to stand in the corner for a time out. Okay?"

"Okay," I responded, trying to sound relieved.

"I promise, I won't hurt you. Just stand there, and do what you are told, okay? I won't ever hit you, okay?"

"Okay," I said happily.

Soon the boy came out of time out and joined the rest of the family for a ride on the ferris wheel.

I watched Jeremy interact with the other characters. He had great patience as he explained things to the boy and his friend. He played very gently with them before saying he had enough of this game, could I play the frog game with him.

We played several other games that afternoon, but none had as profound an impact as the ferris wheel. I knew from his playing, Lindsey and Wayne were the perfect fit for Jeremy. They obviously had already laid down some ground rules for him. I was grateful. The circle of healing had begun.

As we pulled into Lindsey's driveway, Jeremy jumped up and down in his seat, "Can you come in and meet Suzie? Please?"

"Just for a few minutes."

"Yippee!" He jumped out of the car and flew up the stairs, before I even got out of my seat belt.

Lindsey, Timmy, Rusty, the dog, and sure enough, Suzie, the cat greeted us at the back door. Lindsey's home was beautiful. So were her antiques, which filled every room, including the kitchen. After exchanging pleasantries, Jeremy shuffled me off upstairs to his room. On the way, Timmy began vying for my attention. Jeremy, sulking and angry, turned and sharply stated, "She's my therapist and friend, not yours."

Lindsey heard and quickly joined us on the stairs. "That's right, Jeremy. Robyn is here for you. Timmy has Sharon, his therapist and friend, too. Come on Timmy, let's let them have some time alone." She led Timmy back down the stairs.

As we walked into Jeremy's colorful room, he whispered, "Be quiet. Stephen's asleep on my bed. Don't wake him up." Stephen, laid on his pillow, the withered yellow mums placed in a small clear glass on his bedside table. His red patchwork quilt was spread out over his bed. Suzie followed us, and jumped on Jeremy's bed, rubbing her head against his arm, purring as loud as could be. We sat, for a moment, petting Suzie, holding each other.

"This is really great, Sweetie. I'm happy for you. Unfortunately though, I gotta get going."

"Oh, no. When will you come back?"

"I'll see you next Thursday."

"Goodie! I'll walk ya to your car."

"Thanks. That'd be nice."

We held hands all the way there.

"Robyn," he said thoughtfully, "sometimes I have so much love inside of me, I could just close my eyes and stay in here forever. I love you. I hope next week comes fast so I could see you again."

"It will, Sweetie. I'm so thankful that I know you. I love you, too." I kissed him on the forehead and got in my car.

I rolled down my window after starting my car. "Robyn?" Jeremy asked with longing in his big, brown eyes.

"What, Buddy?"

"Do you think one day I can sleep over with you and Jim?"

"If it were only up to me, I'd say yes. I'll have to ask Debra about it. I'm sure it would be okay if we took you out for the day, though. I'll let you know. Deal?"

"Deal!"

As I backed out of the driveway, he motioned for me to honk my horn. I did. He jumped up and down exuberantly.

Timmy stood watch from the back door.

CHAPTER ELEVEN -- MY WISH FOR THE FUTURE

The next few weeks went by smoothly. I picked Jeremy up from school every Thursday, drove to Sharon's office, played with him and talked for a while, then drove him back home to Lindsey's. I'd call during the week, just to check in with Lindsey to see how things were going. They call it the honeymoon... everyone's on their best behavior, everything's going smoothly.

One Thursday afternoon, as I walked toward Jeremy's classroom, I passed through a hallway, its walls plastered with children's essays. All were entitled, "My Wish for the Future."

I arrived a little early, so I walked around reading them. Normal kids stuff... "My wish for the future is that my dad buys a new red Mustang... that I get the new pink party dress I've been waiting for at Christmas...that my family gets to go to Arizona to see my Grandpa..." Most filled a page or two. And then one in particular caught my attention. I should've known it was Jeremy's.

It read, "My Wish for the Future is for everyone to have a home." That was the entire essay. Underneath, he drew a picture of a family of several different sized snails.

I was so absorbed in my thoughts about Jeremy and his essay, time got away from me. The bell rang. Kids swarmed the hallway from all directions. I managed to squeeze through oncoming traffic, and spotted Jeremy standing next to his teacher, waiting. He saw me, and ran toward me as he waved goodbye to his teacher.

"Come 'ere. Quick. I gotta show you something." His eyes glistened as he grabbed my hand, pulling me toward his essay. "Look," he smiled, pointing to his essay.

"What's this?" I asked, trying to act surprised.

"It's my paper, silly. Read it... Isn't it cool?"

"Tell me about it."

"Well, everyone should have a home, and snails always carry their homes on their backs. No matter where they go, they always have one."

"That is so cool."

"Turtles do, too, you know… Leonardo, Michaelangelo, Raphael…" He looked up at me to see if I followed what he said. I pretended not to know what he was talking about. Seeing the puzzled look on my face, he yelled, "Teenage Mutant Ninja Turtles… Don'tcha get it?" He playfully punched my arm.

"Why yes, of course." I rolled my eyes while messing up his hair. I tickled him all the way outside.

Another beautiful fall day surrounded us. I pulled my sweater off as we walked to the car. Trees every color from brilliant reds and oranges, to deep magentas and pinks saturated our view. The smell of burning leaves filled the air.

As we got in the car and started for Sharon's office, we began our usual routine. Jeremy shared his school day. He spoke in a serious tone. "We learned all about duck-billed platypuses today in science class."

"Duck-billed platypuses?" I repeated in a silly tone of voice.

Suddenly Jeremy turned toward me angrily and yelled, "You're not listening to me…You never listen to me…You don't even try…" He turned away, trembling. He pounded on the seat with his fist.

He continued to punch the seat harder, sobbing, quietly repeating, "You never listen to me."

I waited. "Do you wanna talk about it?"

"No." He sniffled, curling his legs upon the seat.

We sat in silence for a while longer. "Are you mad at her?"

"Yeah."

The car filled with quiet. My heart hung heavy. It felt like time stopped.

"That's okay," I said quietly.

Silence continued to fill the air.

"She hurt me bad."

"Yes, she did."

"Why does she do it, Robyn?"

"I don't know, Sweetie. I don't know. I wish I did. I know she doesn't want to hurt you, but she doesn't know on the inside how to make herself stop. That's why the judge took you away from her, for now, so she can learn how to stop."

He started picking at his shoelace, fidgeting with the bow.

"Ya miss her?"

"Yeah... and I miss, Simon, too."

"I bet you do. It must be hard for you to be away from them. Hasn't your mom been bringing Simon to visit with you?"

"Sometimes."

"Well, that's good. How have your visits been going?"

"Okay. I don't wanna talk about that."

"We don't have to."

We drove for a while in silence. When we turned down a residential side street, piles and piles of leaves filled the curbside. Jeremy quietly asked, "How come the leaves fall off the trees and die? Why do they have to die?"

"Dying happens to all living things... plants, animals, people... sooner or later everything dies. When it's our time, no matter how big or strong we are, we die."

"What if you don't want to? What if you're not ready?"

"Well, I think it's when we're finished doing whatever it is we're here to do..."

Jeremy interrupted, "Like Jeremiah. Remember?"

"I do. Just like Jeremiah. We finish the job we came here to do, and then we go back home..."

"Back where we came from? Where God talked to Jeremiah and told him that stuff?" Jeremy asked, as though he already knew the answer.

"You sound like you know a lot about it. Why don't you tell me what you think happens?"

"No, you go first. Please? Then I'll go."

"I envision it kinda like a glove... Ya know how you can slip your hand inside of a glove?" I asked him.

"Yep..."

"Well, the real me, the me that's inside of my physical body, the me that can hear myself talk and knows I have a body... it slipped into this body kinda like a glove. And when my body stops working,

161

when I die, it'll slip back out. Our body provides a home for us while we're on the earth, and when we've finished our job here, we peacefully go back to our real home."

"Yep, and when we're here, we have our guardian angels to watch out for us. And when we go back home, we can play with them and stuff. Remember the time you, me, and Mommy talked about it at Sea World?"

"Sure do."

"Well, I know my Guardian Angels' names. One of 'em is Chief Yellow Sports Car. Another is Chief Yellow Bird. They're gonna drive me around wherever I wanna go. And ya know what else?"

"No, what else."

"When you have a baby, I promise, I'm gonna be their friend and guardian angel, too. And they're gonna have my big eyes and my super long eyelashes, too. Both of them."

"Both of them? Is that so? I sure hope they do, that would be great, Sweetie. Thanks. Jim and I would appreciate that a whole bunch. I don't quite understand, though. How come you think I'm gonna have a baby or two?"

"Just a hunch." He quieted himself for a moment and stared out at the sky. "Yep, you're gonna have two babies. And they're both gonna have my eyes and eyelashes, and I'm gonna watch out for both of them. Maybe I'll even coach 'em howta play baseball! So when it's our time to die, we just go, huh?"

"What do you think?"

"I think so. Can you take me to McDonald's? Please?"

"Ya hungry?"

"Super hungry."

"What would Lindsey say? Isn't it almost time for supper?"

"She'd say it's okay."

"All right, then."

We never did make it to Sharon's office that day.

My Wish for the future
is for everyone to have a home

CHAPTER TWELVE -- THE DIFFICULTIES BEGIN

The night before our next scheduled session, I couldn't get Jeremy off of my mind, so I telephoned him. Lindsey answered.

"Oh hi, Robyn. Jeremy's having a tough time tonight. I'm glad you called. Hold on a sec." I heard her cover the receiver as she yelled, "Jeremy, Robyn's on the phone." Lindsey tried to fill me in, "His mom…" But before she could even finish her sentence, Jeremy picked up the phone extension from upstairs. Lindsey gracefully hung-up.

I heard a faint, "Hi." The tone of his voice went right through me. He sounded so down.

"Hi, Buddy. Everything all right?"

"Could ya come over?" he asked softly, then hesitated and added, "now?"

"I'm sorry, Jeremy, I can't come now. But I promise I'll pick you up tomorrow from school. We can talk over the phone now though, if you want."

He didn't answer. I gave him some time to decide. When he remained silent I asked, "Did something happen with your mom?"

"Yeah," he sighed.

"Did ya talk to her?"

"Yeah."

"Ya feelin' sad?"

"Yeah… and mad."

"What happened, Sweetie?"

"She calls me a lot over here, and she cries. She said she didn't mean to hurt me. Why didn't she know that when I was there? I

164

didn't do anything wrong but she keeps on hitting me. You believe me cuz you saw her in Florida."

"Of course I believe you, Jeremy. It's not your fault, Sweetie."

I gave Jeremy time to catch his breath. In between sobs, he managed to continue, "She said she's sorry and she's gonna stop hitting me. She said when I come home, if she hits me ever again even one time, then I'll come back to Lindsey's. So she won't do it ever again, anymore."

"What do you think about that?"

Just then, I heard Timmy yelling in the background, "Come and get me, Jeremy!"

"Ooh — Timmy just ran by me with my new squirt gun, and I gotta get it from 'im." Jeremy's voice sounded much more upbeat. "No more talk today. Okay, Robyn? That's enough. Let's talk tomorrow 'bout it. I'm gonna go play. All right?"

"Sure."

"Bye. Love you."

"Bye. Love you, too." We hung up.

When I picked Jeremy up from school the following afternoon, he looked lethargic. During the drive to Sharon's office, he stared out of the window, subdued. He said he didn't feel like talking. As we walked into the waiting room, Jeremy ignored the receptionist's "Hello," and strolled down the hallway to the closet full of games. He grabbed two of them, along with a nerf baseball and bat, and proceeded to the office where we always met.

I followed him in and closed the door behind us.

"Would you like to talk more about what you told me on the phone last night?"

"No."

"That's okay. How are things going at Lindsey's?" I asked.

"Fine."

I waited, giving him time to elaborate, and continued making eye contact with him.

"Timmy makes me mad. He keeps doing things wrong."

"Like what kind of things?" I asked.

"Well, like…" and then he stopped and looked away from me. "I never do anything wrong. I'm perfect, ya know." He folded his arms across his chest and leaned against the wall.

"Perfect, huh?" I asked as I cocked my head and raised my eyebrows.

"Yep. Perfect." He squinted his eyes.

"I'm not perfect," I said, "and that's okay. God loves me just the way I am, and so do Jim, and Sammy, and Winnie, too. Even with all the mistakes I make and things I do wrong."

"Do wrong, you don't do anything wrong..."

"Sure I do. Sometimes I get mad and lose my patience with Jim, or Nanny, or even myself. And sometimes I feel like I hate something or maybe the way someone acts. I burned dinner the other night when I was cooking it. And I didn't stop long enough at the stop sign near my house, and a policeman pulled me over and yelled at me..."

"So what?"

"Well, if I was perfect, I wouldn't have done any of those things."

"You wouldn't?"

"Nope. Do ya think sometimes you might do things that aren't so perfect all the time, too?"

"I guess..." He scratched his head and said, "Well, maybe I'm perfect just a little bit sometimes." Jeremy grinned from ear to ear when he said that one. Then he picked up the nerf ball and threw it at me. "Think fast!" he yelled as it whizzed past my head.

We played rough until it was time to go. He needed to be very physical, jumping on me, tackling me, punching the bean bag chair. It helped. He looked much calmer and more like himself during the ride home.

Lindsey called me at home the night before my next session with Jeremy, to tell me she'd hide the key to her house in "Jeremy's secret hiding place," so Jeremy and I could get in and have our session at home. She and Timmy wouldn't be home until early evening — Timmy had a clinic appointment that afternoon. I thanked her for her thoughtfulness.

When Jeremy unlocked the back door the afternoon of his session, Suzie, the cat, jumped into Jeremy's arms and greeted him with a big kiss on his nose. It was obvious, she was in love. As we walked into the kitchen, I noticed an envelope, with my name on it, taped to the refrigerator. When Jeremy went in to use the bathroom, I quickly opened it.

Dear Robyn,

Jeremy visited with his mom yesterday at the agency. He came home extremely upset and was uncooperative with us all evening. He wouldn't tell me too much, except to say that she yelled at him for wearing the same clothes every single time she sees him.

He picks out the same outfit to wear each time he sees her because it's the only outfit he has from her. She's refused to give him any of his own clothes to wear over here because she claims they'll get full of cat hair. So to please her, instead of wearing some of the clothes we've picked up for him, each time he visits with her, he wears the outfit she gave him. He can't win, with her.

She has been berating him for the way I fix his hair. She puts that gel in his hair, but I can't. I tried, and found I'm allergic to it. Twice when she's seen me, she let me have it about his hair, too.

He worked hard all day Saturday drawing a picture for her. I found it in his knapsack this morning, crumpled up in a ball. I just wanted you to know what a rough time he had yesterday. Hope this helps. Thanks.

Lindsey

Jeremy came out of the restroom and took me up the stairs to his room. Stephen, the lamb, sat on his pillow. The bright red quilt was spread out on his bed. I opened the conversation with, "So how'd your visit with your mom go this week?"

"Fine." He turned away and wouldn't look at me. He purposely and loudly dumped all his Legos all over the floor.

"Are you sure?"

He shook his head, no, and still didn't make eye contact.

"Wanna talk about it?" I asked.

He shook his head, yes, and looked up at me. "I got really scared. I thought she was gonna hit me again." He began to shiver.

167

I held out my arms toward him, and he walked in toward me. I wrapped my arms around him and knelt down to his eye level. "Rebecca wouldn't let that happen." Rebecca was his new social worker from the foster care agency, which supervised his visits with his mom.

"Mommy yelled at me for wearing my own clothes. They're the only clothes I have from home. She won't give me any more cuz she says Suzie's gonna get them all dirty. I really thought she was gonna hurt me bad, and I told her, 'Please don't act this way again.' I crumpled up the picture I drew for her and brought it home."

Tears streamed down his face.

"It was a super special picture I drew for her, but I didn't want to give it to her, cuz I was too mad, and too sad, cuz I wanna go back home and live with her and Simon, but I'm scared she's gonna hurt me again." I held him in my arms and comforted him until he stopped wailing.

When he finally came up for air, I said, "I'm so sorry all of that happened, Jeremy. Know that you are safe now and that she won't hit you ever again."

I felt very strongly that God would not ever let Jeremy be physically abused again. I had a knowing, a confidence, deep down that everything would continue to work out for him. I found out later that during some of Jeremy's visits with his mom, his new social worker, Rebecca, observed their interactions through a two-way mirror. I picked Jeremy up, sat down on his bed, and rocked him in my arms until he wanted me to stop.

When he was ready, he said, "Let's play. Come with me. I have something super special to show you." He grabbed my hand and led me up to the attic. "Lindsey said she's gonna build me my own room up here. Isn't it so cool!"

He ran toward the window and grabbed a flute, which was sitting in a black velvet lined case. "This is Lindsey's daughter, Michelle's, flute. She's away at college. She lets me play with it." Just then, we heard Lindsey call for us up the stairs. Jeremy yelled, "Be down in a minute." Jeremy showed me a couple of cubbyholes tucked away in different parts of the attic. "They'd be really good places to hide from Timmy." He looked over at the east wall by the window and said, "This is where I'm gonna put my bed. Lindsay's gonna have to move Michelle's stuff back in the corner to make room for me."

When he was ready, we raced down the stairs and joined Lindsey and Timmy. They had made us some hot chocolate.

CHAPTER THIRTEEN -- THE HEALING

During our next two sessions, Jeremy was able to verbalize just how hard it was to have, "Two moms." He shared that, "Mommy gets mad at me, cuz lately I've been wearing the clothes Lindsey gave me, and Mommy says they're 'used'. I told her it doesn't make any difference and that if she gave me my own clothes I'd be happier, but she still says that Suzie'll make 'em too dirty. I don't understand her." He folded his arms in a huff and plopped down on the chair in Sharon's office.

"I'm really mad at her. She hates the way Lindsey fixes my hair, too. Nothing I do makes her happy." When I walked over toward Jeremy to comfort him, his bottom lip began to quiver, and he abruptly turned away from me.

I pulled a chair in front of him and sat down, saying nothing. He needed time to be angry. After a few minutes, he stood up, picked up the nerf ball and slammed it into the two-way mirror. After several more throws, I said, "Be right back."

I ran down the hall to find the nerf bat. By the time I got back, he had kicked a bucket from a game across the room. I quickly closed the door. "Here, Sweetie." I handed him the bat and got out of the way. He began beating the couch as hard as he could. Within a few minutes, he broke down, bawling his eyes out, yet still managed to remain swinging. After a while, he collapsed onto the floor and called me. "Hold me," he whispered.

I sat on the floor and gently placed him in my lap. As I smoothed his forehead with my hand and whispered, "There now, you're all right," I couldn't help but to feel his sadness, his anger, and

170

his utter exhaustion. What torment my Little Buddy had to endure, and I endured with him. He soon fell asleep in my arms.

He was beginning to feel a little feverish. I didn't know if it was from the physical outburst of his anger, or if he was coming down with something. When he awakened after his short nap, he looked wiped out. He fell asleep during the car ride home. I carried him up Lindsey's stairs, and with Lindsey's help, put him straight to bed.

He ended up missing two days of school and was placed on a strong antibiotic. He had come down with another infection of some sort.

The following week, when I went to the principal's office to sign Jeremy out of school for our next session, the principal came out of her office, as soon as she saw me.

"We've been trying to get a hold of Jeremy's foster mother all day today, but she hasn't been home. Neither is her emergency contact person. Jeremy's been sick all day. His temperature climbed to 104. He's asleep in the nurse's office right now. The nurse wasn't in today, so I had one of the teacher's aides sit with him. I called his hospital and they told me to give him two Tylenol every four hours. His last dose was at 1:00. I'm glad you're here. I'm very concerned about him."

"I don't know where Lindsey has been. You can call me if this ever happens again, and I can pick him up earlier," I said.

"That'd be great. Come with me." She led me to where Jeremy was sleeping. When I looked in on him, my heart sank. He looked awful. He woke up as soon as I walked into the room.

"Robyn..." He reached out his hand from under the covers. He shivered. His lips looked a little bluish in color.

"Hi, Buddy. I'll take you straight home and sit with you until Lindsey gets there, okay?"

"Okay."

I grabbed his coat and put it on him. I quickly scooped him up and carried him, as fast as I could, to my car. My heart raced as I thought, *Oh dear God, please let him be all right.*

I managed to buckle him in his seat belt, as limp as his body was, blasted the heater, and drove like a madwoman to Lindsey's. I carried Jeremy up the stairs, found the hiding place for the key and

171

opened the door. Suzie scooted out of the way as I ran with Jeremy up the stairs to his room. By then, Jeremy's teeth were chattering, and his lips looked blue. His extremities felt ice cold.

As we passed by the spare bedroom, I grabbed three quilts from the foot of the bed and piled them on top of Jeremy. I hurried into Jeremy's room, placed him on his bed, pulled both of our coats off, and without even thinking, jumped into Jeremy's bed. I pulled Jeremy onto my lap with his back resting against my solar plexus, and covered us both up with his bed linens. I piled the three heavy knit quilts on top of us. I snuggled him in as close to me as I could get him, wrapped my arms tightly around his upper body, placing the palms of my hands on his tummy, and my legs gently over his.

I began rubbing my hands up and down his arms and legs, trying to warm him up. I placed the soles of my feet over the tops of his feet. It took a good ten minutes for him to stop shivering and for his teeth to stop chattering. When he finally started to warm up, I began rocking us back and forth for comfort. I prayed silently.

Dear God, please heal Jeremy. Please don't let him die. I'm not ready.

I continued rocking, placed the palms of my hands over Jeremy's solar plexus and started to sing "In the Garden," softly, a favorite hymn of mine. I sang it over and over even after Jeremy fell asleep...

> And He walks with me
> and He talks with me
> and He tells me I am his own
> and the joy we share
> as we tarry there
> none other has ever known...

After about an hour, I heard Lindsey come home. She walked upstairs and found us. I told her what had happened. The sound of our voices awakened Jeremy.

"I'm sorry I wasn't home today, Jeremy. You're not feeling good, huh?" Jeremy looked at her glassy eyed. "I'll go get you two Tylenol and come right back. Do you want something to drink?" Jeremy shook his head in the affirmative.

Lindsey quickly came back. Jeremy chewed two Tylenol and took a sip of 7UP. Lindsey walked out to get the thermometer.

Jeremy, still in my arms, suddenly sat upright and projectile vomited across the room. I screamed, "Lindsey!"

Lindsey came running back in. "Oh, boy!" She helped Jeremy climb out of bed, and I jumped up and ran out of the room, gagging, and apologizing. "I don't handle vomit well, sorry." Lindsey laughed. She calmly carried Jeremy into the bathroom as I stood in the spare bedroom watching from afar, feeling somewhat embarrassed, and hoping I wouldn't add to the mess. I folded my arms and suddenly realized that my clothes were soaking wet from perspiration. I walked downstairs to collect myself and sat in the kitchen until Lindsey called me back upstairs.

When I got back into Jeremy's room, Lindsey, clad in disposable rubber gloves, had just finished bleaching everything down and had stripped the linens from Jeremy's bed. She began putting clean sheets on his bed. Jeremy sat at his child-sized table and chairs playing Legos. "Hi." The color had come back to his face.

"Hi. Feelin' better?"

"Yeah. I feel great! Wanna draw some pictures with me?"

"Sure, I'd love too." I said.

Jeremy ran to his closet shelf and took down a pad of sketching paper and some crayons. "How 'bout I draw a picture of you and you draw one of me?"

"Sounds good."

"Hey, Lindsey," Jeremy yelled.

Lindsey yelled back, "What?" She was in the bathroom, emptying her cleaning bucket.

"I'm hungry! Can I have some bologna and cheese, please?"

Lindsey came rushing in to Jeremy's room. "Did I hear you correctly? Did you say bologna and cheese?"

"Yep."

"Let me take your temperature first, okay?"

"Okay."

Lindsey slid the thermometer under Jeremy's tongue and left the room. She came back shortly and read it. "Oh my. 98.6. Normal. Bologna and cheese coming right up."

Lindsey went downstairs to fill Jeremy's request and in a few minutes brought him back up a plate full of Fritos and his sandwich.

"Thanks! Want some Fritos, Robyn?"

"Thanks, Sweetie," I said, reaching for one.

Jeremy and I sat and drew portraits of each other with crayons. He didn't like the one he drew of me, so he sketched a picture of all four Teenage Mutant Ninja Turtles for me instead.

I handed him my color sketch of him.

"Wow. Where'd ya learn to draw like that? It looks just like me. Lindsey…" He ran down to show her and then ran back up and put it on the bookshelf in the hallway, next to a photo of Lindsey and Wayne.

"I'm gonna keep that one forever. Thanks." He walked over and hugged me.

"I gotta get going, Sweetie." I looked out the window. It was getting dark outside. Jeremy walked me to the back door.

"Thanks for helping me. I feel lots better."

"I'm glad, Little Buddy. I'll see ya next week."

"I love you."

"Love you, too."

I said good bye to Lindsey and walked out to my car, feeling relieved.

Two days later, Lindsey called me at home early Saturday morning. She had taken Jeremy to the hospital late the night before. His fever spiked that evening to 104.3 and nothing she did would bring it down. She said that after I left Thursday, Jeremy felt great. Lindsey had promised Jeremy that if he didn't have a fever Friday morning, he could go to school. His class was taking a field trip to see Santa Claus, and Jeremy desperately wanted to go.

Sure enough, his fever stayed away long enough for his wish to come true. Friday night, he was admitted to the hospital and placed on an IV antibiotic.

Saturday afternoon, my friend, Amy, called me on the phone. When I shared with her my experience with Jeremy from the previous day, she exclaimed, "I didn't know that you were such a vehicle for healing."

"What?" I asked, feeling my face get flushed.

174

"You heard me," she stated emphatically, "You were an incredible instrument for the healing of your little friend."

"I didn't do anything."

"God did it. You were just the vehicle through which it took place. Don't you see?"

I sat for a minute, reviewing that afternoon's events in my mind's eye. All I did was hold him close against me, put my palms on his stomach, and pray and sing my heart out. Then another of his dreams came true, his fever stayed gone long enough for him to see Santa with his school friends.

"Wow, Amy. I guess I would have never thought of that."

CHAPTER FOURTEEN -- THE HONEYMOON'S OVER

Jeremy spent close to a week in the hospital. His fever wouldn't come down, so his doctors had to try several different kinds of IV antibiotics.

When I visited Jeremy in the hospital, I read him a book I had bought for him at a wonderful metaphysical bookstore on Chicago's northside, called Healing Earth Resources. The title of the book was Hullo Sun. It's an introduction to spirituality for children and teaches them about the light each of us have inside.

After I finished reading it, Jeremy asked, "Remember when we were in your car that one day, and I got mad at you about the duck billed platypuses?"

"Yeah..."

"This book's kinda like our talk — remember you said that when we die the real us leaves our body like we take off a glove?"

"Mm hmm."

"We're right. And all the stuff I said about my Guardian Angels, Chief Yellow Sports Car, and Chief Yellow Bird... God is real. And God is right here," he boasted as he pointed to his heart, "and over there and over there," he said pointing out the window. "God is everywhere!"

"Hmm... I...."

Jeremy interrupted, "Robyn, could you go get the portable Pacman game? I wanna beat you at it!"

176

"Hey, who said I want to play?" I asked, tickling him under his arm.

"You do... Please?"

"Be right back."

I wheeled the large game into Jeremy's room. We played for over an hour before I had to leave for a meeting. We said our good byes. I stopped Jeremy's nurse on the way out. She said he had been responding well to the latest antibiotic, and he'd probably be discharged in a few days. I felt relieved.

When I got to work, Connie said that the state was thinking about pulling us off of Jeremy's case, since he now had Rebecca, his new social worker at the foster care agency. The state didn't want to pay two agencies to service the same family. The mere thought of being taken off Jeremy's case left me feeling devastated. Connie agreed to look into it. No one wanted Jeremy to lose the strong and close relationship he and I had. I chose not to mention it until it became official. I hoped it never would.

The next few weeks ended up being extremely hard for Jeremy and for his foster family. The most difficult times seemed to be coinciding with Jeremy's visits with Delilah. Near the end of November, Lindsey telephoned me at home. She was really good at reaching out to me when Jeremy was having difficulties. When I heard her voice, I thought for sure, Jeremy must have been sick again.

"Don't worry, Jeremy's all right," Lindsey stated, obviously hearing the apprehension in my voice. "Physically all right, that is. He's just a wreck emotionally, Robyn."

"What's going on?"

"Things have really been getting pretty unbearable around here this past week. For starters, Jeremy tried to scald Suzie by holding her under the shower with only pure hot water coming out...."

"What?" I blurted, as my heart skipped a beat.

"And twice he told me he had no homework, when he really did. He crumpled up the note his teacher sent home for me and hid it in his book bag. Should I go on?"

"Please do."

"He flunked two spelling tests, started wetting his bed yesterday, and he's been giving Timmy absolutely cold stares of hatred. He doesn't seem even the least bit remorseful for the way he's been acting. We're at our wits end."

"Wow, I'm really sorry. He hasn't told me any of these things. But during our sessions lately, he's been really clingy toward me — more than ever before. He hasn't wanted to talk much about anything. He just wants me to hold him and rock him in my arms. I can't believe he scalded Suzie? Is she okay?"

"Looks like she managed to get out just in time. She scratched the heck out of Jeremy's arm and leg, trying to escape."

The incident at the pool, in Florida, flashed into my consciousness. I remember clearly that Jeremy became petrified of the water. He refused to go in the pool and ended up curling into the fetal position, on a lawn chair next to the pool, shivering and whimpering, obviously terrified. I became suspicious, even then, that he was probably reliving some sort of trauma.

Children who have been physically or sexually abused often act out, with safe objects, what has been done to them. That's why play therapy is so important. And who or what was safer to Jeremy than Suzie the cat, who adored Jeremy's every move ever since he had set foot into their household. It made perfect sense to me. On a deep level, Jeremy was trusting Lindsey and Wayne so much, he was beginning to act out his trauma.

I shared my thoughts with Lindsey.

"I'm sure you're right, Robyn, but I don't know how to handle him anymore. It's like he's trying to provoke us."

"You're exactly right, Lindsey. He probably is. That way, if you guys respond to him the same way Delilah does, by hitting him, then in his mind, he'll be justified in his thinking that she really does love him and care about him. He knows you guys love him, he's told me. And you don't hit him. So, if he can get you to act like his mom, than that means she loves him like you do."

"Oh, my. I tell you, he's been making us so mad, and it sure is tempting to want to spank him. But we'd never hit him... Poor Jeremy." I heard Lindsey take a deep breath.

"Yeah, poor Jeremy. And poor you guys. I'm sorry this is so hard. I'll try to get him to talk to me about what's going on. In the mean time, would you guys like any pointers on how to handle him?"

"I called Sharon, you know, Timmy's social worker. She's Rebecca's supervisor. She gave me a couple of articles to read about difficult kids in foster care. You kind of explained the same things they did — how the child tends to act out what has happened to them and tests the new waters. I've been holding him accountable for his behavior by standing him, in time-out, in the corner. And Wayne and I have both been working hard to help him with his homework."

"All those things are great. I think, too, the more you can explain to him what you're doing and why you're doing it, the more he'll be able to understand his present behavior and begin to sort out the things he needs to work out from his mom, as separate from you guys. I'll help him with that, too. If you guys can tell him honestly how his behavior is affecting you, for example, 'I feel angry when you lie to me', that will help him to see how he's acting. A lot of his actions are unconscious, he's not aware of what he's doing. All of us have to be able to see what we're doing before we can change our behavior. If you, Wayne, and I work on reflecting back to him what he's doing, that'll be a big help to him."

"Sounds good. I'll tell Wayne what you've said. I'm glad I called."

"I am, too. And Lindsey?"

"Yes."

"Thanks again for all you and Wayne are doing for Jeremy. I know it's incredibly hard, and I admire you guys so much for doing it. I really appreciate everything. You've truly been an answer to my prayers."

"Some days, I wonder. Especially these tougher ones. But I know we're doing the right thing," said Lindsey.

"You really are. Thanks. There aren't many people who could do what you and Wayne are doing. Remember, if you need to call anytime, please do. I'd do anything for Jeremy and for you."

"Thanks. I just might take you up on that."

As I hung up, the thought passed through my mind, *Oh God, what if Lindsey and Wayne decide they've had enough?*

I sat for a while, petting my cat, absorbed in my thoughts, when Jim came home. "Hi."

"Hi," Jim answered. "You okay?"

"Sorta."

"Jeremy?"

"Yep." I started to cry. Jim sat down next to me and held me.

"He's really been giving Lindsey and Wayne a hard time lately." I filled Jim in on the details. "What if they decide they don't want to handle it anymore?" My eyes again filled with tears.

"What did ya have in mind?"

"We could take him," I answered. Jim and I both sat in silence a minute and then Jim spoke.

"Graduation's a long time away. What if he got sick? Who'd stay home with him?"

I felt so overwhelmed even thinking about it, yet I felt so strongly that we couldn't not take him. We had to. I didn't feel like I had a choice. I loved him so much. So did Jim, just like we'd love our own child.

"We'd figure somethin' out," I said.

"You're right. We'd figure something out. Maybe my mom could help."

"I don't know if I could ask your mom to help — I don't know if I could ask anyone to help. We'd be making a choice to care for Jeremy knowing his body fluids are deadly, and I don't think I could put that on anyone else just to help us out… Ya know what I mean?"

"Yeah, I guess so. Ya know what though?" Jim placed my chin gently in his hand. "Everything always seems to work out for us… Just when we were desperate for a car, your student loan money came through. And when I got laid off from work, the hospital job came through the next day. I firmly believe that if God wants us to have custody of Jeremy, somehow this will work out, too."

Jim and I embraced as we reaffirmed our commitment to Jeremy — we would walk him through to the end, no matter what it took.

I remained hopeful that Lindsey and Wayne would still come through for Jeremy, too.

The next morning, when I got to work, Connie gave me the bad news. It was official. Carolyn and I were being taken off of Jeremy's case. I'd have to tell him during our session the following day.

CHAPTER FIFTEEN -- THE UNIVERSITY TEAM
BOWS OUT

I felt angry and hurt that Rebecca would now be Jeremy's social worker. I know I should have approached the situation with more distance, after all Jeremy was in foster care and our program was for intact families. But unfortunately, I did take it personally. In fact, I had begun to take just about everything with Jeremy personally. I knew that I would stay involved with him on my own time, it was just a matter of who it was okay to tell about it. I would keep my promise to Jeremy no matter what, and no matter how I had to do it, or how long it took.

Connie called Carolyn and me into her office the following morning. "Given the state's decision, I was wondering, Robyn, if you had any plans for Jeremy?" I glanced at Carolyn, who already knew of my plans, and thankfully Connie continued, "It would be great if you stayed involved with Jeremy. You know, on a personal level. Julie and her supervisor agree with me. We'd be thrilled if you did."

Who would've figured?

"I'm really glad you guys feel that way." I quickly answered, trying not to reveal my prior decision.

"You're really important to Jeremy. He needs you," she said.

"I was having a really hard time with the state's decision. He's become an important part of my life, too."

You stated that very diplomatically.

"Well, good. I kind of assumed it would turn out this way."

Since that was now cleared up, it would be much easier for me to break the news to Jeremy, and to Lindsey and Wayne. I felt more comfortable with the state's decision, to remove me as Jeremy's social worker, since they had given me official "permission," to stay involved with him. Although I have to admit, I was a little miffed that I needed their "permission" to do anything in my personal life. Oh well, at least I wouldn't have to sneak around at work pretending not to know anything more about him.

I didn't think Jeremy would have a problem accepting my new role, I just hoped Lindsey and Wayne would be comfortable, too. After all, I had been with Jeremy through some pretty tough times.

For our session that afternoon, I had planned to surprise Jeremy. Kevin, my hairdresser, had given me $40.00 to buy Jeremy something for Christmas. Of course, I had told Kevin all about Jeremy, without using Jeremy's name. Kevin wanted to do his part to help make Jeremy's Christmas extra special.

When I walked into Jeremy's classroom, he raced toward me, jumped into my arms and announced, "Hi, Robyn. I miss you." He gave me a big smooch on my cheek, which prompted his classmates to break out in giggles.

"I miss you, too, Sweetie," I whispered as I gently placed him on his feet. "Better go sit back down." I could tell by his teacher's expression, she wasn't happy with the disruption of her class.

"You have to finish cleaning up your desk, Jeremy, and then line up like everyone else," she snapped.

Jeremy walked slowly and deliberately back to his desk, his eyes downcast. His teacher approached me. "Jeremy's having a very difficult time adjusting lately. Please tell his foster mother he's bringing home a note today."

"Sure." I answered. Then added, "We're all trying to help Jeremy make this adjustment."

She forced a smile and told the kids to line up.

Indian summer was officially over. Unexpected snow flurries filled the air. "Brrr, it's freezin' out here," Jeremy yelled as we raced down the hill in front of the school to my car. "Could we go see the Christmas lights downtown instead of goin' to Sharon's office today? Pretty please?"

We drove down Lake Shore Drive toward the "Magnificent Mile" on Michigan Avenue to see the Christmas lights and decorations. Jeremy especially wanted to watch the horse drawn carriages, which tour the city and offer a beautiful view of Lake Michigan.

"I have something to tell you, Kiddo."

"What's up?"

"Since you have Rebecca now, I'm officially not your social worker anymore. So guess what that means?"

"I can sleepover and eat pizza with you and stuff?"

"That's absolutely right…"

And before I could finish my sentence, Jeremy yelled, "Yippee! What else can we do?"

"How does play baseball, rent movies, go to the zoo with Jim…"

"Can we go tonight?"

"Not tonight, but soon. Promise."

"Pleeease?"

"Sorry. But I'll talk to Jim and we'll set something up real soon."

"Darn." Jeremy put his head down. After a brief moment, he looked over at me and said, "I like that you're not my social worker anymore."

"You know what else, Sweetie?"

"What."

"My promise to you still holds. I'll still do my best to make sure that you're always safe."

"I know that. Could we go home now so I could tell Lindsey I'm gonna sleep over?"

"Well, I have another surprise for you…"

"What is it?"

"Kevin, the guy who cuts my hair, gave me some money to buy you something for Christmas. Would you like to go to Toys-R-Us and pick something out before we head home?"

"Yeah, yeah, yeah," he said whispering his Ernie impersonation, "Toys-R-Us'rrrre great!" he added sounding like Tony-the-Tiger from the Frosted Flakes commercial.

I pulled over at the first pay phone I saw with a phone book and located the nearest Toys-R-Us. It was just a few miles from Lindsey's house. We drove straight there.

As we entered the store, Jeremy took off ahead of me and raced to the aisle filled with action toys. He quickly scooped up all four Teenage Mutant Ninja Turtles, plopped down on the floor in the middle of the aisle, and started sparring with them. I watched as he acted out each character in a different voice and with a different personality. Unfortunately, $40.00 only bought two figures and some Silly Putty. Jeremy didn't seem to mind. He thanked me and asked me to remember to thank Kevin, too.

We pulled into Lindsey's driveway. Jeremy quickly jumped out of the car and flew up the back stairs. I raced after him. He rushed in the back door and as soon as he saw Lindsey, blurted out, "Mommy, Robyn's not my social worker anymore, so I can sleep over at her house, Jim's gonna teach me how to play baseball and stuff, and they're gonna take me out for my favorite kinda pizza. Isn't that cool!" Since the day he set foot into their house, Jeremy called Lindsey and Wayne, Mommy and Daddy. I think he called them by their first names in front of Jim and I, so we wouldn't get confused.

Lindsey looked surprised. With her eyebrows raised and eyes widened, she responded, "That's wonderful, Jeremy. I can see how happy it's made you. Now she's your friend!" The expression on her face didn't match her words.

"Yeah, now she's my friend." Jeremy came toward me, placed his arm around my back, laid his head against my stomach and closed his eyes. As I wrapped my arm around his shoulder, and cuddled him back, I glanced over at Lindsey who was biting her lip, trying hard to maintain her composure.

"Timmy's watching a Ninja Turtle video upstairs in my room. Why don't you go join him, Jeremy, and I'll bring you guys some popcorn in a little while."

Without hesitation, Jeremy took off toward the stairs. Before climbing them, he turned around and yelled back, "Robyn, wanna watch it with me?"

"No thanks, Sweetie. I have to get going."

Jeremy ran back into the kitchen to give me a hug and kiss and then raced up the stairs.

"You okay?" I asked Lindsey.

She motioned for me to step out onto the back porch. It was pitch dark outside and rather cold. As she stood in the doorway, with the door partially closed behind her, she frantically asked, "What's this all about? Who's going to be Jeremy's therapist?"

"Rebecca is..." And before I could finish my thought, Lindsey cut in.

"Rebecca hardly knows him, or his mother, for that matter, and things are getting harder and harder to manage around here. Wayne's pretty tired of some of Jeremy's behavior. He might be thinking about throwing in the towel."

My chest suddenly felt heavy. "I'm not sure what you mean."

"We really don't feel much like a cohesive family, even though we're adopting Timmy next month. The boys have been behaving so badly lately. All they do is fight and pick on each other. And on top of everything else, Wayne's mother's become quite ill. We don't know how much longer she has to live. We're driving out of state to see her this weekend. Wayne doesn't want to take either of the boys."

"I'm sorry. Like you guys don't have enough on your plate, right now. Jeremy hasn't been acting any better?"

"No, in fact Timmy has started wetting the bed, too. Wayne bought training pants for them both, but neither one has agreed to wear them yet. Jeremy flunked two more spelling tests, and he's still not bringing home all of his homework. His teacher isn't very supportive either."

"No, she's not. I could tell by the look on her face today, when Jeremy greeted me in class. She asked me to tell you that she sent home a note today in Jeremy's book bag."

"Thanks. I'll see if he remembers to give it to me."

"I didn't realize Timmy's adoption had come up so soon," I said.

"Yeah, we've been waiting a long time for this. His mom gave up her parental rights and agreed to the whole thing."

"That should make the process a little easier. I'm really sorry things are so hard right now. I hope Wayne's mom will be all right. This is too much for you guys...." I reached over and touched Lindsey's hand. A tear trickled down her cheek.

"I just don't know what to do anymore. I have to respect what Wayne needs and can handle, but I don't want to give up on Jeremy. I feel so bad...."

Oh my, give up on Jeremy?

When Lindsey's attention returned to me, I managed to pull it together and said, "Your needs are important, too. Don't forget that. Maybe a weekend apart is just what you all need."

"Maybe...." Lindsey sniffled, as she looked away from me, and began picking at the brick wall.

When she finally looked up again, I continued. "Jeremy's really doing his best to test you guys. It'll take time for him to learn that you guys aren't going to hit him. As he sees that your discipline with him remains consistent, he'll start to quiet down."

"Maybe it's perfect timing for you to not be his therapist anymore," Lindsey added. "Perhaps because of your professional involvement, he's been holding back telling you about his mom, so he doesn't get her in any trouble. If he knows he won't lose you, he might open up to you even more."

"And now he'll have me as his friend, and he'll have Rebecca to help him work on his anger. Lately, he hasn't wanted to talk about his mom or what's going on here with you guys, so I haven't been pushing him. He has needed holding, cuddling, and fun from me, so that's what we've been doing."

"I don't want to lose Jeremy, but right now Wayne doesn't have the energy to handle Jeremy's behavior, his impact on Timmy, and the added stress of his mom."

"The boys will survive without you guys for a weekend, and if you need more time, I'm sure they can put Jeremy in respite care or I can see if they'd let Jim and I take him. You guys need to take care of your needs, too."

"Two different sets of friends agreed to take either of the kids for the weekend. We want to keep them separated to give them a break from each other."

"Sounds like a good idea. Feel free to call me from Wayne's mom's, if you need to talk. And please, don't feel bad about needing a break from Jeremy."

"I guess...." Lindsey ran her fingers through her hair and let out a deep sigh. "It'll all work out."

"Yes it will. No matter what happens, no matter what you guys need to do, it will all be okay."

Lindsey let me hug her before I left.

I drove home, feeling completely overwhelmed and sad. The mere thought that Wayne was questioning whether or not they could keep Jeremy frightened me. Things would eventually settle down once Jeremy worked through more of his feelings, but it was possible the worst wasn't over yet, either. I could understand each person's perspective. Jeremy was challenging Lindsey and Wayne's authority, and he and Timmy were trying to work out their pecking order. I felt so helpless. There was nothing I could do to change what each person had to work through. The only thing I could do was try and support each of them through it, and pray.

I so much wanted for everything to go smoothly for Jeremy and for Lindsey, Wayne, and Timmy. I prayed hard and once again put Jeremy's fate in God's hands.

CHAPTER SIXTEEN -- OUR FIRST CHRISTMAS

At 8:30 sharp, Carolyn and I waived our ID cards and bypassed the metal detectors of Juvenile Court. Our first court date, since Jeremy had been placed in temporary custody of the state, had arrived. I met the morning with excited anticipation. Today I could finally tell the judge Jeremy's story. We walked through the crowded hallways and approached the waiting area for Courtroom H. It would be Carolyn's last appearance in court, since Jeremy's case had been taken away from us.

I, on the other hand, intended to show up until eternity, if that's what it took.

We arrived just as court had opened. The waiting area was relatively quiet. A few families, dressed in their Sunday best, sat on the hard wooden benches on the south wall. Carolyn and I took a seat on the benches across from them.

As I set my coat and folder down, Carolyn looked at me rather strangely. "Kinda nervous, huh?" She wore a mischievous smile on her face.

"Is it that noticeable?" I answered, feeling somewhat self-conscious.

"Look down," Carolyn said quietly.

The top button of my blouse was buttoned to the second buttonhole. Carolyn and I burst out laughing.

"Thanks, Carolyn. Be right back." As I approached the women's restroom, Brian, our prosecuting attorney walked toward me.

"You're Robyn, right?"

"Right. Nice to see you again, Brian."

"Judge Hamilton's back. She'll hear your case today. There will be some preliminary business that will have to be taken care of, but it's possible you will be asked to testify today. Are you ready?"

I breathed a deep sigh. "I'm ready."

"Don't forget, she's the really tough one for keeping families together — especially African American families with white social workers as the prosecutors."

"How could I forget."

"Is that other woman who was a witness going to be here today?"

"Hannah? I'm not sure."

"I'll check the docket and see what we're up for, and I'll let you know in a little bit."

"Thanks, Brian."

As I fixed my blouse in the restroom, my hands shook. Brian seemed to know Judge Hamilton well. I got the feeling from him that she might award Jeremy back to Delilah even after hearing my testimony. I couldn't understand how anyone could do that, knowing Jeremy might not have long to live. But who was I to question her authority? I said a silent prayer and again put Jeremy in God's hands.

The night before, I had stayed up late preparing for my testimony. I filled nine jumbo index cards describing all the abusive incidences I had experienced with Delilah. I went back into the waiting room, sat beside Carolyn, and pulled the cards out of my folder.

"Better?" Carolyn asked.

"Much, thanks." I filled Carolyn in on what Brian had told me. As we talked, I felt a tap on my shoulder. Jeremy and Lindsey stood beside me.

"Hi, Kiddo!" Jeremy jumped onto my lap and wrapped his arms around me. "Hi, Lindsey," I said looking up at her, smiling.

"Hi. I'll sit over here," Lindsey pointed behind us," so I'm not in the way." Foster parents don't have any legal say over the foster child in their care.

In no time, the waiting room had filled to capacity. Many people leaned against the walls; others paced up and down the hallway outside the waiting area. Once Lindsey got comfortable, she leaned forward and whispered in my ear.

"I was at the clinic yesterday with Timmy and Jeremy. Hannah wanted me to let you know she had an emergency today and wouldn't be able to meet us here."

"Everything okay?"

"Yeah. Do you remember the little boy from clinic, Danny?"

"The little blonde boy?"

"That's him. Hannah's been making a lot of home visits to him and his dad. His mom just passed away from AIDS, and Danny's pretty close to death, too. Hannah thinks it might be today."

"Awww, I'm sorry. I'll have to call Hannah tonight and see how she's doing. Thanks for telling me." I turned back around and felt a heaviness in the pit of my stomach. Who knew when we'd be saying that about Jeremy, or Delilah? I was glad that Jeremy was at the end of the bench, out of earshot, playing with some kids he had befriended.

I grasped the index cards with sweaty palms and sunk myself into studying them. I reread my notes over and over again, hoping this whole nightmare of court and custody would soon be over. I purposely wrote sentences that would jog my memory in case I needed to look down at them while I testified. I didn't want to draw a blank, or be at a loss for words. There was a lot to remember.

- Jeremy's case was referred when he allegedly fell out of a second story window of the homeless shelter where he and his mother resided. He wore a full body cast for three months.
- Mother missed first two scheduled home visits with our program after agreeing to meet with us. She did not call to cancel or reschedule either appointment. On 2/8/90, during first visit to family, this MSW and Community Worker both observed a large welt under Jeremy's bruised left eye. Mother explained that after hitting Jeremy on buttocks with a belt, the buckle accidentally backlashed and hit him in the face.
- Family has absolutely no support system — completely isolated.

- 3/5/90 This MSW made verbal suicide contract with mother over the phone. Mother was threatening to walk in front of a moving bus just to get this over with.
- 3/27/90 During home visit, Jeremy was unable to sit down. Jeremy stated that his mother "whupped" him after she dragged him to the bathroom because he urinated in the toilet after telling her he didn't have to go. I just learned that on 4/9, 4/14, and 4/19 Jeremy's school had sent his mother a certified letter with forms to sign to get the tutor started for Jeremy, but mother refused to sign for it. Jeremy waited over two months for tutor to begin. The mother told me that it was the fault of the school that the tutor didn't begin immediately.
- 5/11/90 Make - A - Wish Trip: Mother became enraged when Jeremy spilled his milk at pizza restaurant and would have elbowed him in the head had this MSW not intervened. At Disney World, when Jeremy didn't go in the bathroom stall, which his mother told him to go in, she slapped Jeremy so hard on his face, a welt of her handprint appeared on his cheek. His nose bled uncontrollably, he fell and hit his head and chest, and got the wind knocked out of him.
- 5/11/90 Jeremy asked this MSW, "Please help my Mommy, I'm scared. Something's wrong." Later that week, he asked if he could live with this MSW.
- 6/8/90 Held staff meeting regarding this case with state worker — state made decision for this MSW to confront mother one more time to convince her to comply with treatment. Mother had failed counseling since return from Disney trip. She spent majority of parenting group in restroom.
- 6/13/90 This MSW confronted mother on discipline of Jeremy and not complying with the agreed treatment plan. Mother defiantly refused to cooperate and stated, "What's Children Services going to do about it?"
- 6/14/90 Mother admitted to hospital for birth of second child. Did not leave medications for Jeremy or instructions

with live-in homemaker on how to obtain them or administer them.

- 6/20/90 Took Jeremy to visit mother in hospital. Again Jeremy asked this MSW if she could become his mommy and move in with her.
- Mother returned from hospital and fired homemaker on the spot for having a birthday party for Jeremy and allowing him to visit with the neighbors. She was extremely angry and grounded him for a month. She did not allow him to play with any of his toys or with any of the children in the clinic.
- 6/27/90 During a home visit, mother threatened Jeremy when he attempted to sit on the couch between this MSW and the Community Worker. She screamed, "I'll punch you so hard you'll fly through that wall, and I don't care who sees me."
- 7/10/90 Mother agreed to work with team again and made plan to have this MSW pick family up weekly, drive to day camp at hospital and drop Jeremy off, then have a session with this MSW. Mother complied only once over the entire summer.
- Week of 8/22/90 Mother failed three more scheduled home visits with this MSW.
- 9/11/90 Mother withdrew Jeremy from all medical treatment and changed phone to unpublished number.
- 10/8/90 Saw Jeremy for first time since 8/15. He stated mother told him he'd be removed from her by this MSW, and that mother would not touch him from now on.
- 10/11/90 State obtained temporary custody of Jeremy.

As I became lost studying my index cards, Carolyn nudged me with her foot. I looked up and saw Delilah pass by carrying Simon in an infant carrier. Simon was now almost six-months-old. My heart skipped a beat. I quickly looked away. Rebecca accompanied them.

I couldn't bring myself to look Delilah in the eyes. I felt too ashamed. I had just been instrumental in having her son removed from her own custody, which on some level didn't make me feel too good about myself. It wasn't the idea that Jeremy had to be taken away from her that bothered me; I was ecstatic he was finally safe. It was that I had to be the one that took action to make it happen. Although I still held a lot of love and compassion for her, I had to keep Jeremy protected from her, since she wasn't able to control herself.

My heart became heavy as I wondered how much longer Delilah had to live. She had pushed so many people away, I was afraid she'd die alone.

I managed to avoid her until Jeremy's case finally got called, after waiting over two and a half-hours to appear before the judge.

Before we walked from the waiting area into the courtroom, Carolyn and I quickly said a prayer to surround the entire courtroom and everyone in it with the White Light of Christ. We prayed for Divine Order to reign over everyone present. When we got in to the actual courtroom, Brian told me to stand to the right, facing the judge. In Juvenile Court, everyone testifying stands before the judge. Carolyn stood next to me. Delilah stood with her attorney on Carolyn's left. Jeremy played Legos at a little table at the back of the courtroom. Lindsey waited in the waiting room, doing her needlepoint.

None of us were sworn in. The judge had another agenda. She stated that notice had been made to Jeremy's father through the newspaper and asked if the father was present. He was not. The public defender, representing Delilah, stated it was thought that he was deceased. The judge had nothing further at this time and issued a continuance until the end of January. That was it. We all filed out of the courtroom.

Here it was, my first time in front of Jeremy's judge, and she still doesn't know what has happened to Jeremy. And for all I knew, she hadn't even been notified, in chambers, that he had AIDS.

One good thing did come out of the hearing — Jeremy would remain safe with Lindsey and Wayne until the next hearing.

At least I hoped he'd remain with Lindsey. I hadn't had a chance to speak with Lindsey privately, since her talk of possibly needing to give Jeremy up. I knew they had just come back from their visit to Minnesota.

I called her that night. "Hi, Lindsey."

"Oh, hi, Robyn." She sounded better. Lighter.

"Since I really didn't get a chance to talk to you today in court, I thought I'd give you a buzz. How is Wayne's mom?"

"She's doing a little better, thanks."

"I'm glad. Who took Jeremy?"

"Friends of ours. Delilah called Jeremy while he was there and must have said something terrible to him. He hung up the phone, crying hysterically, but refused to talk about it. Our friend was so upset by his reaction, she called Sharon to report the incident and demanded that Delilah not call Jeremy at her home the rest of the weekend. I think it's a shame no one supervises Jeremy's phone calls with her."

"It really is. Jeremy didn't mention anything to me about it in court today."

"Despite the phone call, Jeremy had a great time. They took him to the zoo and out to eat. The time away from us really seemed to do the trick, too. He's hasn't wet his bed since, and he asked for help with his homework twice this week." I could hear the relief in her voice. Hopefully this signified a level of Jeremy's acceptance in the household by all, including Jeremy.

"Wow, that's great."

Since Lindsey didn't say anything more about the possibility of needing to give Jeremy up, I certainly didn't broach the subject. Their weekend apart seemed to be what everyone needed.

"May I please say good night to Jeremy?"

"Sure, hold on a sec." She covered the phone and yelled, "Jeremy, Robyn wants to talk to you." Jeremy picked up the extension upstairs. Lindsey and I said good bye.

"Hi, Kiddo."

"Hi. Me and Timmy are watching Dumbo."

"What a great movie. I heard you haven't been wetting your bed anymore."

"Yep. And I brought my homework home today, too. Me and Timmy got to watch the movie cuz we finished all our homework."

"Super job! I'm really proud of you, Sweetie. I just wanted to say good night."

"Good night. I love you. I'm gonna watch the movie now."

"Okay. I love you, too. Good night."

I hung up and remained sitting, curled up on my couch, beaming, thinking of a plan to reward Jeremy. One quickly came to mind. Good thing, too — I heard Jim walking up the front stairs. Before he even kissed me hello, I bombarded him with my idea. "Jeremy loves surprises...." I thought I'd plant a little seed first.

"Yes..." Jim answered with wrinkled eyebrows and his head cocked to the side. "Whatcha got in mind?"

"He's doing so much better. He stopped wetting the bed and asked Lindsey for help with his homework."

"Go on...."

"How 'bout if we pick him up Friday night, take him to that pizza place we went a few weeks ago where they had all those video games, and then he can sleep over and help us put up our Christmas tree?"

"That only gives us two days to do our Christmas shopping for him and to pick out a tree...."

"So it's a date?"

"It's a date. Now can I take my coat off?" Jim laughed.

I called Lindsey back and she liked the plan. She even said she'd try to keep Timmy and Wayne out of the way, so that Jeremy could eat up all our attention for himself.

On Friday, just before dinnertime, Jim and I drove to Lindsey's house and parked on the street in hopes of Jeremy not seeing our car. We quietly crept up the back stairs and peeked through the kitchen window. Lindsey saw us and winked. She had purposely sat Jeremy with his back to the window and had him busily rolling peanut butter dough into cookies. Lindsey walked to the door, pretending to let the dog out, and let us in.

Jim snuck up behind Jeremy and yelled, "Surprise!"

Jeremy squealed with delight and jumped from his chair. He tried to tackle Jim, who quickly picked him up, flipped him around and lifted him onto his shoulders. "You guys scared me," Jeremy exclaimed as he happily messed up Jim's hair.

"He's all packed," announced Lindsey, laughing.

"Packed?" Jeremy asked, "Where'm I goin'?"

"How 'bout pizza and spending the night with us?"

"Hooooray!" Jeremy shouted, while bouncing up and down on Jim's shoulders, "I get to see your kitties, too!"

Lindsey handed me Jeremy's Mickey Mouse suitcase and reached into the fridge to get his medicines. "The pink liquid and the big white pills he gets every six hours, and the small white pills he gets every eight. He should get one more dose of all three tonight before he goes to sleep. I don't wake him up to take them."

"Ya mean we're gonna sleep?" Jeremy teased, "I thought we'd have a pillow fight and stay up real late."

"I'll make sure he takes them on time," I promised. I gently punched Jeremy in the arm and added, "We'll see who stays up the latest, deal?"

"Deal," Jeremy answered, bending over to slap me a high five.

As we walked out to the car, Timmy and Wayne pulled up in their Jeep. Timmy jumped out of the car and ran to us. "Where ya going, Jeremy?"

"I'm sleepin' over at Robyn and Jim's. See ya, Buddy."

As we got into the car, I heard Timmy ask, "Can I go with 'em?"

"We'll have a fun weekend, Timmy. Jeremy'll be back soon," Wayne answered.

It took us over an hour to drive to the pizza joint, without much traffic. We sat in the non-smoking section and let Jeremy order — an extra large double cheese pizza with sausage and a pitcher of Coke. "Come on, Jim. Let's go play Galactica! I'm gonna win!" Jeremy took off with Jim tailing him, while I waited patiently for the pizza to arrive. It gave me a warm feeling watching the two of them being "kids" together.

When the pizza arrived, I quickly went to find them. Jeremy was busy pounding the button, which shot at the alien ships, while Jim watched in amazement. As I put my hands on their backs, I couldn't believe how they could have worked up a sweat in the middle of a cold December evening. I guessed it was a guy thing. Jeremy had beaten Jim at four different video games. The kid was a whiz.

Jeremy inhaled four pieces of pizza. I was thrilled because lately his belt was on the tightest hole over his favorite blue corduroy pants. His weight loss was becoming more and more noticeable.

I let Jeremy sit in the front seat while Jim drove home. They were doing some heavy-duty male bonding. Jeremy watched Jim's

196

every move. "You're an awesome driver, Jim. I like how you watch everything in the mirror and still drive straight."

"You'll make a good driver someday, too, Jeremy." Jim smiled and winked at me in the rear view mirror.

It's amazing how those few words hit me and quickly brought me into a different awareness. Maybe he'd drive around in his "Chief Yellow Sports Car," as he so eloquently called one of his guardian angels. I wasn't quite sure what he meant by that name, whether the angel was actually a car, or if the angel would drive him around in one. It didn't matter. It was his angel, and he had shared the name with me. I just hoped he'd be able to drive whenever he got there and have fun.

When Jim turned the corner onto our street, I pointed to our apartment. Jeremy was so excited that before Jim even stopped the car, Jeremy had attempted to pull the door open. Thank goodness it was locked. Jim scolded him anyway, just to teach him.

"Sorry, but I wanna see your white kitty, Sammy, real quick!"

"You'll have time," Jim answered. And again, the words hit me. I wish I knew how much time we did have.

Jeremy raced up the stairs to our apartment. As I opened the front door, the smell of fresh pine wafted into the hallway. Jeremy burst in and asked, "Can we decorate your Christmas tree? Pretty please?"

"I hoped you would want to. But don't you wanna see the kitties first?" I asked.

On cue, Winnie came whizzing through the room chasing Sammy. Sammy climbed up the tree trunk and quickly came tumbling down with the tree on top of her. Jeremy rolled on the floor with laughter. Soon after, Jim landed on top of him and they began to wrestle. I sat on the floor, watching them play, absorbing Jeremy with all of my senses. Listening to his laughter, I pulled his coat from the chair and breathed in his scent. I watched his eyes sparkle with his Inner Light and beauty. I hoped to memorize the scene forever.

When they finished roughhousing, Jim showed Jeremy to the attic. They carried down the Christmas decorations. I put my favorite Johnny Mathis Christmas tape on the cassette player. We had fun putting up the lights and hanging the ornaments on the tree. Just before Jeremy hung the last piece of tinsel, Jim snuck out to the kitchen, made us some hot chocolate, and brought out Jeremy's present. He set the present on the table while Jeremy stood in front of him, admiring our hard work.

Jeremy turned around. "Perfect," he stated, "it's just perfect."

"It sure is," said Jim as he handed Jeremy his gift. "Open it."

Jeremy sat down, yanked the wrapper, and with one hard pull, a bright yellow Game Boy fell into his lap. He flipped it on and began pressing away at the buttons. (I had remembered to put batteries in it.) Within seconds he yelled, "Score! And Michael Jordan does it again!" Jeremy sat for the next two hours playing his new basketball game. I snapped his picture, and I have one of the pictures on my fridge to this day.

At around midnight, I brought out the air mattress we use for camping and began blowing it up for Jeremy to sleep on. I placed three pillows next to the couch. As Jeremy lay sleepily on the floor, petting our third cat, Toby, I gently clobbered him with a pillow and all heck broke loose. Both Jim and Jeremy quickly grabbed a pillow and joined in the fun. As we laughed and romped around the room, a lamp accidentally fell and broke. Feathers from the down pillow, which had hit the lamp, floated gently to the floor. We laughed, and ended the pillow fight so Jeremy wouldn't get hurt.

As I made up Jeremy's bed on the floor, Jeremy asked Jim to hold him and read him a story. "Better yet," said Jim, "how 'bout if I make one up for you?"

"Yeah, yeah, yeah!"

"Once upon a time there was a young boy, I think he was seven, who could do anything, he could even fly...."

Jeremy laid down beside Jim and placed his head in Jim's lap, absorbing his every word. After Jim finished his story, around one in the morning, Jeremy asked if we could do our Oreo cookie hug. We did. Jim went to the fridge and got Jeremy's last doses of medicine for the night. Jeremy swallowed them both without a complaint. Jim and I both kissed Jeremy, and we all went to bed.

I laid in bed thinking that the world would lose out if Jim were not a dad. I remember wishing that Jeremy would live long enough to meet our first child, even though we still hadn't committed to having one.

Long into the night, I reviewed the events of the evening as though I had a movie camera in my head, savoring every movement, every breath that Jeremy took. I no sooner dozed off, than Jeremy's uncontrollable coughing awakened me. Jim and I both ran to see if he was all right. He sat up, gasping for breath. It scared me. I picked him up and held him. I rubbed his back while Jim got him some water. Eventually, Jeremy fell back asleep in my arms. Jim and I sat a while, in the dark, watching him sleep before we placed him back in bed.

We spent the next day at home. Jeremy didn't feel well — he awakened lethargic and with no appetite, although he managed to swallow all of his medicines again. I made pancakes and sausage, at his request. He just picked at his food and asked to be excused, so he could lie down. Later in the morning, Jeremy came back to life a little bit. He managed to figure out how to play every game on our computer. I had tried several times myself, but still hadn't figured them all out.

We drove him home late that afternoon. I told Lindsey I had kept my promise to her. Jeremy kept up with his schedule of medicines like a real trooper.

Jim and I were quiet the whole ride home.

CHAPTER SEVENTEEN -- I'VE HAD ENOUGH

I gave my all to each of my fourteen families. I walked around seeing the pain in their faces, in their frightened eyes, living their pain with them, sometimes for them. It got to the point where I worked harder than some of them did at making their lives better. I began to feel it was time to move on.

Since I had allowed myself to experience and eventually be transformed by my own pain from my past, I felt comfortable allowing others' pain to touch me as well. My hope was to meet my families on equal ground where we all suffer — on the human level. I felt strongly that the more I opened up to their pain, the greater the chance that they'd open up as well. So often, a family had been closed off for generations. I felt like I was their last hope. Many of them would die without ever feeling loved, without ever feeling part of anything.

Day after day, I did my best to show my vulnerability by sharing my heart. I'd work on teaching young moms how to make more positive choices for their children, like taking their toddlers for their long overdue immunizations. One time, Carolyn and I waited patiently in the parking lot at Robert Taylor Homes, when it was 20 below zero, to drive two teenage sisters and their three children to the doctor. Finally we got out of the car, and climbed several flights of stairs, which reeked of urine, to the clients' apartment, unable to take the elevator because a drunken man was passed out in his own vomit on the floor. They didn't answer their door.

Carolyn and I gave chance after chance, and demonstration after demonstration, in simple terms, to this same family; how to keep their apartment clean and their kids healthy. And time after time, we'd have to pull our shirt sleeves over our hands as we entered their apartment, so we wouldn't touch the built up gunk on the door knob. We'd witness one of the daughters mopping the floor with a bucket full of filthy dirty cold water with cigarette butts and dead cockroaches floating on top. More cockroaches raced up and down a five-foot high mountain of dirty, rancid laundry, which blocked most of the concrete walled hallway.

Other times, we'd witness toddlers from the same family, the teenage daughters' children, drinking from empty beer cans full of cigarette butts because they were so thirsty and hungry. When the state decided we had given them enough chances to get their act together, I finally had to testify to have all the toddlers removed from their mothers' custody. The sheriff had to escort me to my car, so that the teenage moms would not harm me on my way to the courthouse parking lot.

I didn't know if AIDS had made my clients so apathetic that they couldn't care anymore, or if generation after generation of dysfunction had settled in and become normal for them.

And then the day came, in mid-January. The last straw. The day I made the decision to quit my job without having another one.

Carolyn had called in sick. I spoke with her that morning. Her blood pressure was up, and she wasn't feeling well. She gave me her reassurance that she'd remember to say a prayer for me at 3:00, when I had a home visit scheduled with another of our challenging families, one in which several of the children had not only hemophilia, but also HIV. The purpose of the visit was to discuss possible foster care placement for several of the children with the state child welfare worker and the family.

The Jones', another of my HIV families, consisted of a mother, grandmother and seven children, four boys and three girls. They were African American. The oldest son died of AIDS before we got the case. He and his two younger brothers had been infected with HIV through the blood supply. They were all hemophiliacs except the youngest son, three-year-old, Derek. Derek was not hemophiliac, but autistic. Sixteen-year-old Martin, the oldest living hemophiliac son, stood six feet two inches tall, and had the gang graffiti of one gang purposely carved on the right side of his head, another gang's insignia purposely carved on the left. I had worn out every possibility for help and placement for Martin. Every agency I tried turned me down once they heard Martin's story.

Martin was so full of rage after his brother died of AIDS, that he set his family's kitchen on fire. When that didn't hurt anyone in his family, he placed his HIV infected blood in the cookie jar, and planted used syringes, needles pointing up, in strategic places on the floor with the hope that others would step on them. Martin was an extremely volatile adolescent who upped the ante with every move he made. Nothing would stop him until he hurt someone as badly as he hurt... the antithesis of Jeremy. He spoke in extremely foul language. Neither his mother, nor grandmother, could control him. His grandfather, the only one who could control him, lived over sixty miles away. The entire family was petrified of Martin's every move. He was the most hateful child I had ever met.

I arrived for the visit precisely at 3:00 p.m. I entered the run down home and remembered to watch my step as the warped concrete at the entrance, and in the hallway, made it difficult to walk. I immediately felt uncomfortable, not only because Carolyn was not by my side, but also because the state worker had already started talking to the family without me. I sat down on the ripped-up couch trying to avoid the two springs that protruded from the fabric. The two teenage daughters came into the room once I did, and took their places beside me on the couch. The girls and I gently hugged before we sat down.

The grandmother and mother sat across the room on the radiator cover and listened intently to the caseworker speak. Old sheets, stapled to the wall, covered the broken windows. Despite the structure of the house and the dilapidated furniture, the house smelled and looked like someone had just finished cleaning.

Martin sat several feet away from me in an old, creaky rocking chair. When I politely greeted him, he snarled at me, got up from his chair and came toward me. My heart rate went so high, my face instantly got hot. He bent down, leaned in my ear and whispered, "Fuck you, white bitch," and turned around to sit back down in his chair. This guy had an agenda. I could feel it. The worker, oblivious to what had taken place, continued talking. "Robyn and her colleagues think your children should be placed into different foster homes..."

What? I thought to myself, *what is she doing? We didn't say all of her children, and we were to discuss the possibility of removal, not the definite removal of some of them. What else has she told them? She set me up. That's why Martin is so angry...* And before I could get a word out of my mouth, Martin began to thrust quarters at the side of my head. I looked directly at him and told him to stop. His response was, "Fuck you, you white bitch," as he hurled another one at me. Everyone in the room froze. I looked at the worker, the mother, anyone, to get some help. The worker said in a singsong voice, "Now, come on Martin, stop it."

"No," he yelled angrily, making everyone cringe. "She's gonna pay..." He stood and approached me in a foreboding manner.

I didn't know what to do. So I quickly prayed. "Heavenly Father, Mother God, I wish to serve. Please, if the only way I can get Martin help is to have him hit me, so I can press charges, please don't let him hit me hard. Please, protect me. Thank you. Amen." At that very second came a knock at the door. Martin paused. The four-year-old daughter, who had never uttered a word in her life, ran out from the kitchen carrying a Bible. She sat down next to me on the couch. She opened the Bible to a full page, color picture of Christ, pointed at it and said, "Look at Jesus, look at Jesus." At the same moment, someone opened the front door. The grandfather entered the room, obviously saw what was happening, and ran toward Martin, placing him in a full-nelson hold, pinning him to the floor. I was stunned. I guess I didn't need to be hit after all. I got up from the couch, walked out the door, and ran to my car. I sobbed the whole way home.

When I got there, Jim wasn't home from school, yet. I called Carolyn and was crying so hard, she barely recognized my voice. "Calm down," she said in her reassuring voice, "take some deep breaths, and tell me everything that happened." I did. She couldn't believe it.

"Carolyn, I don't know what to do. I can't go back. This is too much...."

"Girl, you cannot continue to do this job. You're right. This is too much. It's time for you to move on. You've given all you can to these families."

"But I don't have another job. What will I do? Jim doesn't graduate until next year, I'm the only one working."

"Just do it. You know that God will provide. Look, if He got you through today, He can get you through anything. Have faith! You have to quit."

I gave my two-week notice the next day. And Carolyn was right. Once I took the flying leap of faith, I got a phone call three days later from the vice president of an agency I worked at during a summer of graduate school. She asked me if I would be willing to start up a private practice and see court ordered clients under guardianship. She had two clients who needed in home counseling. When I heard the "in-home" part, I panicked. Then I learned both clients were quite wealthy, living in beautiful homes near Lake Michigan.

Thank you, God.

All of this synchronicity made me step back and do a lot of thinking about Jeremy and this whole experience. From a spiritual perspective, I knew there had to be a bigger purpose going on here. Some good had to come from this, or Jeremy wouldn't have to be going through it. He was too good.

I felt that for myself, on a spiritual level, I had taken the job with my families with AIDS in order to meet up with Jeremy and do everything I possibly could to help him. In Jeremiah 1:5 it reads, "Before you were conceived I knew you; before you came to birth I consecrated you...."

If I really allowed myself to become aware of it, and to let what I felt and knew was fate sink in, I was consecrated to help Jeremy. And to eventually write his story so others would know him, too. I'm sure Jeremy was consecrated to show his mother, and the rest of the world, unconditional love, and to teach us about the choices we make, moment by moment, in our internal worlds. Do we live each day in anger, hurt, bitterness, resentment, or fear about a wrong someone did to us? Or do we use each clean page of our life to love and heal others and ourselves, as Jeremy did?

Now that Jeremy's case had been taken away from me, it felt okay for me to quit my job and move on. After all, Jeremy hadn't been taken away from me.

Once I gave my notice, I felt relieved. I'd be able to spend time with Jeremy in a different way — like we were family. In fact, when he was with Jim and I, he often called us Mommy and Daddy.

We were family. It chokes me up now even as I write it. After I quit my job, I'd call Lindsey and Jeremy about once a week, sometimes more, sometimes less, depending on their needs and this time mine. Jeremy spent the day with us a few times a month. Sometimes he slept overnight.

Jeremy had such a powerful impact on both Jim and I. It was like the deeper we loved him and committed our hearts and souls to him, the stronger our commitment grew to each other. After bringing Jeremy home from one particular weekend we spent enjoying him, Jim and I had a long talk on our couch. The incredible amount of love we felt for Jeremy, and from Jeremy, was such a powerful feeling, neither of us could come up with the words to describe it adequately. It was like if you put a word to it, it was much more than that word. His love was like an endless supply from a deep, deep source that would never run out. The more he gave, the more he had to give. Being around him made us want to give as much as he did.

By the end of our talk, Jim and I had found that this incredibly painful situation had dramatically changed us. We had made a decision to become parents in the future. This was a big step for us, as we had both been givers our whole lives. Up to this point, we weren't sure that we wanted to make such a big commitment to giving to parenting what we both felt it took to do it right.

Jeremy changed all that. Through him we were able to see that even if you make mistakes, unconditional love can get you through even the hardest of times. Jim and I have a lot to thank Jeremy for.

Jeremy's third court date was scheduled for the week after I stopped working with my AIDS families. The night before court, I again prepared by studying my index cards. I hoped it would finally be the day I could tell the judge Jeremy's story.

I awakened early in the morning. My stomach had so many butterflies, I couldn't eat. I drank a cup of tea as I drove to court. I prayed on my way, telling God what my needs were — to get this over with— but asking that Jeremy needs be met over mine.

I still had my staff picture ID, so I waived it to the sheriff and walked in. Lindsey, Jeremy, and Hannah were already in the waiting area for Courtroom H. Jeremy ran toward me with a picture he had colored for me and gave me a big hug with it still in his hand. I bent down to look at it.

"It's great, Sweetie. Thanks!" It was an excellent drawing of the Ninja Turtles, each with their mask on and special colored belt.

"I wanted ya to have it. Don't forget to show Jim, okay?"

"I won't forget."

I no sooner sat down than Brian came in to see Hannah and I. He first took me into a corner of the hallway and grilled me on how to answer his questions. I was beginning to see that it was actually Brian that had not done his homework. It seemed that the reason he was so ruthless in his questioning wasn't only because he was convinced that the judge would return Jeremy to Delilah, it was because he had so much to remember to ask me, in order for all of the evidence to come out that he was angry and frustrated as well. He scared me.

In Juvenile Court, the prosecuting attorney has to have enough information to form a specific question to ask the witness. For example, Brian just couldn't ask, "What did you witness with Jeremy the day you first met him," he'd have to phrase it very specifically. "On February 8th, during your first home visit to the Miller family, did you witness any evidence of physical abuse to Jeremy Miller?" Brian probably had hundreds of cases to deal with in a week. As far as I know, for all of them, the state had gone through the regular channels of investigating a family after receiving a call through the child abuse hotline and finding specific evidence proving the abuse. These were "founded" cases of abuse or neglect. Jeremy's was "unfounded." We had to prove our case. Maybe that's why Jeremy's case was a thorn in his side. I had no idea; I just didn't like how irritated he'd get when trying to sort things out with me. It took me three court dates to finally figure this out.

Delilah didn't show up for court this time. We waited two hours before Jeremy's case was called. At least Hannah and I were sworn in this time. But again, neither of us was asked to testify. The judge ordered Delilah to undergo a psychiatric interview and asked Rebecca, who had arrived late, a few questions on how Jeremy was doing in foster placement. Rebecca said he was adjusting well. The judge continued the case until the end of March, awaiting the psychiatrist's report. The fight still wasn't over.

CHAPTER EIGHTEEN -- A MESSAGE FROM A STRANGER

Can one prepare for the beginning of the end? Seems like a strange question to ask. My hope was that somehow preparing would make the outcome easier. I had to begin to let Jeremy go and help him to do the same.

In February, my mom said I sounded like I needed some "R and R," so she bought me a round trip plane ticket to stay with her for a week.

I was grateful. I flew to Mom's the following weekend while Jim stayed home and went to school and his internship.

The evening of my arrival, Mom treated me to Crabby Bill's for dinner. We spent the rest of the night enjoying each other's company out on her balcony. Just smelling the fresh salty air and hearing the waves crashing against the shore instantly soothed my mind and body. It was a beautiful evening, in the lower sixties. I sat and stared at the star coated sky. Nine months had passed since I had shared Mom's balcony with Jeremy and Delilah.

Mom went in to brew us a pot of hot tea. She came back and handed me a warm mug. "You look really exhausted, Little One. I'm so glad you took me up on my offer." No matter how old I was, Mom always called me her "Little One." I'm the youngest of five children.

"I'm glad, too. Thanks, Mom." I leaned over and hugged her. She began to give me a back rub.

"Why don't you unwind, get things off your chest. Tell me what this experience at your job has been like for you. You know, at times I've been frightened for your safety."

"I know. Thanks for not saying anything about it as I went through it."

"I trust you. Now start talking so you can put this all behind you."

"You sure you wanna know?" I asked, trying to give her fair warning.

"If you can handle it, I can. That way you can start with a clean slate tomorrow. You look too serious. You're really burdened by all of this."

"I never could hide anything from you...."

She winked at me and smiled. I took a deep breath as Mom moved her chair so she could look lovingly into my eyes, waiting patiently, until I was ready to start.

"Everyday, I'd see such awful stuff. Such bleakness, and darkness, and hopelessness. Even ugliness. I couldn't take it anymore. I'm not even sure where to start."

"Just pick one, and we'll take it from there."

"You sound like me." I said, laughing. And then I closed my eyes and waited until a memory filled my awareness. "Oh yeah, here's a good example."

"Let's hear it."

"Just before Thanksgiving, Kevin, the guy who cuts mine and Jim's hair gave me $150 to buy turkeys for each of my families. Carolyn and I did the shopping on our own time. We even had enough money to buy fresh sweet potatoes to go with them."

"That was nice of him."

"Yeah, he's had a couple of friends die from AIDS. He said he wanted to try to make a difference for someone who was still living with the disease. Anyway, we drove to one of our families who lived at Robert Taylor Homes to deliver their turkey. I remember it was a 25 pounder because I had to cart it up several flights of stairs, which were filthy and stunk like urine. Carolyn and I walked in on a heated argument, I should say fight, between the mother, who was alcoholic, dying of AIDS and had active TB and her sixteen-year-old daughter. Right in front of us the mother threw a fork into the daughter's forehead and called her a slut. Then she tried to reach and grab for a knife, but she was so drunk, she fell on the floor instead."

Mom shook her head in utter disbelief, "Her own daughter?"

"The fork stuck right in the girl's forehead. Blood trickled down her face. Carolyn and I tried to convince the poor kid to come with us, but she refused. We ran to get out so we could call the police, but as I turned the knob to the only working door in the whole place, it fell off into my hand."

Mom shook her head harder. "What'd you do?"

"We tried to put the knob back on a couple of times, at least enough to turn it, but it didn't work. Finally we said a quick prayer and yelled, 'In the name of Jesus the Christ, open the door!'"

"And it opened?"

"It opened. We ran like heck to my car and drove to the nearest pay phone. I called the police. They told us not to go back in. When they went up to their apartment, the women denied anything happened."

Mom's mouth hung open. "No wonder you had enough. And you have more stories?"

"Mmm hmm." I shook my head in the affirmative.

She shook her head in amazement. "It's hard to imagine." She let out an uncomfortable laugh.

Hearing my own words made me laugh, too. It sounded so ridiculous. Mom must have thought I'd gone off the deep end because I couldn't stop laughing — that nervous, tension-relieving laughter. But my laughter soon turned to tears.

Mom moved in closer and stroked my forehead like she always did to comfort me. "There now, it's all over. Shhh...."

"It was really horrible, Mom. I couldn't stay in all that darkness anymore. I had to get out."

When I stopped crying, Mom had only one more question for me. "Why in God's name did you put yourself through it?"

"I can only think of one answer...."

I looked over at her as we both said in sync, "Jeremy."

"I'm really tired. I'm going to hit the sack. Good night." I got up and gave her a kiss.

"Good night, Sweetie. I love you."

209

"Love you, too." We held each other for a long minute, and I went to bed.

The next morning when I woke up, I felt so achy and chilled, I could hardly move. Mom brewed me cup after cup of "Thera-Flu" with extra lemon. Isn't that the way it often happens when you relax and finally let your guard down on vacation? I slept my way through most of the week.

By the end of my trip, I had recovered from the flu and was slowly gaining my energy back — physically, emotionally, and spiritually.

The weekend after I returned home, Jeremy asked Jim and I to take him to see the movie <u>Kindergarten Cop</u>, with Arnold Schwarzenegger. The coming attractions looked innocent enough on TV. I was mortified. It not only was quite violent, during one of the scenes they show a boy from the kindergarten class being physically abused by his dad. During that scene, Jeremy jumped into my lap and buried his face in my chest. He stayed in my lap the rest of the movie. Jim and I felt awful.

Afterward, when we went to Bressler's for ice cream. Jeremy ordered a strawberry sundae with extra whipped creme. As we sat down, Jim asked, "How's things with your mom, Buddy?"

"She still keeps yellin' at me about my hair not being right and how my clothes look so bad. I hate when she does that. I get scared of 'er." My eyes met Jim's for a brief second.

"I'm sorry, Sweetie." I said, leaning over to pick Jeremy up and lift his skinny body on to my lap. I began smoothing his forehead.

"She acts like she's gonna hurt me again." He buried his head into my shoulder and hid his eyes.

"Is Rebecca still in the room when she does that?"

He shook his head no. "She mostly does it when we're alone." I barely understood him with his mouth smushed against my shirt.

"When are you alone with her?" I was shocked to hear his answer.

He looked up. "At Rebecca's office. She leaves us alone and then after awhile, she comes back. Mama acts better when she's around." I felt the hairs on the back of my neck stand up. Rebecca needed to help Jeremy feel safe.

Court was scheduled for the next Tuesday. I made a vow to tell Rebecca what Jeremy had divulged to me, when I saw her in court.

Early the following Tuesday morning, I reviewed my index cards, preparing one more time for my testimony. I didn't like not having Carolyn with me in court, praying with me and lending me her moral support. I felt too alone and isolated.

I walked into the crowded waiting area for Courtroom H. I spotted Rebecca, sitting alone. Delilah was no where in sight. I greeted Rebecca and asked her to step into the hallway, so we could talk privately.

Before I could share with her what Jeremy had told me, she spoke. "I want you to know that I'm going to recommend unsupervised visits for Delilah with Jeremy. She's been doing so much better. She's made every…"

I interrupted. "Rebecca, please don't take offense at this, but I don't think that's such a good idea. Jeremy told me just last Saturday that he's still frightened of her. He thinks she's still going to hurt him even in your office. Delilah's very good at showing only the parts of herself she wants people to see and know — the surface ones that look like she's got it all together." I gave her a minute to think about what I had said, but she quickly responded.

"I think I know Delilah, by now," she answered, placing her hand on her hip. "And I think she's capable of seeing her son without someone looking over her shoulder, when she does. She's been working hard, Robyn. She started counseling at a mental health center and she's been taking great care of Simon. I don't think you can make a recommendation about Delilah — you haven't worked with her in a while."

"No, I haven't. But she let me in close enough to see what really goes on inside of her, and a few months of therapy isn't going to change someone like Delilah. Jeremy's still scared of her. Doesn't that count for anything? She still needs to be supervised around him."

"Let's let the judge decide." Rebecca turned away, flipped her long hair over her shoulder, and walked off. When I walked back in the waiting area, Delilah held Simon and sat next to Rebecca. Lindsey, Jeremy, and Hannah had also arrived, and were seated in the benches across from them. Jeremy saw me and ran to greet me. We sat down beside Hannah.

Brian walked up. He asked Hannah and I to step into the hallway. "Ladies, I think today's your lucky day. The judge will hear your testimonies today. We have a lot of practicing to do. Robyn, you first. Hannah, if you'd like to sit back down, I'll let you know when I'm ready for you to rehearse." Hannah left Brian and I in the hallway.

I instantly felt nauseated. Brian began drilling me on my answers. "You can't elaborate," he scolded. "Just answer my question. I'll lead you where you need to go." But the more he questioned me, the more he didn't lead me anywhere except to tears of frustration. He continued to leave out some of the dates of abuse.

"We're gonna lose," were the last words he said before I let him have it.

"With that kind of attitude, Brian, we just might. I didn't work this hard, for this kid to be sent right back to his mother. It's got to work. It's going to work!" And with that, I stormed toward the women's restroom. I had to pull it together. If this guy was going to be on our side, the responsibility was on Hannah and me to make sure it worked.

After I composed myself, I walked back toward the waiting room. I saw Brian coming out of the men's room. I quickly warned Hannah of his mood.

After playing what felt like our hundredth game of tick-tack-toe, hangman, and dot to dot, the sheriff announced, "Court will adjourn for lunch and resume at 2:00." I let out a deep sigh and looked down at my watch. I couldn't believe it. It was already 12:45 and we'd have to come back again?

Hannah, Lindsey, Jeremy, and I walked to my car. I drove us all to a great deli close by. Jeremy had a huge kosher hot dog, and the three of us ordered hot corned beef sandwiches on rye. Even after finishing every bite, I still felt drained.

We got back to court right on time, and waited, and waited. At 4:00, Hannah announced she was leaving. She needed to make a home visit across town, and get there before five. Good thing she didn't wait around any longer — at 4:30, Brian informed us Jeremy's hearing had been rescheduled for the first week of May.

The last week of April, I had signed up for a week of classes at a spiritual retreat outside of Indianapolis. I was really looking forward to going — this would be my second week of respite to refuel and reward myself, since I had quit my job. A few days before I was ready to leave, I got a call from Lindsey.

"I just called to let you know that Jeremy's court date has been moved up. It's next week."

"Oh no, I have plans to take classes out of town...."

"Sharon told me it's for a progress report on his foster care. I don't think they'll be needing you." I guessed it still wasn't the right time for me to testify — it wasn't in Divine Order.

"Are you sure you don't need me there?" I asked, needing Lindsey's reassurance.

"Positive."

Once I heard that, I felt more comfortable with keeping my plans. I'm glad I did.

A social work grad student had introduced me to this retreat. Different topics of spiritual interest can be studied there, from metaphysics and clairvoyance, to world religions and Native American philosophy.

I drove the three and a half-hour trip filled with mixed emotions. I was pregnant. I knew it. Seven days to be exact. Jim had felt it, too. It was hard to leave him to take the trip, yet I was very excited to have this opportunity to study and take classes toward my spiritual development.

I'd call Jim every night, sometimes more, to report. I had already started to have morning sickness.

One particular class met in the chapel on the campgrounds. We had been learning about different gifts of the Spirit; healing, prophecy, and on this specific day, our third day of class, we were to practice whatever our gift might be, even if we weren't sure we had one. A woman, whom I had never met before, stood in front of the class and began giving clairvoyant messages...

"I am receiving the name of a young boy, Jeremy, who is wise beyond his years..."

213

My knees tremble as I write this memory, almost as much as they did when I first heard her.

"Would this sound familiar to anyone?" I managed to raise my hand, though I could not speak. "Jeremy is preparing to make his transition to the spirit world..."

I choked back my tears, as my heart raced, and I tried to maintain my composure enough to hear the rest of her message. My chest shook, as I gasped for breath.

"Jeremy knows how much you love him, and he comes here today in hopes of helping you begin to prepare for his death. You need to be able to let go of him, so that it will be easier for you to help him be comfortable with dying, with letting go of the physical world. He has suffered tremendously, and his spirit says it's time to go home. He struggles with wanting to finish something left undone. He needs your help."

She even used his words, "time to go home." I bolted past my classmates, out the chapel door. I ran through the woods and down a hill until my legs could carry me no longer. I collapsed under a tree. "I'm not ready, God. You can't do this. It's not fair. He can't die. I can't lose him..." I cried until there were no more tears, nothing left to say.

It was dark when I came back to the present enough to realize that it felt like the mosquitoes were eating me alive. I got up and made my way back to the cafeteria to get a cup of hot tea and to try and sort out what I had just experienced.

I sat, sipping my tea with shaky hands, pondering her words, Jeremy's words, "It's time to go home."

I knew the day would come when I'd have to begin to let Jeremy go. I also knew that I'd have to help him to let go... of life. To be comfortable with death. That was going to be hard, he was so good at living it one moment at a time.

I'd have to give him up and help him to give me up.

Before I took this job, I knew what I was in for, at least with respect to death and with helping my clients come to terms with it. And I was going to hold myself accountable to the promise I had made to Jeremy, to help him through to the absolute end.

The time was now, or so I'd been told. I was beside myself. I wanted to help him. I knew I could. I would. But I didn't want it to be him that was dying. It just wasn't fair.

I went for a walk and tried to come to terms with what I had been given. I'd have to be there for him wholeheartedly, 110%, encouraging him to let go, to die, when it was time. I promised myself I would do it, I promised Jeremy I would be there.

Obviously, I had a lot of my own work to do to be able to truly be free of my needs for him, so I could support him in his needs, unconditionally.

In a way, I was grateful for this message from the stranger. I didn't fully realize until that moment how much I really wanted Jeremy to live, and how much I was holding on to him with every ounce of my being. On the other hand, I hated knowing.

CHAPTER NINETEEN -- ANOTHER INTERVENTION FROM ON HIGH...

Later that evening, I walked to the phone booth outside of the chapel and telephoned Jeremy. No one answered. I tried several more times that night. I needed to hear his voice. I never got an answer.

The next day, I called many more times. After not reaching anyone, I finally let it go. Maybe they went on vacation or something. I'd make it a point to see him soon after I returned home from my retreat.

It's funny sometimes how things work out. When I got home, I looked in my phone book and realized I had been dialing the wrong phone number. This was very strange for me — I had dialed the correct number at least a hundred times before, from memory.

I guessed I needed the distance from him at the moment.

My first night home, Jim and I talked in depth about my experience receiving the clairvoyant message from my classmate. We both agreed; I had to believe her. She knew too much accurate information for me not to believe her.

When I saw Jeremy for the first time after receiving the message, I tried hard to begin the process of letting him go. Jim and I picked Jeremy up from Lindsey's early the following morning, on Saturday, for a sleepover. Jim wanted to take him to a fun park on Chicago's southside, called Haunted Trails, where they have a few carnival rides, a video and game arcade, and batting cages.

During the ride there, Jeremy sat on the seat in between my legs, with my seat belt wrapped around both of us. As I smelled his hair, and felt the warmth of his legs and back against my body, I kept trying to psych myself out by telling myself it would all be okay. I could love him with all of my heart and still let him go. I could set him free, and he'd be all right. I had spent so much of the last year working hard to protect him and keep him at only an arm's length, and now I'd have to be completely vulnerable and trusting and let him go forever.

Jeremy and Jim told jokes and made up silly stories most of the ride there. I stayed quiet much of the time, listening and absorbing Jeremy.

"You okay?" Jeremy asked, turning his head far enough back so he could see my eyes.

"Yes, why do you ask?" I said.

"Cuz you're quiet."

"Oh. I'm just thinkin'."

"'Bout what?"

"'Bout you."

"'Bout me?" he asked with a grin on his face. "What about me?"

"How much I love you. And how much I love to be with you."

"And how much fun we have when we're together?" He asked with a big grin.

"Yes."

"What else?"

"You think there's something else, do you?" I asked tickling his belly.

"Stop," he said laughing, "tickle me right here." He pointed to the top of his knee and showed me exactly how he liked it done. Then he leaned over and tickled Jim the same way. It was a good thing Haunted Trails was just around the corner. We were laughing so hard, I couldn't see. It was the sadness I felt, mixed with my happy tears, that had blurred my vision.

After Jim parked the car, Jeremy ran ahead of us after spotting the batting cages. "Ooooh look, Jim! Cooool! Can I try?"

Jim and I looked at each other, puzzled. The bat probably weighed more than he did.

"How about I help you. Bats are pretty heavy, you know."

217

"I know. Maybe just the first coupla times. Then I can do it myself."

"Have you ever played before?" Jim asked.

"Sorta." I wondered where he had had the opportunity, since Delilah was so strict with his play. "But never in one of those cage things!" Jeremy's eyes lit up as he pointed to the cage.

"Okay then, get in line, and I'll go pay," said Jim.

"Awesome, thanks!" Jeremy slapped Jim a high five as he walked by, and continuously jumped up and down in line until it was his turn to bat.

I felt a little scared. The balls really whipped at the batter. In my opinion, this wasn't a batting cage for a child weighing less than 40 pounds. Jeremy didn't seem to care. As soon as Jim showed him where to stand, and how to hold the bat, he slugged the first ball with all his power. He put his entire body into it. The ball flew high and long, and crashed into the back fence. Jeremy screamed with delight, jumping for joy. In his excitement, the next ball whizzed right by him. He quickly regrouped and slammed the next one.

He was a natural. Pretty soon, a crowd gathered to watch our slugger. He was quite a sight to see — this skeleton of a body slugging what could have been home runs each time. He rarely missed a pitch. He developed quite a cheering section. He continuously hit for sometime. He was soaked with perspiration and asked for something to drink.

His cheering section applauded his performance. Jeremy bowed, grinning from ear to ear.

We walked in to the air-conditioned arcade and before even getting a drink, Jeremy spotted one of those picture booths where you can have photos taken for a dollar. "Let's go in, guys. Please?"

The three of us crammed in the booth. I sat on the stool with Jeremy on my lap and Jim stood behind us. The pictures came out great. Jeremy looked a little puffy. He was on Prednisone again for his breathing. He always looked swollen when he was on that drug. We took two sets of pictures, one for Jeremy to keep and one for us. We keep ours in a magnet frame on our refrigerator.

We spent the next hour and a half playing games in the arcade. Jeremy quickly won a huge pile of tickets and redeemed them for a baseball, of course.

By the time we got back to our apartment, we were exhausted. The three of us took a nap on our bed. It was great. Jeremy slept in between us. When we woke up, Jeremy swallowed his three pills, and we drove to our favorite pizza place for supper. Jeremy and Jim played every video game there. This time, Jeremy barely ate any of his favorite double cheese and sausage pizza.

That night, Jeremy's cough was the worst I had ever heard. We ran the humidifier for him and rubbed him down with Vicks. He liked that. He fell asleep by 9:00 in Jim's arms. We brought him home the following morning because he still felt miserable.

When I saw Lindsey, I told her about the terrible night Jeremy had.

"His cough has been getting worse. The Prednisone does help, but the side effects are pretty rough." Lindsey's face reflected the sadness she felt.

"I forgot to ask you, how'd the last court date go?"

"Good. Nothing big. The judge asked Rebecca how Jeremy was doing, and she got the psychiatrist's report on Delilah. She didn't share any specifics from it."

"Rebecca didn't say anything about unsupervised visits, did she?"

"No."

"Thank goodness." I let out a sigh. "And what did she say about Jeremy?"

"That he's fine, adjusting well."

"Did they give the next court date?"

"Let me go grab my appointment book." I followed Lindsey into the dining room. "July 23rd." She wrote it down for me.

"I sure hope I get to testify. I want to get this over with," I said as I slipped the piece of paper in my pocket.

"I don't blame you. I hope so, too. Judge Hamilton seems pretty tough, though."

"Yeah, that's what they say. I've heard rumors that she even brings families back together who have been apart a long time, if the parent shows any inkling of cooperation with the state."

"Yikes." Lindsey squinted her eyes and shook her head.

"We'll just keep praying. That's all we can do."

219

Jim and Jeremy came down from Jeremy's room, and we all hugged our good byes. "See ya, Kiddo. Love you." The three of us did our Oreo cookie hug. Jeremy gave us both an extra squeeze that morning.

"Love you, too. See ya. Thanks." He walked us to our car.

On the way home, I sat in silent prayer for Jeremy and for court. July seemed like forever, even though it was only two months down the road.

The following Friday, I happened to pick up a Chicago Tribune while waiting for my doctor's appointment. I skimmed the front section and stopped when I got to Mike Royko's column. The title grabbed my attention: "Why is this judge in Juvenile Court?" My heart raced as I read further. He had written a letter to the Chief Judge of Cook County Juvenile Court asking him, "Why in the hell is someone like Judge Morgan Hamilton sitting in Juvenile Court?"

Yes! She's Jeremy's judge.

Mr. Royko cited a recent case of a three-year-old girl who was murdered by her mother's boyfriend. The boyfriend poured boiling water over the little girl after he raped her and her two sisters, while the mother was in bed with all of them. The mother went to work and left the girl home with burns over 75% of her body. The girl died. The article describes more abuse that the girl and her sisters had suffered.

The boyfriend went to prison, but the mother didn't have to. The article goes on to say, "The prosecutors hoped she would testify against the boyfriend and didn't bring charges against her. When the boyfriend copped a plea, her testimony was unnecessary, and she was off the hook." Her two living daughters were placed in foster care.

"Which brings us to Judge Hamilton in Juvenile Court," Royko continues. "People who work in that court say that Judge Hamilton is a strong advocate of bringing families back together. Some say she is almost obsessive about it."

You could say that again!

"It appears so. Judge Hamilton recently decided that the mother should be granted unsupervised visiting privileges with her daughters. That means that mom takes the children home and spends a few hours with them each week. Not everyone involved in the case was pleased. The lawyer who represents the children protested. She says that when mom and her daughters get together, 'There's an underlying tension. No warmth, no love.'

I wonder why? What's a little rape, brutality, and murder when it's all in the family? The prosecutor was upset, too. She says the visits amount to, 'restoring limited custody to the mother.' And when visitation rights are granted, it usually means that the next step will be for the mother to ask that she be declared fit as a fiddle and get her children back."

Absolutely right! You tell them!

Royko continues by lambasting the mother and the system, then later in the column asks, "So if it is necessary for Judge Hamilton to be a judge, why don't you find a more suitable court for her?" Mr. Royko suggests traffic court. He also suggests that if the chief judge does not straighten this mess out, he'll humbly suggest that the voters do.

Wow. This is great.

I felt a renewed sense of excitement. I'd have to get a Tribune the next day to see what ramifications his article had for the judge, if any. I sure hoped it would.

Thank you Mike Royko.

The next day, the following article appeared in the Tribune. It read, "A Juvenile Court judge whose rulings often have frustrated prosecutors who feared she jeopardized the lives of abused children was transferred Friday to the 1st Municipal District."

Transferred Friday! Thank you, thank you.

I continued reading. "Associate Judge R. Morgan Hamilton's transfer came the same day that she was the subject of a column by Tribune columnist Mike Royko, who attacked her for allowing unsupervised visits between a mother and her two daughters after a third daughter was scalded to death by the mother's boyfriend."

Thank you, God. And thank you again, Mr. Royko. I am forever grateful. I felt like a ton had been lifted from my shoulders.

221

CHAPTER TWENTY -- FINALLY!

I couldn't wait to see which judge would be assigned to Jeremy's case. The days to Jeremy's court date seemed to drag on forever. In anticipation of it, I became impatient and restless, hoping everything would be over soon, praying I'd be able to finally place the burden of Jeremy's custody battle onto the judge's shoulders and off of my own. We had been in court close to one year by now, and I had yet to tell Jeremy's story.

Jim and I didn't see much of Jeremy over the summer. He was very busy having fun being a kid. Lindsey initiated an action-packed, kid filled, summer vacation for him. He went fishing with Wayne and Timmy, spent a week at Vacation Bible School, went camping in Wisconsin, played baseball, learned how to fly a kite, and skateboard with the neighbor kids. Every time I called, he was out of breath from rattling off what an adventurous day and week he had had. Or at least I wanted to believe that was why he was out of breath. Each time we spoke, his cough sounded deeper, wetter. He often had to stop talking in order to gulp for air. It didn't seem to bother him, though. He just kept going, living moment by moment, filling each breath he took with his vim and vigor for love and for life.

Jim and I did manage to spend a day with him in June and another one in July. And then July 23rd rolled around, Jeremy's court date in front of the new judge.

I prayed hard the night before and asked God to show me in a dream anything else I needed to know for court the next day. When I woke up the next morning, I didn't remember even having any dreams. I hoped that was a good sign.

I lived close to Juvenile Court. I got in my car at 8:15 a.m. and drove to the court parking lot. If you wanted to get a space there, you had to arrive early. I pulled out my old staff picture ID card and trudged toward the entrance. Even though it was hot and humid outside, I felt numb. I had done this routine so many times since the previous October, when Jeremy was placed in temporary custody, I had just about lost all hope that this hearing thing would ever be over with.

The ID card did the trick. I avoided the long lines at the metal detectors, took a deep breath, and walked toward Judge Hamilton's old courtroom. I looked around for a familiar face, but saw none. I sat on the hard wooden bench I had acquainted myself with so well, the one near the middle of the rows facing the north wall. I silently said my ritual of prayers and went into somewhat of a meditative trance, listening for some last minute guidance from within. When Hannah tapped me on the shoulder, I about jumped out of my skin.

I looked up to see Jeremy standing next to her. Lindsey, of course, stood right beside him. We said our hellos. While hugging Jeremy, I quickly glanced across the room to where Delilah usually sat with Rebecca. Sure enough, they were right there. Simon wasn't with them. Delilah stared at the floor. As I put Jeremy down, Delilah's state caseworker, Debra, ran up to me and summoned me to the hallway.

"Judge Brownfield's been assigned to hear Judge Hamilton's cases today. He's a supervisor to the other judges. We're definitely on to tell Jeremy's story."

Her words thundered through my mind like a rockslide.

"You okay?" she asked.

"Yes, thanks. I just can't believe it. It's finally here. Are you absolutely sure, Debra?"

"Positive. Are you ready? Your moment has finally come."

"I've been ready," I said, emphasizing "been."

"Good, I'll go find Brian."

I told Hannah and Lindsey what was going on. Debra came running toward us and grabbed my arm. "Brian's gone. We've been assigned a new state's attorney. You and Hannah need to come with me."

Amen!

Hannah and I quickly followed her. She took us into a small room and closed the door behind us. Within seconds a woman walked in. "Hi. I'm Shelly. I'm the new prosecutor on Jeremy's case. Debra told me about this little guy. I'm sorry about his AIDS."

"Me, too," I mumbled.

"And you are…"

"Robyn. I'm the social worker that worked with him and his mom last year."

"Great. Debra told me about you. And you must be the nurse," she said as she turned toward Hannah.

"I am," Hannah answered. "I brought the report I wrote up when Jeremy was first removed from his mother."

"Great. May I see it?" Hannah handed it to her.

The longer we sat in the room, the harder my heart pounded. It was beginning to really hit me. This was it. After today, at least according to what Brian had told me our last court date, Jeremy would either be continued in temporary state custody, or he'd be returned to Delilah.

Shelly read Hannah's report. Debra handed Shelly a manila file folder. She pulled out and began reading the original report I had written to get Jeremy removed from Delilah. When she finished, she said, "Robyn, you'll testify before Hannah, but Debra will testify before you."

I had my trusty index cards in hand when Shelly asked, "What are those?"

"My cheat sheet. I recorded all of the dates and descriptions of incidents which I witnessed against Delilah."

"Perfect. This'll help me tremendously. May I see them please?" I handed them over. "This is great. All I have to do is read the dates from the cards and prompt you on what happened that specific day. This should be a piece of cake.

Now why hadn't Brian made it that easy?

"Let's practice," Shelly said. "You first, Robyn." I nodded my head in the affirmative. We no sooner got started than we heard a knock on the door. The sheriff walked in.

"Shelly, judge is in. He's already ruled on three cases. You're next."

Oh my God. Next? For us?

224

Shelly stated, "Okay ladies, we've got nothing to worry about. Judge Brownfield is great. Let's go." I guess my question was answered.

I took a deep breath and squeezed Hannah's hand for luck. We walked out of the room and into the courtroom. As I glanced around, I saw Jeremy sitting at a table, filled with Legos, at the back of the courtroom. Lindsey sat in the second row of benches inside the courtroom, doing her needlepoint, pretending to mind her own business. She winked at me as we walked by to stand in front of the judge.

Shelly stood at the farthest right, facing the judge's bench. She instructed me to stand on her left. Hannah stood on my left and Debra stood next to Hannah. Next to her was the GAL, Guardian Ad Litem, the attorney assigned to protect Jeremy's rights and interests. It wasn't Lisa as it had been, the woman who visited Jeremy in the hospital the day after he was placed in temporary custody. I had seen this woman talking with Jeremy, alone, earlier that morning. Next to the GAL stood Delilah. Rebecca stood somewhat behind her, and on Delilah's left was the public defender, Delilah's attorney. I thought it was interesting, we were all women standing in front of the judge.

I kept taking deep breaths and saying silent prayers in my head for Divine Order to reign over the entire courtroom and all in it. I surrounded everyone with the White Light of Christ for about the hundredth time. I wondered if the judge had been informed about Jeremy's AIDS. Just as that thought entered my mind, Shelly asked that the three attorneys meet with the judge in chambers. They did.

Thank you, thank you.

When they returned, the bailiff spoke. "Will the first to testify please raise her right hand?"

Shelly motioned for Debra to start. The bailiff swore her in and Shelly began her questioning. "Please spell your name for the court."

"D-e-b-r-a J-o-h-n-s-o-n."

"How long have you been working with the Miller family, Ms. Johnson?"

"Approximately one year."

"How did the family originally become involved with the state?"

225

"Jeremy fell from a second story window of the homeless shelter where he and his mother were staying. A child abuse hotline report was filed at that time."

"And was the evidence against the mother founded?"

"There were no witnesses, so no evidence for abuse was found against the mother. A worker was assigned to the family at that time because of the extenuating circumstances surrounding their case and because the mother was cited for lack of supervision of her son."

"Did the state make a referral to a private agency at that time?"

"Yes. We made a referral to a private program, which is under our contract, to provide more help to the family than we could offer."

"Thank you, Ms. Johnson."

"The state's attorney's office asks that Ms. Accetturo, our next witness, be sworn in at this time." I looked over at Shelly. She smiled and nodded her head at me. I raised my right hand and was sworn in. My whole body shook.

"Please spell your name for the court."

"R-o-b-y-n A-c-c-e-t-t-u-r-o."

"And you are the social worker that worked closely with the Miller family, correct?"

"Correct."

"Please tell the court the reason the Miller case was referred to your agency."

"The state hired us to provide in-depth counseling and case management services to the family."

"Can you please spell out for the court what that means?"

"I'd be glad to. I worked as a team with my co-worker, Carolyn Mitchell, whose title is Community Worker, to help Ms. Miller and her children cope better with their situation. If there was a service they needed that we couldn't provide, we connected them to an agency that could provide it. We assisted them in getting their rent paid for three months, helped them apply for AFDC and SSI, took them to and from doctor appointments, got clothing and baby items donated for Ms. Miller's new baby, intervened with the Board of Education when Jeremy was suspended from school, provided crisis intervention…"

"Thank you. That gives us a clearer picture of the services you provided. Did you make your initial visit to the family on February the eighth of 1990?"

"Yes, I did."

"What took place during that visit?"

"Ms. Mitchell and I introduced our program to Delilah Miller and her son Jeremy."

"Did you notice any evidence of physical abuse on Jeremy that particular day?"

"Yes, I did."

"Tell the court what you saw."

"Jeremy had a large welt on his face which covered his eye and part of his cheek. His face was badly bruised."

"Did you ask his mother where the welt came from?"

"Yes."

"What was her answer?"

"She said that he forgot his homework, in first grade, so she 'whupped' him with a belt on his buttocks and the belt accidentally backlashed and hit him in the face."

As I heard the words coming from my mouth, I got a little choked up. I took a deep breath and clenched my fists to give me strength.

"Did you inform Ms. Miller that using a belt on her son, on any part of his body, is unlawful?"

"I did."

"Did Ms. Miller agree to work with you during that first visit?"

"She did."

"And on March the fifth, did you have to make a suicide contract with Ms. Miller?"

"Yes."

"Please tell the court the situation surrounding your contract."

"I had spoken with Ms. Miller over the phone that night, and she had said that she felt like getting things over with by walking in front of a moving bus. I asked her if she thought she might act on that feeling, and she said no. I made a verbal agreement with her to call me anytime of the day or night, if she ever felt like acting on it, and she agreed she would."

227

"She had access to you after office hours?"

"Yes. She had my home phone number and Ms. Mitchell's home phone number."

"And you made seven visits to this family during the month of March?"

"Yes."

"On March the twenty-seventh, another incident took place, is that correct?"

"Yes."

"Please tell the court what happened."

I went alone for a visit to the family and when Jeremy walked in after school, he walked with a limp and had difficulty sitting down. He looked frightened."

"Did you ask him what was wrong?"

"Yes. I had his mother explain."

"And what was her explanation?"

"She said that he had been playing Nintendo for a while, and was jumping up and down like he had to use the restroom. She asked him if he had to go, and he said no. When he continued to jump up and down, she took him to the restroom and told him if he urinated, he was in trouble for lying to her. He did urinate, and she beat him with the belt." My voice cracked several times during the explanation. I could feel my tears rising up in my chest, moving closer toward my throat.

"You visited the family seven times in April?"

"Yes."

"And in May you escorted them on a trip to Florida sponsored by the Make – A – Wish Foundation?"

"I did."

"Why did you have to escort them?"

"Make – A – Wish wanted them to have an escort because the mother was ready to give birth to her second child and in case she needed to rest, or went into labor early, they wanted someone to be there with Jeremy. The family didn't have anyone else to accompany them. If I didn't go, they couldn't go."

"And another incident occurred while you were at Disney World?"

"Yes."

"Please tell the court what happened."

"While in the women's restroom, Jeremy didn't go into the stall his mother told him to go into, so she followed him into his stall and hit him so hard on the face, a welt of her handprint appeared there..." I started to cry. I couldn't maintain my composure any longer. Hannah handed me a tissue. I felt like a jerk. I couldn't help myself. It was such a release to be finally telling his story, uninterrupted, that I started to completely unravel.

The judge asked, "Are you able to finish this one incident and then we can recess until you're able to continue?"

"Okay." My chest was heaving as I did my best to pull it together so I could speak. I felt grateful to be standing in front of a judge who had compassion and reacted like a kind human being.

Shelly said, "Please, continue."

"His nose bled uncontrollably, he fell and hit his head..." Tears poured from my eyes. "He got the wind knocked out of him. He let out a blood curdling scream and came running around the corner, with blood pouring from his face, to find me." I blotted my tears with tissue.

The judge spoke. "I've heard enough for now. Court will adjourn for a ten-minute recess. Bailiff, please get Ms. Accetturo a box of tissue and a glass of water. Ms. Accetturo, if you need more time, we will take it. Thank you." He pounded his gavel and got up and left.

Hannah approached me and held my hand. Shelly dragged a chair over for me to sit down. I felt embarrassed. I was unable to stop crying.

I had held onto Jeremy's story for so long, it had become my own.

The judge came back in ten minutes. The bailiff announced, "All rise. Court is back in session."

I wiped under my eyes, trying not to smear my mascara, and took a deep breath.

The judge asked, "Are you ready to continue, Ms. Accetturo?"

"Yes, Sir," I answered.

He glanced over at Shelly and nodded his head.

"And on that same day of the Disney World incident, did Jeremy ask you if he could live with you?"

"Yes, he did."

"Did he also tell you he was scared?"

"He did."

"And did he plead with you to help his mommy?"

"Yes."

"Did you make a total of eight visits to this family in May?"

"Yes."

"And four visits in June?"

"Yes."

"On June thirteenth, did you make another home visit to the Miller family?"

"Yes."

"And what took place during that visit?"

"Ms. Mitchell and I confronted Ms. Miller about not complying with the agreed service plan. She had missed several parenting groups and counseling appointments. I also confronted her on disciplining Jeremy and reminded her that corporal punishment was unlawful."

"How did she handle your request?"

"She defiantly refused to cooperate and said, 'What's the state going to do about it?'"

"On June fourteenth, when Ms. Miller was admitted to the hospital for the birth of her second child, did she leave Jeremy's medication with the homemaker to administer to him?"

"No."

"Did she leave his medical card with the homemaker?"

"She did not leave his medical card, either."

"Did he get his medications filled?"

"Ms. Hanley, who is standing next to me right now, made arrangements to have them filled at the hospital pharmacy. I took Jeremy to pick them up. I also explained to the homemaker how to administer them, when I drove him home."

"On June twenty-seventh, did you make another home visit to this family?"

"Yes."

"Did anything unusual occur during that visit?"

"Yes."

"Please, tell us what happened."

"When Jeremy attempted to sit between Ms. Mitchell and I, on his couch, his mother threatened him and said, 'If you don't sit over here, I'll punch you so hard you'll fly through that brick wall, and I don't care who sees me.'"

"Did you make only two visits to the Miller's in July?"

"Yes."

"Tell the court what Ms. Miller agreed to do on July the tenth."

"Ms. Miller agreed to have weekly counseling sessions with me while Jeremy attended daycamp at his hospital. I was to provide transportation to and from daycamp for the whole family. Ms. Miller and I were to have our sessions after dropping Jeremy off, and then we were supposed to pick him up together and I would drive them all home. Ms. Miller only followed through once. Our agreement was for nine weeks."

"Did you attempt to make four more visits to the family during the month of August?"

"Yes."

"How many did Ms. Miller keep?"

"Only one. She failed the other three."

"Was that your last contact with Ms. Miller?"

"Yes, it was."

"Once Jeremy was placed in protective custody with the state, in October of last year, did you provide individual counseling for him regarding his adjustment to foster care?"

"Yes."

The judge spoke. "I've heard enough testimony from Ms. Accetturo. Please call your next witness."

Thank you, Judge Brownfield. Thank you, God. It's finally over. I don't have to hold onto one more story.

My head pounded so hard and my heart raced so fast, I felt like I might vomit. Hannah was the next witness. I felt so overwhelmed and sick to my stomach; I barely heard one thing she said. I kind of came back to life at the end of her testimony, when she said that Delilah withdrew Jeremy from all medical treatment and changed her phone number to an unpublished one.

After Hannah's testimony, it was the public defender's turn to highlight Delilah's progress. Rebecca said how good Delilah was doing with her visits with Jeremy and how well she cared for Simon. She said that Delilah was following through with her counseling at the mental health center.

When Rebecca finished testifying, it was Delilah's turn to testify. The bailiff swore her in. But before Delilah's attorney, the public defender, even got a chance to ask Delilah any questions, Judge Brownfield spoke. "This case has been in court since October of last year, when Jeremy was placed in protective custody. Since that time, have you ever interviewed Ms. Accetturo or Ms. Hanley?" He was speaking to Delilah's attorney.

"No, Your Honor, I..."

"That's what I thought. And you, Ms. Miller, do you deny any of the things these two women have said about you?"

Delilah hung her head low and quietly mumbled, "No."

"This case has been in court almost a year, with this much evidence against this mother, and you have never bothered to obtain any evidence other than the mother's. This is deplorable. And your behavior, Ms. Miller, is inexcusable. I am very sorry that the court took so long to hear the details of this case. Jeremy Miller will remain in protective custody with the state of Illinois. We will reconvene in one year. During that time, I suggest, Ms. Miller, that you work extra hard in counseling if you wish to get your son back. If not, he will be placed for adoption at that time. Thank you all for your testimony."

The sound of his gavel sent goose bumps up and down my entire body. It was finally over.

CHAPTER TWENTY-ONE -- IF ONLY I HAD KNOWN

Words don't do justice to describe the relief I felt, now that the burden of responsibility for Jeremy's safety was finally placed where it belonged — in the hands of someone with the power to do something about it. Judge Brownfield so eloquently told Delilah and her attorney just what he thought of their behavior. I couldn't have been more pleased.

As victorious as I felt, a part of me felt sad for Delilah. I could see by the shock in her eyes that she had no idea this was coming. She still believed she was "just disciplining him." I remained concerned about her. Would this news somehow affect her health? After all, our emotions have an impact on our physical health, especially the immune system. And could the judge's decision change how she cared for Simon? I hoped, with all of my heart, that she wouldn't begin to treat Simon the way she treated Jeremy.

I also hoped that I wouldn't have to see Delilah face to face. It was too painful for me to look into her eyes. I had tried every way I knew to help her, but still ended up having to take Jeremy away from her. A part of me felt I, too, had failed. Perhaps that's how Jeremy also felt — like he had to try one more time, and one more time after that, and so on and so on, until he melted away her walls of rage, hatred, and fear, with his love. AIDS and Jeremy's safety had taken the luxury of time away from me, and time was what Delilah needed if she was ever going to break through the reality she had built around herself for her own protection.

Late that evening, just as the judge's decision was beginning to sink in for me, the phone rang. I answered it. "Hello."

"Hi, Robyn. It's Lindsey. Is this a good time to talk?" The tone in her voice sounded ominous.

"Sure, what's up?"

"I just put the boys to bed, and I wanted to tell you what Jeremy shared with me this afternoon after court."

"Go on."

"We stopped at a park on the way home because Jeremy seemed so down. I asked if he wanted to talk about it. He said we don't know the whole story…"

I felt my whole body get flushed as I anticipated the rest of her words…

"He said that before Delilah would give him a beating with the belt, she'd go over and shut all the windows and curtains, even in the heat of summer, so no one could hear him scream for help."

I felt like a ton of bricks had landed on my chest. "Oh my God," I whispered.

"He said it happened a lot. He wouldn't say much more than that. I told him it would never happen again — that he's safe now with us. The judge made sure of that today."

"How'd he respond?"

"He remained quiet, so I reassured him that he'd still see his mom and his brother regularly, just like before court. He at least looked up when I said that."

"You handled it really well, Lindsey. Are you okay?"

"I hate what Jeremy went through. I'm just thrilled the judge finally ruled on all of this."

"Me, too."

We said our good byes. I felt sick to my stomach when I hung up. Picturing Delilah purposely closing the window infuriated me. She completely stripped him of all his power. At the moment, I couldn't even stand to think about it. It made me feel like I didn't want to see Delilah for a long, long time.

Dance With an Angel

With the judge's decision behind us, everyone involved with Jeremy wanted to make his life the most enjoyable possible. Lindsey, Wayne, Timmy, Jim, and I tried to focus on the present, living out each moment we had with Jeremy to the fullest.

My family and I threw Jeremy a birthday party on a Sunday afternoon. It was actually a month after his eighth birthday, but my sister, Susan, who was visiting from Georgia with her family, wanted to meet this child who had become such an important part of my life. My sister, Rosemary, and her husband, Alan, hosted the party at their home in Glen Ellyn. My brother, Ron, also came to meet my, "Little Buddy."

As Jim turned off of Lake Shore Drive to pick Jeremy up for the festivities, I got butterflies in my stomach. When we made that familiar turn into Jeremy's driveway, I thought my heart might jump right out of my chest. I so much wanted the day to be perfect. After all, who knew how many more birthdays we'd be able to celebrate together. The love and commitment that Jim and I felt for Jeremy was the kind of love that hurts so deeply, yet it's the kind of love that can heal your soul.

Instead of waiting at the kitchen window and greeting us by bolting down the back stairs, this visit began void of Jeremy's usual rhythm. As Jim and I stepped into the kitchen, we found Jeremy in a rocking chair, clutching his knapsack, waiting. The dark circles under his eyes looked puffy. He made little eye contact. He sat with his thin, 34-pound frame slouched slightly forward, his head tilted down. I knew three-year-old children who weighed the same. I could see and feel his fatigue, his physical distress. The sound of his deep, wet cough, echoed through my soul. My chest ached, literally, in empathy for Jeremy... everything he had lived through... and with. How I wished I could make him well. Thinking back now, I realize he was beginning his withdrawal from us, in preparation of what was to come. I wasn't able to allow myself to think it back then.

Lindsey handed me a bag full of medicines along with a handwritten schedule for when each medicine had to be taken. The pink liquid every four hours, the big white pills every six, and the small white ones every eight; his own mini pharmacy to be doled out on time, just like the last time he slept over.

235

Jeremy asked to please sit on my lap in the front seat for the ride there. He wanted me to hold him, so we could cuddle. The seat belt smushed us together in our, "Oreo cookie hug," as Jeremy would say.

Jeremy extraordinary quietness that day made my heart sink. I had never seen him so exhausted. Within minutes, he fell asleep in my arms. Except for his deep, wet chest cough, the three of us rode in silence. Each time I glanced over at Jim, our eyes met and filled with tears. Jeremy's soft brown curls rested upon my chest. The rhythm of our breath at times was synchronized. I bent my head down to smell his curly hair and smooth his forehead with my hand. Sadness filled my heart. Something felt different that day, although I couldn't put my finger on it. I should've felt happy. After all, Jeremy did not suffer through anymore beatings with the belt... or full body casts from "falling" out of second story windows... or welts of Mom's handprint on his face. Nope, only safety from now on.

As we drove to the ice cream shop where I had ordered Jeremy's favorite strawberry ice cream cake covered in Teenage Mutant Ninja Turtles, Jeremy awakened to ask Jim to turn off the air conditioner. It was a hot August day. Even though our bodies generated much heat between us, Jeremy's teeth began to chatter and his body shivered. He soon fell back asleep.

Jeremy awakened as I carried him out of the car, up Rosemary's driveway. He was still groggy. When he was ready, I introduced him to my family. Even the pile of presents on the table didn't excite Jeremy like I thought it would have.

Still withdrawn and clinging to me, I tried to find out what was going on inside my Little Buddy. So I sat at the table on the deck, plopped Jeremy onto my lap and gently whispered in his ear, "You're pretty quiet, Sweetie, are you all right?"

He nestled his head into my shoulder, saying nothing. I was really concerned; this was so out of character for Jeremy. I put one arm around him and stroked his back with my other arm. Rosemary, Susan, and my niece, Christina, joined us at the table. Each time Jeremy coughed, all eyes turned toward me, filled with sadness. It broke our hearts as we watched him helplessly survive another coughing fit to catch his breath.

The deck was covered with potted annuals, every color of the rainbow. Rosemary had decorated with streamers and balloons in bright yellow, Jeremy's favorite color. My brother, Ron, who brought his guitar, plopped down next to Jeremy and began strumming, singing a silly tune. He made up a song about Jeremy. Giggles resounded from Jeremy's belly.

"Where'd ya get *that* song?" Jeremy inquired sheepishly.

"Oh, a little birdie must've whispered it in my ear," responded Ron, winking at him.

"Can he whisper another one, do ya think?"

"I bet he can," answered Ron. "He even takes requests. Gotta special song you'd like to hear?"

"Wind Beneath My Wings."

"I don't know all the wor..." began Ron.

"That's okay," Jeremy interrupted, "I do." And with that, Ron began strumming away.

"That's my favorite," Jeremy whispered as he scooted over to touch Ron's knee. The song ended with "Thank you, thank God for you, the wind beneath my wings." Jeremy squeezed my hand and cocked his head to lean against my chest. He seemed like he was back from wherever he had retreated, to join in the fun.

Sometimes when Jeremy and I were together, he'd sink into a trance-like state, as though his spirit needed to take off for a bit of a respite. When he'd return to his physical awareness, his eyes would sparkle and I could feel his strength and love emanating from his being. He often showered me and others in his presence with strength, calmness, and peace.

Alan, my brother-in-law, had barbecued some of Jeremy's favorite foods including hot dogs, hamburgers, and buffalo chicken wings. Jeremy barely ate, but he managed to swig down a mouthful of his pink medicine and swallow his small white pill with a sip of ice cold lemonade. After dinner, we sang Happy Birthday and cut the cake. Jeremy didn't touch his piece.

I thought opening his presents might cheer Jeremy up, so we quickly cleared the table and piled it with lots of gifts. Of all the gifts he had received, a remote control car, hand held video games, and a tape player among others, his "bestest" one was the wiffle ball and bat given to him by Rosemary and Alan. It had been Alan's since he was a kid.

Suddenly, Jeremy came back to life, jumping for joy, grinning from ear to ear.

"This is the bestest present I ever got! Thanks!" he yelled exuberantly, whipping the ball to Alan. "Let's play!" He ran down the stairs into the back yard. We all followed.

"I'll pitch," I yelled.

"I'll catch," yelled Rosemary running up behind Jeremy, tickling him. Everyone else stood in the outfield.

"You guys better back up," announced Jim. "This guy can really hit! Right Jeremy?"

Wham! Jeremy hit the ball with mighty force. "YES!" he screamed, jumping up and down as he watched Alan and Glenn, my other brother in law, race for the ball clear into the neighbor's yard. The outfielders each took several steps backward to adjust to the slugger's moves.

"Holy cow! What a hit!" exclaimed Ron.

"Great hit, Jeremy," shouted Rosemary.

"High five, Kiddo," I yelled, running toward him, arm raised.

"I wanna hit again, can I, can I? Please?" he asked, looking at me.

"Sure, Slugger," I answered, turning around to the outfield. "Look out guys, Slugger's up again!" Jeremy beamed.

He continued to jump up and down with excitement as I pitched another fast one. "Strike one," yelled Rosemary.

"Ooh, slowing down are you, Slugger," I teased, pitching another fast one.

"Watch this," Jeremy quipped, slamming the ball with such force, it literally brought me to my knees. The ball whizzed by me, knocking my left pierced earring out of my ear and me to the ground. The ball then landed on the neighbor's deck.

"Whoa!" I yelled, laughing, clutching my bright red ear lobe. Jeremy fell to the ground, in seventh heaven. The neighbors, Lisa and Steve, applauded him. Lisa was wearing a White Sox cap. She walked over, returning the ball, placing her cap on Jeremy's head. "Anyone who can hit that good deserves my special cap," announced Lisa. "Where'd you learn to hit like that?"

"Jim. Taught me a coupla months ago."

"You're great," responded Lisa, walking back to resume her position on the deck.

Jeremy yelled, "Save me a hot dog from the bleachers, will ya?"

Steve responded, "Hit me a homer, Slugger, so you can autograph the ball!"

"You got it," yelled Jeremy. With that, he hit the ball so hard, it cracked in half. Glenn ran to Jeremy and handed him a pen. Jeremy signed both of them and ran and gave half to Lisa. Alan got another ball from the garage.

As the game continued for quite some time, one by one, each of us dropped out from exhaustion. Jeremy was the only player left standing. He continued to hit balls by himself, running to retrieve them. I had to interrupt him when it was time for his big, white pill. He swallowed it and continued playing.

Before Lisa even completed her sentence, Jeremy went running toward her. She had invited him over to play. Jeremy spent over an hour there. They had a water fight, and when it ended, Jeremy was completely soaked. Lisa walked Jeremy back over to Rosemary's, wrapped in one of her towels, with her arm around him. "Anytime you're visiting, please come by and visit us, too. We haven't had this much fun in a very long time. Thank you." Lisa gave him a kiss on the cheek and a big hug.

Jeremy blushed. "You're welcome, and thank you, too."

I held Jeremy, wrapped in a blanket, while Rosemary put his clothes in the dryer. We read stories until they were dry.

Jeremy slept the entire way home. He awakened as we pulled in his driveway.

"Can you guys come up for a little while? Please?" he asked with his shining, big brown, puppy dog eyes.

Although Jim and I were both thoroughly exhausted, we couldn't turn him down. "Okay," I said patting him on the head, "Just for a little while. I'm really pooped." I was almost four months pregnant.

"Yippee!" he screamed, running up the back stairs.

As we walked in, Timmy raced into the kitchen to greet us.

"Hi, guys! Did you have fun, Jeremy? What'd you get?" he asked, grabbing a box from under Jeremy's arm.

"Oh, lots of stuff," Jeremy responded low key. "Come on guys, let's go up to my room." He grabbed my hand and pulled me toward the stairs.

Wayne was upstairs rewinding a video for the boys.

"Please, can you watch this video with me. Please?" Jeremy pleaded.

"No, Sweetie, I'm sorry. It's almost 9:00. I'm really tired. We have to get going soon," I said.

"Please?"

"Another time, okay?"

"Promise?"

"Yep. Promise."

Jeremy jumped up into my arms. "I love you," he said, looking directly into my eyes. "I had lots of fun today, thanks."

"I love you, too, Jeremy," I said. Jim joined us in an "Oreo cookie" hug with Jeremy in the middle. "Don't forget me," chimed Jim. "I love you, too, Jeremy."

"Before you go, can you guys come into my room and play Legos for a few minutes?"

I looked at Jim to see what he wanted to do. He smiled and answered, "Sure, we can, for a few minutes."

"Goodie!"

We stayed until Jeremy and Jim built a "heliport within a magical city," as Jeremy called it. It looked like something out of Star Trek.

As I now remember the good byes we said to Jeremy that night, my heart flutters. The remaining days of August brought vacations for all of us. The week after Jim and I made Jeremy the promise to watch a video with him, Jeremy spent a week with Timmy and Lindsey at a ranch with other HIV infected children. Jim and I left for Wisconsin the week after Jeremy got home from camp. During our long drive home, we planned a special sleepover with Jeremy for the weekend after Labor Day. We'd rent some videos, take him out for his favorite pizza, and go downtown to see Buckingham Fountain and walk by Lake Michigan, if Jeremy was up for it.

Soon after we got home and unloaded the car, Jim went downstairs to throw in some laundry while I went to call Jeremy to tell him of our plans. Our answering machine light was blinking. I'll never forget pressing the button to retrieve the messages. The first one was from Lindsey.

"Brace yourself, Robyn." The words are etched into my memory. Even now, my chest tightens as I allow them to become ever present again..."Jeremy was admitted to the hospital with an extremely high fever. He's in intensive care. They have him in an induced coma so that he won't fight the ventilator that is helping him breathe. He looks terrible." There was a long gap of silence. "I know he's still in there, Robyn, because I told him that he has to get better so he can go to your house to play baseball again. He opened his eyes when I said that. Please, call me."

CHAPTER TWENTY-TWO -- PLEASE... NO...

Oh my God, this is it...

Without even realizing it, I had drawn my knees up toward the rest of my body and was holding them tightly, rocking myself, while my shirt became wet with my tears. When Jim came up and saw me, he knew immediately it was Jeremy. He sat down beside me and I managed to get out, "Lindsey said he's in a coma and on a ventilator." Jim held me as we both sobbed.

"It'll be okay," he whispered, "no matter what happens, we'll get through it together."

When we had no tears left, Jim and I prayed together. I began, "Heavenly Father and Mother God, we wish to serve. Please surround and fill Jeremy with the White Light of Christ..."

I started to cry again, so Jim finished the prayer. "We pray for healing for Jeremy, and for Lindsey, Wayne, Timmy, and Delilah. Please give us the strength to get through this, and may your will be done. Thank you. Amen."

"Thanks, Jim." I slowly got up and walked over to the phone. Jim stood beside me as I dialed Lindsey's number. It rang four times and her answering machine came on — darn. "Hi Lindsey. It's Robyn. I..." Lindsey picked up the phone.

"Hi," she said in a subdued voice.

"Hi."

"I take it you got my message."

"I did. We just got home. How is he?"

"He's still in a coma. When we got back from the movies on Saturday, Jeremy vomited. He just didn't look right, so I called his doctor. He told me he'd meet us at the emergency room. None of us wanted to take any chances since Jeremy had just gotten out of the hospital on Wednesday for a high fever and vomiting. On the way to the hospital, he decompensated very quickly. By the time we got there, he couldn't even hold his head up, so I carried him inside. The doctor took one look at him and wheeled him right up to intensive care. They did an arterial blood gas. It read 32. While they ran further tests, Jeremy asked for Timmy, so Wayne and Timmy took the train in. Just before they hooked Jeremy up to the ventilator, Jeremy held Timmy's hand and said, 'I want to thank you for being my brother and helping me at home.'"

An oppressive gap of silence hung heavily in the air. Lindsey continued. "You guys can go see him. Wayne and I have been there all afternoon. We'll go back after supper. Timmy's seen him a couple of times, but he doesn't like it. He wants him to wake up."

"Me, too," I mumbled.

"No kidding," replied Lindsey.

"We'll go see him in a little while," I said.

"You and Jim really need to prepare yourselves for this. He doesn't look good. He's on this medicine called Pavulon, which actually puts him into a coma like state so that he doesn't fight all of the tubes they have in him...." Lindsey continued talking, but I zoned out for a minute, unable to take in anything more she said. I came back when I heard her say that they had taped his eyes shut because they were partially opened and watering so much. They thought he'd be more comfortable if they were closed.

When I hung up the phone, I felt sick to my stomach. I went into the bathroom and vomited. I was 18 weeks pregnant. Not even morning sickness had made me feel this ill.

Jim waited outside the bathroom door. "You okay?"

"Okay as I can be. You ready to go?"

"Are you?" Jim answered.

We were. We anxiously drove in silence to the hospital. When we entered the lobby, Jim asked where intensive care was. "Fourth floor. Take the elevators down that hallway."

"Thanks."

As Jim pressed the up elevator button, I got butterflies. I said another silent prayer in my head. When the elevator door opened at four, my heart raced so fast I feared it might jump out of my mouth. Jim grabbed my hand as we began our walk through the double doors to intensive care. I didn't look around at first. I couldn't. We approached the nurses' station. A nurse stopped writing on the chart and asked, "May I help you?"

"Yes, thank you, we're looking for Jeremy Miller."

"Who are you?"

"His friends."

"Intensive care is for family…"

"I was his social worker."

"You should have said so. Lindsey called and told me you'd probably be coming when you got home from vacation. Hi, I'm Cindy. I'm Jeremy's nurse for this shift."

"I'm, Robyn. This is my husband, Jim."

"You're the one he plays baseball with," she said, smiling. "I understand he's quite a slugger."

"He is." Jim smiled.

"Step over here, and I'll show you how to dress so you can go see him."

She took us over to the sink and had us step on a foot pedal on the floor, which turned on the water. She showed us how to press another button to spray some foam soap onto our hands and arms. Then she handed us each a gown and a mask.

"You have to put these on. We don't want to pass any more germs onto him."

I guess we were ready. Physically, anyway. She walked us past a newborn baby who breathed with a ventilator and several other machines and contraptions attached to him. The baby's mother and father sat on chairs beside their precious bundle, looking absolutely exhausted. The nurse led us to Jeremy and patted me on the back. "If you need me, I'll be right over here."

Oh, Dear God, please… no…

It didn't even look like him. I gently took his limp hand in mine, brought it up to my lips and held it there, kissing the back of it. "Hi, Buddy," I whispered. "It's, Robyn," and Jim added, "and Jim. We love you, Buddy." Tears streamed down Jim's cheeks. I tried with all my might to hold it together.

Two IV poles stood beside Jeremy's bed. I counted seven bags of liquid being pumped into his veins. He had tubes inserted into almost every orifice of his body. The hissing of the ventilator sent shivers down my spine, as the machine breathed for him, sending puffs of air, at a specifically calibrated rate, to fill his lungs. The heart monitor, which gave a reading of his blood pressure, oxygen level, pulse, and number of respirations sat on a portable shelf above and to the left of his head. A gooey lubricant covered his eyes, which were taped shut.

I gently placed his hand down on the bed and held mine over his. I bent down to talk softly in his ear. "We love you, Buddy. Whatever you need to do is okay with me."

"And with me," Jim added. "Know that you'll always live on in our hearts, Little Buddy, forever. Chief Yellow Sports Car awaits you whenever you're ready."

"You can let go whenever you need to, Buddy. It's okay to go to the Light. It'll be all right. I'll take good care of your new baby brother, or sister, whoever's in my belly, and don't forget, you said you'd be their guardian angel. I'm gonna hold you to it." I patted his hand. I stood back up and stroked as much of the top of his arm as I could without disturbing all of the tubes.

Back when Jeremy found out I was pregnant, he said it was, "Our baby, yours, Jim's and mine. I'm gonna have a new baby brother and sister cuz don't forget, we're gonna have another baby, too."

Jim asked if we could trade places so he could get closer to Jeremy. Jim bent down to talk softly in Jeremy's ear, "Ya know, Little Buddy, you're the best baseball player I know. Boy, you really know how to hit that ball. Even Babe Ruth would be proud..."

I lost it and had to walk away. I quickly fled out of the double doors, down the hallway, until I saw a door marked as a restroom. I pushed my way in, locked the door behind me and stood, doubled over, sobbing.

"Oh Dear God, please help me do this. Help me..."

Someone knocked at the door and asked, "Are you okay in there?"

"I'll be okay." I heard them walk away. A minute later, I heard Jim outside the door.

"Rob?"

I unlocked the door and walked out into the hallway. We embraced.

"Oh, God, this is so hard," I said to Jim.

"It is. Lindsey and Wayne are in with him now, and right after you left, Delilah came. I guess she's been here everyday."

I took a deep breath. Sooner or later, I knew I'd have to face her again. "What should we do?" I asked Jim.

"Well, since they only let two people in at a time, let's wait down here in the waiting room. Lindsey knows we're here. She said she'd meet us in a few minutes.

We walked down the hallway and found the waiting area for intensive care. It was empty. I sat for a few minutes, but felt so antsy I had to get up and walk around. I peeked through the window in the door to intensive care and saw Lindsey, Wayne, and Delilah all standing around Jeremy. Jeremy always wanted Lindsey and his mom to be "friends." This was about as close as I had ever seen them come to one another without Delilah giving Lindsey a hard time. Maybe Jeremy still had time to have his wish granted.

Lindsey happened to look in my direction and saw me. She waved. Delilah didn't turn around.

I went back into the waiting room and sat beside Jim. Lindsey and Wayne came out to meet us. We said our hellos, and Lindsey and I hugged. I started to cry. We all sat down.

"Is he in a coma?" I asked.

"They put him in one to make him more comfortable," answered Lindsey.

That's comfortable? I thought to myself. "What does that mean?" I asked.

Wayne answered. "He's on Pavulon. It's a drug that completely paralyzes the body. The ventilator does the breathing for him."

"So without the ventilator, would he still be alive?" Jim asked.

"The Pavulon paralyzes every part of his body. Without the Pavulon, we aren't sure what would happen. They put him on the ventilator so he'd get enough oxygen, and so they could treat whatever caused his collapse. If he doesn't try to fight the machines, and just lets them do the work for him, he could get off the stuff. But

I'd imagine that'd be pretty hard and too scary for him right now. Once he got on the ventilator, Lindsey and I explained to him what was happening with all the machines, especially the ventilator. But who knows if he even understood us?"

No one spoke. And then Lindsey added, "On the Pavulon, it's hard to tell when he's asleep or when he's awake. Although when you watch the heart monitor, his blood pressure and heart rate change when you talk to him. He can hear us and knows we are there. I've been reading to him every night, and his mom has been playing his favorite tape, 'Wind Beneath My Wings' to him every time she visits."

"Wow," was all I could think of to say. My heart ached as I pictured Delilah sitting beside him, playing the tape. It amazed me to think that a cold and calculating instrument could witness and measure that our tenderness, love, and compassion were getting through to Jeremy, even through all that machinery he was plugged into.

"Delilah's been a trooper. She visits Jeremy everyday and stayed with him overnight a couple of times. She drops Simon off at a shelter, and he's cared for there while she stays with Jeremy."

"How are you guys doing?" Jim asked.

They looked at each other and Lindsey spoke. "We're okay for now. The doctors are trying everything they can to treat whatever's causing this so they can take him off the ventilator, and we can bring him home. Although the longer he's on it, the harder it is to wean him off when the time comes." Lindsey paused.

I took a deep breath and stared at the floor. I wasn't so hopeful the time would ever come.

After a moment of silence, Lindsey continued. "The doctors are very hopeful that he'll recover. Why don't you guys go back in and spend a little more time with him, if you want. Wayne and I'll stay here until you're finished."

"Delilah's still in there. Don't they only want two people at a time?" I asked.

"They won't mind. Go ahead."

Jim and I walked back in to intensive care, rescrubbed, and approached Jeremy's bed. We stood across from Delilah, who refused to look at either of us. She did not speak.

"I'm so sorry, Delilah," I said. "You and Jeremy are in our prayers."

She muttered, "Thanks," but she still didn't make eye contact. She quickly ran out of the room.

Jim moved around to where Delilah had stood so that we were across from each other. We both placed our hands over Jeremy's body and Jim began to pray. "Father, Mother God, please fill Jeremy with healing energy. Heal his body, mind, and spirit. Amen."

The nurse approached and asked to speak with me. Jim stayed with Jeremy, and she and I walked toward the nurses' station.

"Lindsey and Wayne are great foster parents. They couldn't tell me much about Jeremy's mother, they said I should talk to you." She paused and my heartbeat began to race. She continued. "Do we need to be concerned about the mother? She's awfully cold toward everyone. She wouldn't hurt him, would she?"

The thought hadn't crossed my mind. "Oh, gosh, I hadn't thought of that." I stayed quiet a minute, thinking how to handle this. So I said, "Since the last time we were in court, just a few weeks ago, her visits with him have still been supervised. They've been supervised for almost a year now, so I suppose that should extend to here, too. I don't think she would do anything to hurt him, but you bring up a good point."

"Well, he's always supervised while he's here. I just wanted to get your opinion," she said. The nurse really caught me off guard, which made me think, could Delilah hurt him here? Would she? I felt a pinge of guilt for disclosing this information to the nurse, but I decided I had to keep my tunnel vision and not allow myself to feel remorse or guilt over Delilah's needs or feelings, even at this late stage. At least I convinced myself I had to. I feared that if I did let my guard down to keep Jeremy safe from Delilah until the end, and God forbid, somehow she did lose control of herself and hurt him, I would never be able to forgive myself. After all, I never knew when her rage would take over, and she would attack next.

Just then, loud beeping went off near Jeremy. The nurse rushed over to him. "It's all right, Jeremy. We're going to have to suction you. Hold on just a minute." She turned toward Jim and I and said, "You guys might want to step out for this or at least step back."

We stepped back. I wanted to see what she was going to do to my Little Buddy.

She put on her protective gear; goggles with a windshield over her mouth and nose, and another gown over the one she already wore. She unhooked the tube at his mouthpiece, and squeezed some sort of liquid down the tube that went into his lungs. The panic in his face showed how terrified he felt, even though he couldn't move. She let him have a little more air before she stuck this skinny suctioning tube down the big tube and suctioned up the gunk that was down in his lungs. The nurse had to not only cut off his oxygen while she suctioned his lungs, the suctioning tube itself sucked up whatever oxygen was left inside the bigger tube. It was a torturous procedure to watch.

When she finished though, Jeremy seemed much more comfortable. Jim and I stood on either side of him and talked some more to him. "You did a great job, Buddy. It's over now," I said.

"You're a brave, young man. I always knew that about you," said Jim.

"Whatever you need to do, Jeremy, is great. If you are ready to let go, I support you. If you still want to fight to get better, that's okay, too. I'll love you forever. You'll always be my Little Buddy. I'm grateful that I know you. You're my hero." I started to cry.

"I'm grateful too, Buddy. And I support you, too. You do whatever it is you need to, and we'll always be there, no matter what. Promise. You're my hero, too." Just then, Lindsey and Wayne walked in. It was time for Jim and I to leave.

We both kissed Jeremy good bye and said, "I love you." We told him we'd be back again to visit him real soon. We said bye to Lindsey and Wayne, and left the hospital.

I wanted to talk, but found myself unable to speak. Jim must've felt the same way. We drove in silence the whole way home.

CHAPTER TWENTY-THREE -- TIME GOES ON...

Images of Jeremy on the ventilator kept both Jim and me tossing and turning all night. I don't know how Jim got up to go to work the next day. Jim had graduated with his Masters Degree in Social Work and had just started a new full time job.

When I finally crawled out of bed, I prayed for Jeremy first thing. Then I quieted my mind in meditation and asked God to give me any messages I might need in order to do my best to help Jeremy. I no sooner asked, than a song popped in my head. I find that Spirit often uses songs to get through to me when I'm unable to quiet my mind enough to receive guidance. I immediately recognized the tune as "Against All Odds," by Phil Collins. This is what I heard:

> How can I just let you walk away
> Just let you leave without a trace
> When I stand here taking every breath with you...
> Cuz we've shared the laughter and the pain
> We've even shared the tears...
> You're the only one who really knew me at all...

I could hardly handle my emotions when I heard the next line.

> Take a look at me now
> There's just an empty space...
> But you coming back to me
> Is against all odds
> It's a chance I've got to take...

My sobbing had brought me out of my meditative state. So I pulled myself together, closed my eyes again and asked, in my mind, what I was supposed to get from this message. The answer came to me in the form of a strong feeling: Against all odds, Jeremy was letting me know he needed to fight to stay alive, on the ventilator, before he'd be able to let go to die. I asked for confirmation of my message, but got none. Not yet, anyway.

I rubbed my eyes, stretched, and got out of bed. I walked into the kitchen and put the kettle on. I sat at the table, planning my day around a visit to Jeremy. I'd stop at the hospital and spend time with him between my two counseling sessions with my private clients.

I found it amazing that seeing two clients daily, for private counseling sessions, provided Jim and I with more money than my full time job with my AIDS families. And not only that, it was almost as if the Universe had rearranged my life so I had the time to spend with Jeremy that we both needed during this difficult process.

On my way to the hospital after my first session, my heart raced in anticipation of seeing Jeremy again. It about killed me to see that machine breathing for him, but Lindsey and Wayne seemed to think he'd come off of it in the near future. I wasn't so sure.

If only I knew what Jeremy wanted...

To distract myself, I turned the radio on in the car. A commercial and then the music began... "How can I just let you walk away, just let you leave without a trace..."

"Against All Odds," by Phil Collins. I was so overcome with emotion, I had to pull the car over and stop. I put my flashers on and sat in my car, a few blocks from the hospital, listening to each word of the song. I couldn't believe how much they applied to Jeremy. I felt like his spirit spoke to me directly through every word, answering my question, telling me what he wanted; to go against all odds and take a chance that he might get through to his mom and help her to feel his love through all of this.

When the song ended, I took a deep breath to collect myself. Just as I put on my left turn signal and looked into my mirror to pull out into traffic, "Wind beneath My Wings" was the next song that came on the radio.

I guess I must've needed more confirmation. And of course, I sat there and bawled my eyes out.

Thank you, Universe, thank you.

I waited until the song ended before I continued on my way to the hospital. The lyrics to the next song that played were, "I Wanna Know What Love is, I want you to show me, there's so much love... I wanna feel what love is, I know you can show me..."

I felt strongly that through this song, Jeremy was confirming for me that he wasn't finished teaching his mom about love, and that maybe somehow, in the process of his dying, he thought that he would get through to her. I hoped he was right for both their sakes.

I prayed for the strength to do what Jeremy needed me to do and to not infringe my needs over his. I parked my car and slowly trudged my way to the hospital. I dreaded seeing my Little Buddy in the condition he was in. I felt like I was being tortured right along with him. As I stepped off of the elevator onto the fourth floor, I saw Timmy sitting in the waiting room. I walked in and said hi. He was with one of the volunteers from the clinic.

"Where's your mom, Sweetie?"

"She's in there." He pointed toward the double doors of intensive care.

"How are you doing?" I asked. I kneeled down to be at his eye level.

"Fine," he said quietly as he lowered his eyes to the floor.

"Ya sad?"

"Yeah."

"Me, too. Do ya wanna talk about it?"

"No."

"Okay. I'm gonna go in and see Jeremy. I'll see ya later." I patted Timmy on the head and walked toward the double doors.

I took a deep breath and walked in. Both Lindsey and Delilah stood at his bedside. I did the washing and gown routine and joined them.

"Hi," I said, addressing both of them. Delilah wouldn't look at me.

"Hi," Lindsey answered.

"How's he doing today?" I asked. Delilah stormed out the door.

"Obviously I make her uncomfortable," I said.

Lindsey ignored my comment and said, "Come over here for a minute." We walked out of Jeremy's earshot. "They put him on a new medicine today, a really strong antifungal treatment called Amphotericin. We call it amphoterrible because it has such horrible side effects."

"Like what?" The words came out of my mouth before I could even decide if I wanted to hear the answer.

"It has to be monitored frequently through blood draws because it's so toxic to the system. They know at each draw if he's tolerating it or not. It can cause high fever, pain in the joints and muscles, headaches, renal distress, it affects the body's potassium level. It can also cause vomiting, diarrhea, cramping, anemia..."

"That's enough, thanks."

"They want to try it to see if it will help his fever go down. His thrush has gotten so bad, it's all inside of him, too." Normally, Jeremy had thrush in his mouth and down his throat.

Lindsey and I went back to Jeremy. Lindsey said, "Jeremy, I'm going to go get Timmy some lunch. Robyn's here. I'll be back after I take Timmy home. See ya." She bent down and kissed his forehead.

"How long do you think you'll be?" I asked.

"I'll try to be back by 3:00." I looked at my watch. It was 11:30.

"I have to leave at 2:00 to go see another client, but I'll be back tomorrow," I said.

"Great. I'll see you tomorrow then." We hugged and Lindsey left.

I pulled a tall stool beside Jeremy's bed. My ankles were beginning to retain water. My obstetrician didn't want me standing for long periods of time. Before I sat down, I kissed Jeremy's cheek and said, "Hi, Buddy, it's Robyn." I looked up at the monitor. His blood pressure and heart rate both went up. I guessed he woke up in there. I remained standing to be closer to his ear.

"Jim's at work. He says hi and sends his love. Our baby is doing great. I had an ultrasound the other day and the doctor asked if we wanted to know if the baby is a boy or girl. We want it to be a surprise. I wish you could've seen the baby's hands and feet, and it's beautiful round head. It's perfect. I know one day, whether it's here or in the spirit world, you'll meet your new brother or sister. I'll be looking forward to that moment. Knowing you, you probably already have. You're so important to me, Little Buddy, I love you." I put my face down on his, and kissed his forehead. It didn't even smell like him. I touched his hair and caressed his cheek gently. "I want to do the right thing for you. I think your spirit is letting me know what you want. So if you need to fight more to hold on a little longer, I'm with you all the way. And when you're ready to surrender, I'll be with you every step of the way then, too. Remember? I promised. Back at the zoo on Earth day, I promised I'd see you through till the end and keep you safe. I keep my promises. Except for the video… last month… well, I would if you could. I just hope and pray that you're not hurting anymore. I don't want you to suffer anymore…." I was so absorbed in our conversation, I didn't hear the nurse come up beside me.

"Hi. You must be Robyn."

"I am." I sat down.

"I'm Susan, the charge nurse. I appreciate you talking to the nurse last night about Jeremy's mother. We made note in the chart of the court order for supervision. Jeremy is resting more comfortably today. The doctor increased his morphine to eight milligrams. He shouldn't be in any pain. We need to snap a chest x-ray. Would you please step out for a minute?"

"I'll be okay." The nurse pointed at my round belly. "Oh, yeah," I answered, feeling embarrassed. "I'll step out now, thanks." I leaned into Jeremy and whispered, "Hey Buddy, they're gonna take an x-ray of your chest. I'll be back when it's finished. I love you."

I smiled. I saw Stephen, the lamb I gave him, tucked on the side of his pillow.

I stepped into the hallway. Eight milligrams of morphine seemed like a lot to me for an eight-year-old child who probably didn't even weigh 35 pounds. The average weight for an eight-year-old boy is between 55 and 60 pounds.

When the woman driving the mobile x-ray cart passed me in the hallway, I went back in and sat beside Jeremy again.

"Hi, Sweetie, I'm back. I don't want to tire you out too much. So I'll be quiet for now and just sit here with you. Know that I'll always love you."

I adjusted myself on the hard stool, trying to get comfortable, but found it next to impossible. I held Jeremy's hand and closed my eyes. I asked God to surround Jeremy with all the colors of the rainbow for healing. I held the palm of my other hand over his solar plexus area and asked God to send healing energy throughout his entire body. Suddenly an alarm on some machine of his went off.

Susan came over and said, "He needs to be suctioned, please, excuse me."

"I'll be right over here, Buddy. Hang in there."

Susan put her goggles, mask, and gloves on and began the excruciating process. Even though I knew what to expect with the suctioning, since I had seen it the night before, it wasn't any easier to watch this time around. I felt so helpless and frightened. There was nothing I could do to make it better for him, except not have him go through it alone.

Dear God, please don't let him suffer, I silently begged.

Susan no sooner finished and had taken her protective gear off when another series of alarms sounded. She quickly called for another nurse to get more medicine, and gently fiddled with his tubing as she connected yet another IV up to him. In a matter of minutes, she had everything running smoothly.

"It's okay, Jeremy. Everything's back in order now. Try and rest," Susan said. She soothed his forehead. "He should get some rest now. The cafeteria's downstairs if you'd like to grab a bite to eat."

"Thanks, I have to leave in awhile. Is it all right if I sit here quietly? I won't disturb him." I hoped she wouldn't make me leave.

"That'd be fine. I'm going to lunch now. Peggy will take over for me while I'm gone if you need anything."

"Thanks. He is certainly receiving tremendous care."

I sat beside Jeremy for the next hour and a half before I had to leave. I continuously sent him love and asked for healing to be sent to him, no matter where that healing needed to take him. It was much too painful to see him like this, but I had to keep repeating to myself, *in his time, not yours.* I prayed for the strength to see him through.

At 2:00, I leaned toward Jeremy and whispered, "It's Robyn again, Sweetie. I have to go for now, but I promise I'll be back tomorrow. I love you. Do whatever you need to do, Buddy. See ya." I kissed his cheek and stroked his hair. I walked away and took my gown off.

Susan approached me. "Probably on Thursday, if his chest x-ray comes out okay, the doctor is going to start to wean him off of the Pavulon and see how he responds. Do you think you can be here that day?"

"Sure will. What time?"

"After lunch would be good. He responds well to your voice."

I smiled a faint smile and walked away. I very easily could have started to sob. Underneath my smile, I felt so devastated and powerless. Neither my smile nor voice could bring Jeremy the comfort he needed and deserved now. Nothing I could do would take his suffering away, nothing.

As I walked out to my car, I passed the hospital groundskeepers who were busy pulling out all the petunias and impatiens and planting yellow mums in their place. It had been almost a year since I had picked the yellow mums for Jeremy and wrapped them in his quilt when I gave him Stephen, the lamb.

I never thought a year later would bring this. I knew Jeremy would eventually die. But I never imagined the end of his life would be this dreadful.

CHAPTER TWENTY- FOUR -- RECONCILIATION

I visited Jeremy on both Tuesday and Wednesday of that same week. By Wednesday his fever had finally started to drop, thank goodness. I guess that amphoterrible stuff did the trick. The rest of his status hadn't changed. The ventilator continued to breathe for him. He now had eight IV bags dripping into him, and the electrodes from the cardiac monitor were still taped all over his chest. I had to use it as a guide to let me know when he was awake, but I talked to him even when he was asleep. People in a coma can still hear.

Evidently his chest x-ray came out all right. I happened to pass Lindsey at the elevator on my way up to see Jeremy as she was leaving that afternoon. She gave me the good news; "They're going to take Jeremy off of the Pavulon tomorrow. He should be able to communicate with us!" I remembered they had attempted to take him off of it near the end of his first week on the ventilator without success. He'd fought the ventilator too much.

"Wow," I answered. I didn't quite understand this Pavulon drug.

"You coming to see him?" Lindsey asked.

"I wouldn't miss it for anything. Is noon okay?"

"Great, see you then."

By the time I got to the hospital late Thursday morning, the Pavulon had already begun to wear off. I quickly scrubbed and ran over to Jeremy's crowded bedside. Lindsey signaled for me to stand beside her. I could tell by Lindsey's wrinkled clothes she had been there since the previous night. She placed one finger over her mouth as if to say, "Shhh." She began talking to Jeremy and the two nurses who stood on the other side of Jeremy's bed. "Ya have to get better, Kiddo, so you can go to Robyn's house to play some more baseball." She lifted her head and looked at the others. "This one time Jeremy hit the ball so hard it knocked his friend Robyn's pierced earring right out of her ear, and she fell to the ground." The two nurses and another woman, who I later found out was Lindsey's friend, laughed out loud. Then Lindsey added, "Remember, Jeremy?"

Jeremy's eyes opened wider than I had ever seen them. *Oh my God, he's really in there...* I leaned over and said, "Hi, Buddy." I smiled from ear to ear as I leaned down to kiss him. One of my tears fell onto his cheek. "Everything's all right, Sweetie. I love you." He closed his eyes.

The nurses left to give us some privacy. Lindsey said, "Robyn, I'd like you to meet my friend, Tina."

"Hi. Nice to meet you," I said.

"Nice to meet you, too." Tina turned to Lindsey and said, "I need to take off, Lindsey."

"Hold on, I'll walk you out. Since I stayed the night with him, I'll give you some time to be alone with him. Will you be able to stay a while, Robyn?"

"Sure will."

"Great. I'll be back later this afternoon. I need to run home and shower before I have to take Timmy to go see Sharon. I'll talk to you later." Lindsey and I hugged. She said her good byes to Jeremy and left. I didn't know how Lindsey handled all she did as a foster mom. She was absolutely amazing. So was Wayne, her husband.

Jeremy seemed to be resting well. I sat and held his hand and caressed his face. I kept whispering, "You're gonna be okay no matter what happens, Buddy, I promise. I love you."

Twice, the alarm went off on his ventilator. The nurse had to come over and talk to him. "You have to let the machine breath for you, Jeremy. As the medicine wears off more, you'll get more feeling in your body, and it's important to not fight the machine. You'll be okay."

Easy for her to say.

The nurse patted him on the arm and left. I could tell he was getting more and more agitated as the medicine wore off. At one point, he looked at me with panic in his eyes and closed them again.

He anxiously tried to pick his hand up, but couldn't because they had him in restraints so that he wouldn't pull all his tubes out. He started to gag. The alarm went off again.

The nurse came right over and attempted to calm him again by doing more explaining. But the more she spoke, the more restless he became. His blood pressure began to skyrocket, and so did his pulse. The nurse quickly left and grabbed the phone at the nurses' station, directly across from Jeremy's bed. I helplessly watched Jeremy as he lay stricken with terror, and prayed for God to help him. He desperately tried to lift his head off of the pillow, while his arms and legs flailed about, as he fought the restraints. The nurse came right back and administered a shot of something directly into one of Jeremy's IV tubes. I assumed it was more Pavulon. It must have been pretty concentrated, because it quickly knocked him out again. She explained to me the need for her to take immediate action so that Jeremy wouldn't hurt himself by ripping out his tubes. She mentioned that earlier they had given him Valium, in combination with the morphine, in order to try and keep him calm. I guess it wasn't enough.

I needed to get out of there for a moment and collect myself. I told Jeremy I'd be right back. I took the stairs to the cafeteria. I felt relieved that he had been put back on the Pavulon. It was too painful for me to see him panic, struggling to breathe, especially when I could do nothing to help him, but I felt grateful to share a brief moment together with him. After drinking a glass of orange juice, I went back up to spend a little more time with Jeremy before I had to say good bye to him. I told him that Jim and I would be up to visit tomorrow.

Jim and I returned Friday evening and again on Sunday afternoon. Jim struggled with seeing Jeremy in this condition as much as I did. It tortured us both to see our vibrant Little Buddy in such misery. I'm grateful I had Jim to lean on during this whole ordeal. We couldn't share what was going on with many people. No one knew all the details of Jeremy's story like we did. It was not only incredibly painful for us to tell them, it was too painful for others to hear as well.

By the following Tuesday, Jeremy had been in intensive care and on the ventilator for two weeks. The doctors had to increase the amount of oxygen being given to him tremendously. They also increased the PEEP of his ventilator almost daily.

As I understand it, the PEEP, which stands for positive end expiratory pressure, is the amount of pressure we need in our lungs to keep our lungs inflated, so they don't collapse when we exhale. It's kind of like a balloon; if you let the air escape all the way out, it's harder to blow up than if a little air is still in it. When we breathe normally on our own, our epiglottis blocks our trachea and keeps it closed when we exhale, so our natural amount of PEEP is maintained and our lungs don't deflate completely when we breathe out. But when a person has a tracheal tube placed into their lungs to connect them to the ventilator, the tube pushes the epiglottis out of the way and our natural PEEP is lost. So, the ventilator has to provide PEEP for the person so their lungs don't collapse after every exhalation.

Late that evening, Lindsey called to tell me Jeremy's doctors had made a decision to try a different type of ventilator. They ordered a high frequency, or "jet" ventilator for Jeremy, which they were having flown in from a hospital in Philadelphia. The current ventilator no longer maintained Jeremy's blood gases adequately. Even with both the increased levels of oxygen and PEEP being pumped into him, the oxygen level in his blood remained very low.

In the entire country, at that time, only several jet ventilators existed. Jeremy's doctors found one not in use.

Why are they doing this to him? When will they be able to let him go?

Lindsey sounded hopeful over the phone. I kept my feelings to myself.

I kept praying for God's will to be done. After all, who was I to judge what was too much for my Little Buddy? I knew one thing: I couldn't take much more of this. Watching him in this condition was too devastating.

The following day, the jet ventilator arrived and the respiratory team connected Jeremy to it. Jim and I visited that evening. As we exited the elevator, I glanced in the intensive care waiting area. Delilah, Lindsey, and Wayne sat chatting with each other. As soon as we walked in, I sensed their excitement. The mood in the room had lightened up considerably. Wayne shared the reason for their optimism. "If anything can turn Jeremy around, this ventilator can. His doctors think this is just what he needs. It will give his lungs more time to heal."

I certainly didn't share their optimism. I held my reaction in check.

I asked a respiratory therapist, not involved with Jeremy, what this all meant. She explained that the jet ventilator pumps oxygen into the body much faster than the regular ventilator. It shoots quick bursts of air into the lungs at a very high frequency, anywhere from 200 to 800 breaths per minute, in hopes of increasing the blood's oxygen saturation. She said the increased PEEP and the new ventilator were both indicative of damage to the person's lungs, and that the elasticity of the lungs, which allows them to expand and contract as breaths are taken, was also probably damaged.

The next day, during my afternoon visit, they transferred Jeremy to a private room in intensive care — a quarantine room. It was way off in the corner, down an isolated hallway. I didn't know how to interpret the move. My gut told me the hospital staff expected a long haul from here.

Transferring Jeremy to his new room was quite an ordeal. A team of five nurses handled all of the procedures. First, he had to be unhooked from the jet ventilator and his endotracheal tube had to be hooked to a hand-held balloon pump, which breathed for him. Then Jeremy was carefully transferred onto the gurney in order to be wheeled to his new room.

Timing was everything. Once the ventilator wasn't breathing for him, one of the nurses had to continuously pump oxygen into his lungs by hand. She rode on Jeremy's gurney with him and explained to him what was happening every step of the way. Two other nurses pushed his gurney, another pushed the ventilator, while another dragged his two IV poles along side. They all did a fabulous job, efficient and professional. I walked swiftly behind them, carrying some books and a tape player, which Lindsey had left at his bedside. I also carried Stephen. Every bump and dip of the floor made each one of us cringe.

The nurses worked together quickly to transfer Jeremy onto his new bed and hook him back up to the jet ventilator. His new bed was a special-order bed, which is used to prevent decubiti, or bed sores. Once he settled in the right position, of course, they had to suction him.

After the ordeal Jeremy had just been through of being transferred to his new room, I couldn't stand to watch him being tormented even one more time with the suctioning. I ran out of intensive care to the bathroom I had found as my safe haven, the first night we saw Jeremy. I slammed the door, leaned against the wall, and sobbed and sobbed, begging God to end Jeremy's suffering. Forget God's will and wanting Jeremy's wishes to reign. I wanted all of his suffering to be over. Now. Right now. I couldn't take much more, and I wasn't the one hooked up to the ventilator.

Crying it out helped me to gain my perspective again, and I went back into Jeremy's room to be with him. When I got there, Delilah sat next to him. No one else was there. I walked in, said hello to her, and sat down on the chair opposite to her.

Delilah gave me the dirtiest look she could muster and said, "I know what you did, Robyn."

I looked up at her, shocked. What the heck was she talking about? "What did I do, Delilah?"

"You told the nurses I can't be alone with my own son. Some of them look at me like I'm a criminal."

My heart raced. I quickly developed a lump in my throat. "I only answered their questions, Delilah. The court order said Jeremy should be supervised when he's with you. That's all I told them."

"Like I'm going to hurt him while he's in here."

"I did what I had to do as a professional social worker." *And I'd do it again.*

She ran out of the room and let the glass door close swiftly behind her.

I had mixed emotions. I could understand Delilah's anger at me for revealing the court order to the nurses. I really didn't think she would hurt Jeremy at his bedside. And I did feel compassion for her — my God, Jeremy was her son. But on the other hand, especially after I heard what Jeremy had said about Delilah closing the windows so no one could hear him scream, I wanted the nurses to know. What if she lashed out at him in her anger, maybe because he was dying? I never knew when Delilah would flip to her rageful self. I couldn't live with myself if she did something to him. I would honor my promise to keep Jeremy safe until the end, even if it meant "telling" on Delilah at her son's deathbed and alienating her more from me.

I stayed with Jeremy a while longer, singing, "In the Garden" to him and softly touching the back of his hand. I knew this wasn't the last time Delilah and I would cross paths. She seemed to be visiting Jeremy almost daily and so was I. One thing became clear in my mind — we both truly loved him.

Jim and I visited Jeremy again on the weekend. I only saw Lindsey in passing during the week. She and Wayne visited together every evening. Lindsey spent many long nights at Jeremy's side. She didn't want him to be alone during the night. Delilah often joined her.

During the next week, week four of Jeremy's coma, things began to get worse. Very quickly, almost daily, Jeremy started retaining fluid. Somedays his face would be so swollen that if I didn't know it was he lying there, I probably wouldn't have recognized him. When I walked into Jeremy's room on Monday, the atmosphere felt heavier than usual.

Three hospital personnel I had never seen before stood around him. The nurse didn't even look up when I said hello. She remained fiddling with a tube, which came from somewhere underneath Jeremy's covers, obviously coming out of his body at some location. The tube drained into this contraption which was divided into three sections and taped to one of the legs of his bed. Water filled one of the compartments, which the tube's end sat in. Dark colored, gross looking fluid partly filled the others. I asked the nurse, "Did something happen?"

"The jet ventilator caused a pneumothorax in his lower right lung," she answered, without looking up. She couldn't even say Jeremy. Maybe it made it too personal.

"Would you please explain that to me so I can understand it?" Hearing the word pneumothorax sent shivers down my spine.

"I'll try. A pneumothorax is caused when the ventilator sends a burst of air into the lungs, and the burst of air actually breaks through the lung tissue and leaks into the chest cavity. Part of the lung in that area then collapses...."

I couldn't listen to anymore of her words.

In other words, the jet ventilator had blown a hole in one of Jeremy's lungs.

As I looked at my Little Buddy, part of his chest was much higher than the rest, as though that part had been inflated. He was beginning to look like a balloon. When I could focus enough to listen, I took a deep breath and asked her another question. "How do they treat a pneumothorax?"

"The doctor put in a chest tube." I raised my eyebrows as if to say, "What the heck is that?" And she answered, "He opened Jeremy's chest with a small incision in the shape of an "x" and pushed this plastic tube into the area where the hole is in his lung. The tube helps reexpand the lung by allowing the excess air and fluid to escape. That's what's in that new container down there. The end of the tube sits in water so that no other outside air can exchange with the air already in the tube."

Oh my God, that horrid stuff is from his lungs.

"Thanks," I said to her, feeling a little queasy.

"Sure." She continued working with his tubing.

I asked no more questions.

When Jim and I visited on the weekend, I noticed two more drainage tubes coming out from under his covers. I was afraid to ask the nurse what had happened, but didn't want to assume the worst.

The worst possible explanation did happen. The jet ventilator blew two more holes out of Jeremy's lungs. His entire chest was swollen and puffed up.

Jim and I sat across from each other, on either side of Jeremy. We each held one of Jeremy's hands, and one of each other's, so that the three of us formed a circle. In that very intimate moment, together Jim and I spoke to him. "Hi, Sweetie, it's Robyn."

"And Jim. Hi, Jeremy, we love you."

"I'm so sorry you are going through this." My eyes filled with tears. "If there was any way I could make it better for you, I would."

"I would, too, Little Buddy," said Jim.

"It's okay to go to the Light, Jeremy," I said. "Everyone here will be all right. I promise I'll keep in touch with your mom when you're gone, just like you wanted me to do."

"We'll miss you, Buddy, but we'll be okay, too. Chief Yellow Sports Car will be waiting for you."

"And Chief Yellow Bird," I added. "It's okay to let go." Jim and I stood, looking into each other's eyes, with tears falling from our cheeks, as we both gently squeezed Jeremy's cold and limp little hands.

Sometimes people need permission to die before they are able to let go. They need to know that it's okay to proceed with what they have to do. It's okay to not wait for anyone else's needs but their own. "To thine own self be true."

I did not understand why Jeremy still held on through all of this.

Delilah began visiting every weekday afternoon at almost the same time I'd be getting ready to leave. I remained as supportive to her as she'd allow me to be, but up to this point she continued to keep her distance. I'd ask how she was holding up, how Simon was, and she'd give me her usual one-word responses.

Several times, I noticed Delilah standing in the hallway, watching me as I held Jeremy's hand, singing to him. She'd never come in during those times, though she'd continue to watch me from the hallway and give me time alone with him.

On Thursday of week four, as I was getting ready to leave, Delilah came in the room as I was visiting, pulled up a chair, and sat down beside me.

She looked me straight in the eyes, softly brushed her hand against mine, and spoke softly. "Hi."

"Hi." I answered.

"Can we talk?" She maintained her eye contact with me when asking her question.

"Sure," I said, feeling surprised, and somewhat leery.

I took a deep breath and sat back in my chair.

"Are you doing okay?" I asked.

"As okay as I can be. How about you?" She asked with genuine concern in her voice.

"Some days are too hard."

"They sure are."

"How's Simon?"

"He's great."

"And how's your baby?" Motioning to my round belly, she smiled.

"Just fine."

An uncomfortable silence fell between us. I purposely remained silent to give her time to speak.

"I watch you, Robyn, day after day, standing by Jeremy's side, loving him." She paused. "That really means a lot to me."

I started to cry. I never expected her to acknowledge anything from me. I reached my arms out toward her. She stood up and we embraced. As we stood there, holding each other, I imagined Jeremy smiling at us. Or maybe I didn't just imagine it.

She broke our embrace, took a step back and placed each of my hands in hers. She took a deep breath, looked me right in the eyes and said, "I'm so sorry for everything. Dear God, I never wanted to hurt him. I thought I was teaching him — disciplining him — he's such a free spirit. You know how hard he is to keep under control — he's always so boisterous."

The dam broke inside of Delilah. The floodgates that I'd been waiting for so long to open, "Against all odds." Her truth began pouring out of her. She continued, "And you, Robyn, you loved us both from the beginning. No matter how I acted, I always felt your love and your compassion. I still do even through all of this. I know you've done your best to protect him from my outbursts, and Jeremy is always sure of you. He can always count on you no matter what. I'm so glad he has you. Thank you for helping us…" I cried so hard, I couldn't see. Delilah cried right along with me as we held each other.

This must have been the moment Jeremy had been waiting for. In the process of his death, Delilah had finally allowed herself to open up and feel something real — to let in some light. Jeremy's love for her, and her love for him, and I'd like to think my love for both of them, had finally penetrated Delilah's walls of protection. The amount of love Jeremy held inside of him was like an explosion, and the burst of his explosion could be felt by all who had the honor to be in his presence. A love bomb.

Delilah and I sat and talked for a couple more hours. She talked about Disney World. She said that sitting around Give Kids the World, and seeing other families with sick children, "kind of put me over the edge. From the moment we stepped on the grounds of the place, I felt myself losing control. I couldn't stop myself."

While at Give Kids the World, Delilah and I had attended a support group for parents and families, while Jeremy and the other kids, whose parents participated, watched videos and ate popcorn. As part of the support group, everyone had been encouraged to share what they and their child were dealing with. I couldn't imagine that back in 1991, Delilah or anyone with HIV or AIDS, would feel comfortable about sharing in an open group of families and dying children that they had AIDS. I'm sure some parents would have caused quite a ruckus if they knew their terminally ill child shared a swimming pool with someone dying from AIDS. Unless you know about HIV, you wouldn't know that you couldn't catch it in a swimming pool, especially back then.

None of the other kids had AIDS. Delilah left the group before it came her turn to share.

Delilah spoke in more detail than ever before about, "The big dark thing that takes over." She even confessed she felt jealous of any time I'd spent with Jeremy. "I wanted you to spend it with me. I didn't have anyone either."

Dear God, if she only wouldn't have been abusive to Jeremy, I would have spent more time with her and supported her through to the end, just like Jeremy...

Toward the end of our talk, she caught me off-guard when she asked, "Would you be willing to share your dreams and stuff with me? Have you had any recently about us or about Jeremy?"

"I'm not sure what you mean," I said.

"You know, those premonitions you get sometimes. Remember, you told us in Florida a little about how you get messages and knowledge from, I think you called it, Spirit? Remember?"

"I do. I'm surprised you do."

"Are you kidding? I pray I could do that. In fact, could you tell me or show me how to pray? Don't you think it's about time I work on my own spirituality?"

I didn't answer, but smiled at her.

"If for nothing else, I'll do it for Jeremy," she said. "I'm ready."

There actually was light at the end of the tunnel.

CHAPTER TWENTY- FIVE -- THE MEETING

On Monday of the fifth week of Jeremy's coma, I walked past the waiting area and saw Delilah, Lindsey, and Wayne sitting together on a couch. Lindsey casually did her cross-stitch while Wayne and Delilah chatted. One of the volunteers from the clinic held and played with Simon. I hadn't seen Simon in months. He had grown so big. He had Jeremy's big brown, puppy dog eyes. Sharon, the foster care supervisor, also sat with them.

"Hi, Robyn," Delilah said, as I entered the room. She sounded more upbeat than ever. She stood up to give me a hug. We held each other for a long moment. When we finally let go, Sharon and Lindsey came over to us. Lindsey pulled something out from her bag and hid it behind her back.

"I have a present for you," Lindsey said with a silly smile.

She pulled out a white tee shirt and handed it to me. I unfolded it. It read, in Jeremy's own handwriting, "My wish for the future is for everyone to have a home."

Underneath the words were Jeremy's snail drawings.

I looked up, with tears in my eyes, but before I could form my words to speak, Sharon said, "Our agency had them done in Jeremy's honor. We had his original essay printed right on the shirt. I can order more if you'd like some. The proceeds go to our kids with AIDS."

"They're awesome…." I said.

Lindsey interrupted. "Wayne and I wanted to give you one as a gift."

I felt greatly moved by their gesture. "Thank you so much. This really means a lot to me. Thank you." Lindsey and I hugged and then Wayne and I did, too.

Wayne didn't usually visit during the day, except on weekends. I wondered if something was up. I soon found out what was going on. While Lindsey spoke, Delilah sat down on a chair kitty corner from the couch. "The doctors asked us all to be here today, so we could meet with them and talk about Jeremy's status. The meeting's supposed to start in a few minutes."

Just then, Hannah walked in. She greeted each one of us with a hug, and she and Lindsey went out into the hallway. Delilah motioned for me to sit beside her. Then she asked me, "Would you please come into the meeting with me? Lindsey has Wayne... I don't have anyone. It would mean a lot to me if you sat beside me."

Wow. My heart fluttered. "I'd be honored, thank you for asking."

I'd no sooner answered Delilah, than Lindsey came running in announcing, "They're ready for us." I took a deep breath and said a quick prayer. Wayne and Lindsey walked swiftly ahead as Delilah grabbed my hand, and we followed through the double doors into intensive care. My heart raced. I got butterflies in my stomach.

Wayne followed the nurse into a small, bleak meeting room that lay hidden behind the nurses' station. He sat down, with his back to the door, at a large round table. Lindsey sat beside him. Delilah took her place across from them. I sat on Delilah's left. In a few minutes, two physicians, a woman and a man, walked in and closed the door behind them. I could hear myself take another deep breath. Both physicians sat down on the chairs between Wayne and me.

"Good afternoon. I'm Dr. Young, Jeremy's attending physician. This is my colleague, Dr. Larabee. He's a pulmonary specialist. Would you please introduce yourselves?"

"I'm Wayne Ross, Jeremy's foster dad."

"I'm Lindsey Ross, his foster mom."

"Delilah Miller, his mother."

"Robyn Accetturo. I used to be Jeremy and Delilah's social worker."

Dr. Young continued. "The purpose of our meeting is to discuss Jeremy's status in general and then to hear from Dr. Larabee how he's doing on the jet ventilator. I'll begin. When Jeremy came to us, he was cyanotic. His breathing was labored and shallow. His lungs were unable to produce the amount of oxygen his body needed. We intubated him immediately and put him on Pavulon. His white blood cell count...." She continued rattling off all kinds of medical terms and phrases.... This rate of such and such was up but this rate was severely decreased. And as this rate worsened slightly, his blah, blah, blah, did this. She completely lost me. Some of the information she gave sounded hopeful. But the more hope I heard, the more I shut down and blocked out what she said. I didn't believe her. It angered me that not only did she sound hopeful after all Jeremy had been put through, she appeared to be instilling hope in Delilah, Lindsey, and Wayne. When would this ever end? When would everyone, including the hospital staff, be able to let Jeremy go?

Delilah and I held hands under the table. For a brief second, I glanced at Delilah, Lindsey, and Wayne. They all listened intently. I had to wonder if they really understood what the heck she said, or were they hanging on to the unspoken feeling behind what she said, which I interpreted as Jeremy could still pull out of this. Lindsey had the edge over the rest of us because of her nursing background. I sat, staring at the blank walls. The coldness and sterility of the room, along with what was being said, made me feel sick.

When Dr. Young finished, Dr. Larabee took a turn. He explained how the jet ventilator worked. He said that Jeremy's oxygen levels were more stable on the jet ventilator than on the original ventilator. He explained that the jet ventilator was more capable of allowing Jeremy's lungs to heal because his lungs didn't have to work as hard to give him oxygen. He didn't say that they would heal, and I don't remember him mentioning the pneumothoraxes.

I felt relieved when Wayne asked, "And what about the pneumothoraxes?"

Dr. Larabee quickly replied, "That happens sometimes. They will heal as his body heals."

And then Dr. Young asked the million-dollar question, "What would you like to see happen with Jeremy at this point?" Considering the circumstances, the state had acquiesced to Delilah's decision making. Delilah did allow Lindsey and Wayne's opinions to weigh heavily in her decision process. My opinion was never asked for by anyone.

Wayne spoke first. "What do you, as his physicians, think should happen? What will his quality of life be if he comes out of this? Will he be able to play baseball again? Will he be able to run around like the free spirit that he is? Will he have to be on oxygen?"

Good for you, Wayne. I felt glad he had the courage to speak up.

Dr. Young answered. "We really don't know at this point. We've seen some children really surprise us and do well after being weaned off of the ventilator."

I saw Delilah's eyes light up at the implication that this could happen to Jeremy.

Yeah, but did those children have AIDS? I so much wanted to speak my mind. But I couldn't. The only reason I was even in the meeting was to support Delilah. It became obvious to me that these doctors were going to continue to do everything possible to keep Jeremy alive, no matter what they had to do to him.

Delilah squeezed my hand as she spoke. Her voice shook. "So, you're saying that it is possible for Jeremy to still turn around and get off of the ventilator?"

"And resume some sort of normalcy in his life?" added Wayne.

"It's not impossible. Time will tell," answered Dr. Larabee.

"Then I vote to keep going with the current course of treatment," stated Wayne. "I think Jeremy would want that."

"I agree," added Lindsey.

"Me, too," said Delilah.

"Okay," answered Dr. Young. "I will inform the staff to continue with the current course of treatment and ventilator settings. Let's reconvene in one week and see if there are any changes in his status at that time."

Delilah, Lindsey, and Wayne all agreed next Monday would be fine to meet again. The doctors instilled plenty of hope in everyone. Everyone except me. I hated it.

When we went back into the waiting room, Delilah told Sharon the "good news." I went in to see Jeremy for just a few minutes. I hadn't seen him since Jim and I had visited on Saturday. I covered my mouth and shook my head in sorrow when I saw him. He was almost unrecognizable. His frail body was so swollen with fluids and his chest was so inflated, he looked twice his normal size. Even his lips were swollen. His hands felt ice cold.

The sound of the ventilator nauseated me.

I kissed his pallid forehead, picked his hand up and held it, and whispered quietly, "Whenever you're ready to let go, Buddy, it's okay. Everything will be all right. It's okay to go to the Light. Your mom will be okay and so will Simon. I love you with all my heart and all my soul, Jeremy." I sat in silence and held him for a few more moments. I kissed his hand and said, "I have to go, Buddy. I love you. I'll come back again tomorrow."

I drove home and completely disintegrated emotionally. I felt like this hell would never end.

CHAPTER TWENTY- SIX -- MEETING NUMBER TWO

Week six of Jeremy's ordeal brought many changes in him. The nurses and respiratory therapists had to suction him more and more often. Despite the drainage tubes, his lungs began to fill with fluid. I overheard one of the nurses telling another nurse that his chest x-ray showed a lot of increased whiteness. This was indicative of more damage to his lungs, and not of healing as the doctors hoped for.

I couldn't feel Jeremy's presence anymore. Not only physically, but also emotionally and spiritually as well. It didn't even feel like he was in the room anymore. I imagined that his spirit was off somewhere, away from his body, being healed of all the torment he was being put through.

On one afternoon, Carolyn Mitchell, my former coworker when I worked with my AIDS families, came to visit. She had called me the night before to find out what time I'd be there. It was an emotional reunion for us both. I saw Carolyn walking down the hallway to intensive care toward Jeremy's room. She didn't see me. I watched as she glanced through the glass door and looked at Jeremy. She glanced back at his nameplate on the wall, made the sign of the cross, and closed her eyes for a moment before she walked in.

When she saw me, she said, "My God, Robyn, I don't even recognize him. I had to look twice at his nameplate to make sure I had the right room. I'm so sorry..." She put her arms around me to comfort me. I began to sob. "It's okay," she said in her most soothing voice, "It will be over soon. He'll let go when he's ready. I think he's very close."

"I hope so," I whispered between cries.

When I stopped crying, Carolyn stepped back from me, rubbed my pregnant tummy, and approached Jeremy. "Hi, Jeremy. It's Carolyn. You're hanging in there, huh? It won't be long now, you'll be able to let go and let God. Don't be afraid, Jeremy. A much better life awaits you." Carolyn turned back around toward me.

"Girl, this is terrible," Carolyn said to me. "He looks so big... so blown up. What's it from?"

"His body's filling up with a lot of fluid. Plus the ventilator blew three holes into his lungs, so his chest is really blown up."

"All we can do is pray. I'll be praying for you, too." Carolyn and I sat together in silence. It felt good to have my friend at my side.

Carolyn stayed half an hour or so. "I have to go. Court."

"Thanks for stopping by, Carolyn."

"You take care, now. Get some rest." Carolyn and I hugged and she left.

I pulled my chair up to Jeremy. I placed his cold, lifeless hand in mine. I stroked it and began singing "In the Garden," again to him. I didn't know what else to do. I found comfort in the words and hoped Jeremy did, too.

I come to the garden alone, while the dew is still on the roses

And the voice I hear falling on my ear, the Son of God discloses

And He walks with me and He talks with me, and He tells me I am His own

And the joy we share, as we tarry there, none other has ever known...

I stopped when the nurse walked in. It was perfect timing because just as she did, two alarms sounded, one on his IV pump, the other on the respirator. "Time for suctioning, Jeremy," she said gently. She looked at me and faked a smile, but said nothing. She had seen me in Jeremy's room many times before.

I walked out into the hallway and saw Lindsey walking toward me. "Hi," she said, as she held out her arms to hug me.

"Hi." She had dark circles under her eyes. Her breath smelled of coffee. She handed me a manila folder and said, "Open it."

A 5 x 7 black and white photo of Jeremy's smiling face greeted me. Underneath that was one of Timmy. And another of Timmy and Jeremy. Without saying another word, Lindsey gave me a roll of scotch tape, and together we taped the photos all over the door and walls of Jeremy's room.

All around us, Jeremy glowed. His smile could brighten even the darkness inside intensive care.

"I have to go pick Timmy up from Sharon's office. I'll be back later to spend the night. See ya."

I sat back down in my chair, and continued singing softly to Jeremy...

I'd stay in the garden with Him, though the night around me is falling

But He bids me go, through the voice I know, the voice to me is calling...

Delilah walked in, and I immediately stopped singing. I felt embarrassed. "Please go on, finish," she said. I love to watch you be with him.

"That's okay."

She sat beside me and kissed Jeremy's cheek. As she gazed at him, she started to cry. "Oh, God, are we doing the right thing?" Delilah asked. I felt my eyes fill with tears. Delilah continued. "He looks so awful. I know he's not hurting though, they turned his morphine up to eighteen milligrams yesterday because his face grimaced while they suctioned him. It's important that he's not hurting."

I didn't answer her. I sensed from her she didn't want an answer from me, only a sounding board.

By now I literally begged God to take Jeremy. Everytime I visited Jeremy, I whispered in his ear, during a private moment between us, "It's okay to go to the Light, Buddy. You don't have to wait. Your mom will be okay. I'll keep in touch with her, for you, I promise. Jim and I and our new baby will be okay, too. There's nothing more you can do here. Chief Yellow Sports Car awaits you.

Chief Yellow Bird will be there to welcome you. It's okay to let go on this end."

In my exasperation at the doctors and at the ventilator, I found myself in a desperate mental frenzy. I've never experienced anything more dreadful than watching this machine blow puffs of air into Jeremy's lungs day after day to keep him alive. *Why?* Each dawn brought another dreaded day as I waited for Jeremy to die. I waited for them to take him off of the ventilator. And day after day they kept him on it.

Every evening when Jim got home from work, I'd debrief from my day, and he would listen attentively and support me. It was the only way I could keep going back each day.

After every visit, I called Sally, our minister, in order to debrief some more from what I had just seen Jeremy go through. I had to be able to go on — to be able to continue to function. And everyday, she'd find the words to comfort me and help me find the strength to carry on, to be with Jeremy, to finish what I had agreed to do.

Sally told me to not be afraid to have regular fireside chats with God, to tell God exactly what I thought and felt about what was happening to Jeremy, and to me.

I did. Every night I'd lie in bed and plead, *Dear God, how can you let this happen to him? Don't you see how much he is suffering? How can you let them keep torturing my Jeremy — your Jeremy, day after day after day? Where are you in all of this? Please God, make them stop... let Jeremy die with some sort of dignity left in him... please... I can't handle one more day of this. It is too much. Do something... I feel like I am at Christ's crucifixion.*

And I called Rosemary and Alan, after every visit and sobbed a little more, in order to let out some of my grief.

And finally Monday rolled along, the day to meet with the doctors again to reassess where to go from here. I prayed the entire ride to the hospital for Divine Order to reign. I added my desire that this be the day they'd take Jeremy off of the ventilator.

I sighed deeply and stepped off of the elevator onto the fourth floor. I walked to the waiting room. Lindsey, Wayne, Timmy, Delilah, Sharon, Hannah, and the volunteer from Jeremy's clinic sat waiting. As soon as Delilah saw me, she asked me to step into the hallway. I did.

"I don't want you to come with me today into the meeting...." My heart sunk. I felt instantly sick to my stomach. She continued, "It will be too hard for me with you there. I don't want to cry." She walked away and left me standing alone.

I ran to the bathroom, closed the door, and completely fell apart. I felt angry and hurt. I felt powerless... again. And at the moment, I couldn't understand Delilah's wishes. When I gathered myself together, I walked back into the waiting area and had no sooner sat down than the nurse said the doctors were ready.

Lindsey, Wayne, and Delilah got up and slowly walked into the meeting room behind the nurses' station. The door closed.

I tried to sit in the waiting room with Timmy and the volunteer, but I felt like I might jump out of my skin. Sharon and Hannah had left. I got up and started pacing up and down the hallway outside of intensive care. I continually asked for the White Light of Christ to surround and fill everyone involved in the decision process. I prayed hard for God's will to be done and for Jeremy to be sent healing energy. After what felt like forever, I went into Jeremy's room, sat down beside him, and continued praying.

Twenty minutes later, Delilah and Wayne walked single file into Jeremy's room. No one spoke. Delilah dabbed her eyes with a tissue. Wayne came toward me and said, "They're going to unhook him. They think it won't take long after that." He walked away and stood by himself.

My whole body felt heavy. I was overcome by so many emotions — fear, sadness, and sorrow. Yet I also felt a nervous kind of excitement — Jeremy's suffering would finally end. In a way, I felt happy for him — he could finally move on.

Thank you, God. Thank you. It'll be over soon.

I walked over to Delilah and touched her hand. She held mine, but remained somewhat rigid and distant.

Dr. Young and Dr. Larabee both walked in. They approached Jeremy's bed. Dr. Young spoke, "Sometimes it can take a while. I don't think it will take him long." She pulled the curtain around Jeremy's bed to give him privacy. Although none of us could see anything, I felt sick to my stomach when I heard the whirring of the ventilator come to a stop. The room became completely silent. They pulled the tracheal tube out from Jeremy's throat. The doctor reopened the curtain. Each one of us held our breath, waiting to see what would happen next.

Jeremy finally looked at peace.

His blood pressure started to drop. His chest rose and fell with many gaps in between each shallow breath, spaced far apart. We all watched anxiously as his blood pressure slowly reached 86/51 and then were surprised when it stayed there with little fluctuation.

Both doctors left. The nurse looked at Delilah and said, "If you'd like, I can get you a rocking chair and you can sit and hold him."

Delilah quickly answered, "I'd like that." And then she looked at Wayne and added, "Unless you want to first."

"You go ahead," Wayne answered.

The nurse left the room and quickly came back with the chair, several blankets, and two more nurses. She placed the rocking chair next to Jeremy's bed and instructed Delilah to sit in it and place the blanket over the arm of the chair.

All three nurses picked Jeremy up, wrapped him in two heated blankets, and placed his limp body onto Delilah's lap. His IV's and chest tubes were still in. The nurse placed the extra blankets under his head, legs, and under Delilah's arm so that Jeremy's body would be supported and he'd be the most comfortable. In the solace of his mother's arms, Jeremy's blood pressure rose a few degrees.

Delilah asked Wayne to press play on the tape player. "Wind Beneath My Wings" sung by Bette Midler, began to play. So much emotion welled up in my chest as the words to the song echoed throughout Jeremy's room. Delilah rocked Jeremy in her arms and stroked his hair.

> It must have been cold there in my shadow
> To never have sunlight on your face
> You were content to let me shine that's your way
> You always walked a step behind
>
> So I was the one with all the glory
> While you were the one with all the strength

A beautiful face without a name, for so long
A beautiful smile to hide the pain

Did you ever know that you're my hero
And everything I would like to be
I can fly higher than an eagle
For you are the wind beneath my wings...

Fly... fly... fly high against the sky
So high I almost touched the sky
Thank you, thank you, thank God for you
The wind beneath my wings

I couldn't contain my tears. Neither could anyone else. Wayne left the room. It was a very painful, yet powerful scene to be a part of.

I walked over and placed one hand on Delilah's shoulder and the other on Jeremy's shoulder. Another circle of healing and of love had been completed. After over an hour passed by, I kissed Delilah good bye. And I kissed Jeremy good bye for what I thought might be the last time, while he lay lovingly and serenely in his mother's arms.

His presence had come back to him. I felt him smiling.

CHAPTER TWENTY- SEVEN -- A BEAUTIFUL ENDING

At 3:04 a.m. the phone rang. As soon as I heard Hannah's voice I knew. It was finally over. Jeremy had finally let go. I told her we'd be right there.

Jim and I threw on some clothes and sped to the hospital.

We raced to Jeremy's room. Delilah wailed as she sat in the rocking chair holding Jeremy's body in her arms as she had when I left. Lindsey, Wayne, and Timmy sat in a semi-circle of chairs, which had been placed facing Delilah and Jeremy. The nurse brought in two more chairs for us. We joined, to complete the circle, and cried right along with everyone else.

After a long while, Timmy asked if he could hold, "his brother." Delilah stood up with Jeremy still in her arms, while Lindsey and Timmy sat in the rocker together. Delilah gently placed Jeremy in their lap. Timmy began to sob and talk to Jeremy. Wayne kneeled at their side. It was heart wrenching. Even the nurse cried. She kept passing the Kleenex box around.

Lindsey asked if Jim or I wanted to hold Jeremy to say good bye. Neither of us did. I had said so many good byes to Jeremy before that moment. I had said everything I ever wanted to say to him.

As time passed on and we continued grieving, it was almost as though life was beginning to come back to all of us... Timmy made us laugh with stories he told of Jeremy and their friendship and brotherhood together. By 5:00 a.m., the nurse had brought up coffee, orange juice, and donuts and set them out for us on a table in Jeremy's room.

Hannah had come in and out of the room at different times and at around 6 a.m., had to leave to go home, shower, and get ready to come back to work.

I saw Wayne walk alone out into the hallway in front of Jeremy's room. He stood, alone. I walked up and stood near him, but remained quiet. And then he spoke, "I came really close to hitting Jeremy one time. I wish I had never felt that way."

I waited a minute before I spoke to see if he needed to say anything else.

"It's not your fault, Wayne. Jeremy really tested you guys a lot. In a way, he wanted you to hit him. Then he'd think that everybody who loved him, hit him, just like his mom did."

"Did you ever feel that way toward him?" Wayne asked.

"No, but I was in a different kind of relationship with him. He didn't live with us. Who knows? Maybe if he did, he would have tested us in the same way. I know one thing though; Jeremy really loves you and Lindsey, and you guys were certainly an answer to my prayers. Thank you."

Wayne smiled sorrowfully and walked away.

I looked down at my watch. It read 6:45. I had a 9:00 appointment with my obstetrician.

I walked back into Jeremy's room. Jeremy's body had been placed back in his bed. The nurse was getting ready to wheel him away.

Jim and I took a moment and said our final good-byes to Jeremy. Then we hugged everyone and headed home.

I felt so relieved. Jeremy could finally heal. He was finally "Home," as he once called it. I envisioned Chief Yellow Bird, driving Chief Yellow Sports Car, and together they picked Jeremy up at the end of the tunnel.

CHAPTER TWENTY- EIGHT -- WHAT A POWERFUL CHILD

Neither Jim nor I touched our dinner as we prepared to go to Jeremy's wake. I felt sick to my stomach the entire ride there.

Before opening the ornately - carved oak door to the old greystone funeral home, in one of Chicago's northside neighborhoods, Jim gave my hand a firm squeeze and kissed me on the cheek. "We'll get through this together. I love you." I took a deep breath and followed him in. Jim hauled a huge three and a half-foot bright red teddy bear behind him.

The day Jeremy died, Sally, our minister, called and asked if I would like to have this bear. It had belonged to her granddaughter. She told me I could do whatever I wanted with it, keep it for my own child or pass it on. She even delivered it to our apartment. As soon as Jim and I laid our eyes on it, we both knew its new owner... Timmy. It would be perfect for him. It could be his new big brother.

My mom had sent me a note of support in which she had enclosed a poem to help soothe me and help me grieve. The poem touched me so much that I typed it on our computer and dedicated it to Jeremy.

<u>TO THOSE I LOVE AND THOSE WHO LOVE ME</u>

(author anonymous)

When I am gone, release me, let me go
I have so many things to see and do

You must not tie yourself to me with tears,
Be happy that we had so many years.

I gave you my love. You can only guess
How much you gave to me in happiness
I thank you for the love you each have shown
But now it's time I traveled on alone.

So grieve awhile for me if grieve you must
Then let your grief be comforted by trust
It's only for a while that we must part
So bless the memories within your heart.

I won't be far away, for life goes on
So if you need me, call and I will come
Though you can't see or touch me, I'll be near
And if you listen with your heart, you'll hear
All of my love around you soft and clear.
And then when you must come this way alone...
I'll greet you with a smile and "Welcome Home."

In loving memory of Jeremy B. Miller, God's Gift to Us All...

With all of our love,

Robyn and Jim

I carried a stack of copies of the poem with me into the funeral home. We stepped into the hallway. I heard Jim take a deep breath at the same time I did. As I looked up, I saw beautiful mahogany crown moldings lining the ceiling of the room. Lots of dark wood and rich, dark forest greens and velveteen burgundies flooded my senses. The room smelled musty and old. We slowly walked toward the chapel marked, Jeremy Miller, and entered.

Lindsey greeted us with a hug. "What's this?" she asked, looking at the bear with a big smile on her face.

"It's for Timmy. We thought he might like it. Maybe he could pretend it's his new big brother." Lindsey called Timmy, who was over talking to Wayne. Timmy practically ran us over once he saw the bear.

"Who is that for?" Timmy asked, out of breath from running so hard.

Jim handed it to him. "You..."

And before Jim could say anything else, Timmy said, "I'm gonna call him Jeremy, my new big brother." We laughed. Timmy took the bear and started walking him up and down the aisle, playing with him and talking with him as though he was real.

"These are the poems I told you about," I said to Lindsey.

"You can put them right here." She placed them on a table at the back of the room, where we stood. "Please excuse me," said Lindsey. She needed to greet the couple who came in behind us. I recognized the woman as one of the nurses from Jeremy's hospital.

A lovely, ivory-colored lace tablecloth covered the table, which was filled with memories of Jeremy. A blue plaster mold of his "three-year-old" handprint was out for all to see. I placed my hand over his and started to cry. *It isn't fair that he's dead. It's just not fair.* I wanted Jeremy back. I wanted to touch his warm hands and look into his tender brown eyes. I wanted to feel him snuggle into my shoulder like he always did.

When my attention came back to the room, my eyes were led to a collection of photos of Jeremy, at various ages of his short life, which were arranged on a bright yellow poster board. The photo essay leaned against the wall at the back of the table.

His four-year-old handprints, in green paint, hung next to the photos. On the same paper, underneath the handprints, was a poem, which most of us with children would recognize:

> Sometimes you get discouraged
> Because I am so small
> And often leave my fingerprints
> On furniture and walls.
> But everyday I'm growing —
> I'll be grown up someday
> And all those tiny handprints
> Will surely fade away.
> So here's my final handprint

Just so you can recall
Exactly how my fingers looked
When I was very small.
Love,
Jeremy

My whole body flooded with grief.

Everywhere I looked I saw a piece of his life. Two of Jeremy's dinosaurs and the Teenage Mutant Ninja Turtle he had picked out at Toy's R Us that one Christmas sat on the table. Alongside them was the Lego design Jeremy and Jim had built. His "heliport within a magical city."

Several stacks of red programs sat at the edge of the table. Its front cover housed Jeremy's snails — his essay from school last year. The back cover showed a small replica of the green handprint plaque with the poem. The program explained the agenda for the evening.

For a moment I became lost in my emotion of all the memories. I took a deep breath and came back to my awareness of my surroundings and myself. I grabbed Jim's hand and squeezed it. I needed some courage to look ahead into the softly lit room.

Oh, God...It's an open casket.

I immediately looked up at the ceiling, closed my eyes and shook my head, *No!* Every cell of my body screamed out in pain. I didn't want to see his body. I wanted to remember it the way it was. And not only that, Jeremy was gone. He had finally gone "Home." I wanted to think of that and not see his poor dreadful body and what AIDS had done to it.

I looked away to the rows and rows of chairs, which filled the long, rectangular room. The room was immense — I counted ninety chairs. Delilah sat in the front row on the right hand side. Simon's father sat beside her. I recognized him from the hospital.

"There's Delilah," I said to Jim. "Let's go greet her." We walked, hand in hand, to her.

"Hi," I said.

"Hi," she answered, as she stood up. She put her arms around me and kind of collapsed. She began to sob.

"I'm so sorry, Delilah." We held each other. After awhile, I whispered, "I'm glad he's at peace."

"Me, too," she whispered back.

When Delilah and I parted, Jim and Delilah hugged. Delilah turned and said, "I'd like you guys to meet Joel, Simon's father. Joel, this is Robyn and Jim. They're friends of Jeremy's."

Joel shook Jim's hand, and then Delilah and Joel sat down.

Jim looked at me and whispered, "You ready to go up?"

"I guess..." Jim and I excused ourselves.

We walked up, still hand in hand, to pay our respects to our Little Buddy, Jeremy B. Miller. Stephen, our lamb, lay sweetly on Jeremy's tummy, cuddled under Jeremy's left hand. This was such a powerful gesture for Jim and I. It really meant so much to us. We turned, looked at each other and fell into each other's arms, sobbing.

When we were ready, we let go of one another's embrace and looked back at Jeremy. His face and chest were still puffy. He wore his navy blue sport coat and his freshly pressed white oxford shirt. Delilah must have spent hours ironing this one... it looked perfect.

A huge bouquet of long-stemmed red roses covered the lower half of his casket. "For My Son," was written across the large white satin ribbon, which held them together. A few more arrangements stood on either side of him.

I said to Jeremy, "I'm so glad you're finally home, Buddy. You did such an awesome job here. I'm so proud of you..." I started to cry again.

"Time for you to heal, Buddy, time for you to heal," said Jim.

I looked over at Jim, squeezed his hand, and said, "It's finally over. Forever and ever over. Amen."

"Amen," Jim added.

While we continued squeezing each other's hand, Sally and Bruce, our minister and her husband came up behind us. Sally put her arm around me. "It is finally over. You did a wonderful job with your Little Buddy here." She leaned toward me and kissed me on the cheek. I completely fell apart and blubbered away in the comfort of Sally's arms. When I looked up I whispered, "Thanks for coming. I couldn't have done this without you."

"I told you I'd see you through to the end, just as you saw Jeremy through."

Bruce had his arm around Jim as they stood, looking at Jeremy. When the four of us turned around to find a seat, I was astounded at how quickly the room was filling up. Over half of the seats were already taken. We sat in the fifth row, on the left side of the room. I glanced around to see if I could recognize anyone. Many more people from Jeremy's hospital had come — volunteers from the clinic, families with other HIV infected children who Jeremy knew, inpatient nurses, outpatient nurses, even the receptionist from his Tuesday Clinic was there.

It was amazing and very powerful for me to see all of the people Jeremy had touched during the last two years of his life.

When I looked to the back of the room, my sister, Rosemary and brother-in-law, Alan, stood viewing the memory table. Rosemary dried her eyes with tissue. I raced to greet them. Rosemary held me in her loving arms as we both fell apart together. "It's finally over, Robyn. You did it! I'm so proud of you."

I was so full of emotion, I couldn't speak. Hearing my oldest sister say those words, and feeling safe and protected in her arms, really made things hit home for me. It really was over. She and Alan had seen us through until the end, too, and I was grateful.

When we were ready, Jim showed us to our seats.

By the time we got back to them, the rest of the row was filled to capacity. Rosemary and Alan took our seats next to Sally and Bruce, and Jim grabbed the only two seats left in the row in front of them.

As I looked around the room, I was flabbergasted — almost every seat in the house was filled. More and more people poured into the room.

"I'll be right back," I said to Jim. I walked over to Delilah. I thought it would be nice if she met my family. I consider Sally and Bruce family, too.

"My family is here. Would you like to meet them?" I asked.

"I would, thanks."

She got up and we walked over to meet everyone. I could tell Delilah felt uncomfortable. As soon as I finished introducing everyone, she looked down at the floor and quickly left to sit back down.

I whispered to Jim that I needed to use the restroom. I leaned around to Sally and Rosemary and asked if they needed to use it, too. Neither of them did. Jim decided to walk with me to find it.

As we descended down the stairs to the basement, we smelled fresh coffee. Trays of cookies covered one of the tables. As I looked to my right to see if the restroom was along that wall, Jim stopped cold in his tracks. I ran smack into him.

"Look!" he said, sounding shocked. He pointed to the pictures on the wall. Before my eyes stood two paintings, side by side. A yellow Ford Thunderbird, and a painting of an Indian Chief.

"Oh my gosh, it's Chief Yellow Sports Car and Chief Yellow Bird!"

"Yep. Just like Jeremy said," Jim said. We couldn't believe it.

We raced back upstairs and grabbed Rosemary and Alan, and Sally and Bruce, and said, "Come with us!" They did.

None of us could believe it. What confirmation!

Thank you, thank you.

By the time we got back upstairs, all the seats were taken. Some people stood at the back of the room. Others leaned against the walls. As I went to take my seat, Julie, the HIV program liaison from the state and her supervisor, Shirley, passed me and greeted me. Julie patted my tummy and congratulated me on my pregnancy. It was nice to see them there.

We all took our seats and waited for the service to begin. Sally tapped me on the back and handed me a pocket-sized package of Kleenex. "Thanks," I said.

The chaplain from Jeremy's hospital, who knew Jeremy well, began speaking. He greeted everyone and thanked us for coming. He talked about his own personal experience knowing Jeremy. He led us in singing "Amazing Grace," and in reading the Twenty Third Psalm aloud, which was printed on the inside of the red program.

Then he played, "Jeremy and his mom's favorite song," on the cassette player. Of course, "Wind Beneath My Wings" began playing. There wasn't a dry eye left in the room.

Hannah did a reading from the Bible: Ecclesiastics 3:1-8 "To everything there is a season, and a time and a purpose under heaven…." When Hannah finished, the chaplain asked all the kids present to come forward and sit in a circle on the floor. About a dozen children, with Timmy and his new bear, "Jeremy," leading the pack, sat on the floor in a large circle.

The chaplain dumped the contents of a brown paper sack into the middle of the children. Dried autumn leaves, every shade and shape imaginable, fell into a big pile in the center of the floor. He then started to read the story by Leo Buscalgia, The Fall of Freddie the Leaf, aloud to all the children. It's a story of how Freddie the leaf changes with the seasons and struggles with letting go of life at the end of the season. It very lovingly illustrates the delicate balance between letting go of life to make the transition of death.

The room was completely silent as he read the whole story. The kids got a chance to ask questions and played with the pile of leaves.

After they returned to their seats, the chaplain gave everyone an opportunity to stand up and share whatever they wanted to about Jeremy.

When no one else went first, I took a deep breath and stood up. My legs shook under me. I started talking. "Jeremy Miller has had a profound impact on my life. He is the most loving soul I have ever known. I will miss him greatly. One time, when I picked him up from school, Jeremy and I had a similar conversation about death. It was a fall day and Jeremy asked me why the leaves had to die in the autumn. He started asking questions about death and ended up giving some really creative answers on the subject, himself. Jeremy has depth way beyond his years. He was a great teacher to me. I am grateful that I had the opportunity to know him." I had to sit down. If I continued talking, I would have started to bawl my eyes out.

Jim stood. He told about the exuberance Jeremy had while playing baseball in the batting cage at Haunted Trails. Jim added that Jeremy had exuberance for life that Jim had never experienced before.

Person after person stood and shared about a special time they spent with Jeremy and how much of an effect he had had on them. I can't even begin to tell their stories. I was so overcome by my own emotion from hearing each one of them; I truly don't remember any specifics. Except for one story.

A grandmother, whose grandson, Danny, had died at home from AIDS at the age of four with the support from his dad and an in-home hospice, brought the entire room to tears. Jeremy and Danny had become friends. They shared the same Tuesday clinic day at the hospital.

"I can't begin to tell you how grateful I am that I, and my entire family, knew Jeremy Miller. He was like a song in my heart. The courage and strength he gave to me, to all of us, is beyond words. My daughter, Lisa, Danny's mom, died of AIDS just last year…" She started to cry, but managed to continue. "Jeremy gave us all love without any strings attached. He brightened up every room he would walk into. I couldn't have made it through some clinic days without him…." She sat back down.

As I witnessed story after story of how much Jeremy had influenced people's lives, I felt so proud of him. I was grateful that he was finally being recognized for who he really was: the brightest light I have ever seen in my life.

Jeremy managed to get all of his living done quickly.

The service closed with another song, "Bring the Children."

As people started to leave, Timmy and some of his friends brought "Jeremy Bear," to the back of the room. They took turns wrestling with him, just like they used to do with Jeremy. Jeremy would've wanted it that way.

It was a healing sight to see… life continuing. I placed my hands on my tummy as I felt our baby kick.

As we walked out to get our coats, Lindsey whispered in my ear, "Isn't it incredible? I counted over one hundred and fifteen people here tonight. Only Simon's father and Delilah's family, who were here, were part of Jeremy's past. The rest of the people had only known him since his diagnosis two years ago. What a powerful child he is."

"He certainly is," I answered, "he most certainly is."

CHAPTER TWENTY- NINE -- THE FINAL DAY

The next morning, Jim and I drove to Jeremy's funeral. As we pulled into the parking lot of the funeral home, I recognized Lindsey and Wayne's car. My heart fluttered when I saw Sally's car. I felt honored that she wanted to be there for Jim and I, and also there for Jeremy. Even though she had never met him in person, I had talked so much about him that she really did know him.

When Jim hauled open the large heavy oak door, I saw several people standing in the lobby. Lindsey had introduced me to them the night before as her friends who kept Jeremy the weekend when Lindsey and Wayne went to visit Wayne's Mom.

I hugged Lindsey, who greeted us as we entered the room where Jeremy's body still lay in the open casket. We said hello to Wayne and Timmy. Wayne asked, "Jim, we'd be honored if you'd be a pallbearer for Jeremy."

Jim got choked up. "I'd be honored, thanks." Wayne handed Jim a pair of white gloves.

Jim and I walked toward Delilah, who sat alone in the front row. We both hugged her and sat down beside her. The room was peaceful and still. I felt anxious in anticipation of what was to come, yet I felt relieved. It would all be over soon.

A handful of people I didn't know was scattered near the front of the room. Hannah walked in a few minutes after we did. Sharon and Rebecca arrived moments later.

Within a short time, the chaplain from the funeral home greeted everyone. He recited the Twenty Third Psalm and continued on with a very simple service. I held Delilah's hand through the whole thing. When it was time to get up and say good bye to Jeremy before they closed his casket, Jim and I waited with Delilah until everyone except Lindsey, Wayne, and Timmy had finished saying their final good byes.

When the last person, except family, left the room, in a very intimate moment, Jim and I said our final good byes to Jeremy. We left so that Lindsey, Wayne, Timmy, and Delilah could have time to be alone with him.

As we stepped outside into the bright morning sun, I could hear Delilah wailing as she said her final good bye to her son. Sally came up to us, and we took a little walk away from the building. Hearing Delilah's pain was too much for me to handle.

I looked up to the crystal clear, blue sky and inhaled deeply. It was a perfect, warm fall morning. Indian summer had again arrived.

"I'm sorry, I'm not able to go with you to the grave site. I have another commitment," Sally said.

"That's okay." I said. "Sal, there are no words to express how grateful I am that you stood by me throughout this whole two years. Thank you..." I cried in the support of my dear friend's arms. "I couldn't have seen Jeremy through to the end without you."

"I'm glad I could help." Sally hugged us both before she left.

A little while later, Wayne came out and asked all of the pallbearers to step inside. In a few minutes, Jeremy's casket was carried out by Wayne, Timmy, Jim, Leonard, the guy who took Delilah to have her VCR fixed that one time, and two of Wayne's friends.

Timmy held his head high and looked so proud to be carrying his big brother. Nine cars followed the hearse to the cemetery. Delilah rode with Lindsey, Wayne, and Timmy in their car.

When we got to the gravesite, Delilah had regained her poise and appeared strong. She held it together well. I asked her permission to pick a long-stemmed rose from the beautiful arrangement she had gotten Jeremy, so I could bring it home, dry it, and keep it forever. I told her I'd get one for her as well and show her how to dry it.

She liked the idea so much, she wanted everyone to have one. So at the end of the funeral, Delilah walked up to each person at the gravesite, and handed him or her a lovely dark red rose, in Jeremy's honor, and gave them each a hug. It was a powerful gesture on her part.

The social service agency that Sharon worked for held a luncheon afterward, at the home of Sharon's supervisor. He and his wife had set out a lovely array of foods which they had made themselves; several kinds of salads, from tuna and chicken to pasta and fruit salad. I thought it was really nice of them. Delilah stayed with Jim and me throughout the whole luncheon.

When it was time to go home, I asked to speak with Delilah privately. She walked outside with Jim and me.

I took her hands in mine, looked her in the eyes, and said, "I promised Jeremy I would stay in touch with you. He wanted me to. And I want to, too, if that's okay?"

Delilah started to cry. "I'd like that very much."

"Good," I said. Delilah and I held each other.

After a moment, we parted, and Jim, Delilah and I walked back into the house. Jim and I said our good byes to everyone. Delilah walked us back out to the front porch. "Thanks again for everything, Robyn. You too, Jim."

"We're glad we could help." We hugged her, got in our car, and drove home.

I rolled down my window to get some fresh air. We rode much of the way in silence. Jim broke the silence when he looked at me and said, "You did it, Sweetie. It's finally over. He's finally at peace."

"We did it, Jim. I couldn't have done any of it without you. Thank you." We both cried.

Jim smiled and said, "I imagine him driving around in his Chief Yellow Sports Car, having a blast."

"Me, too. And I bet once he rests up enough and heals, he'll probably teach his Indian Chief how to play some baseball." We both laughed. And cried some more.

When we got home, we both felt so incredibly drained, we slept away much of the rest of the afternoon.

CHAPTER THIRTY -- THE FUTURE

- During the fall of 1992, Delilah Miller refrained from suffocating her two-year-old son, Simon, with a pillow, when Simon would not stop crying. Delilah immediately brought Simon to the shelter run by the state and voluntarily gave up her custody of him to the state. She then, for the first time in her life, had herself admitted to a psychiatric hospital for evaluation. Delilah Miller passed away from AIDS in December of 1993, in an inpatient hospice in Chicago.
- Simon, Jeremy's brother, went into foster care in the fall of 1992. His loving foster parents permanently adopted him in 1995.
- Lindsey and Wayne Ross continue to provide foster care to abused and neglected children with HIV and AIDS. Since they adopted Timmy, they have also adopted four other children. One of the children has AIDS, two others seroconverted and are now perfectly healthy children. Some of their foster children stay only temporarily overnight or on a short-term basis, others stay for months and years at a time. God bless them.
- During the planning of Jeremy's funeral, Delilah, Lindsey, and Wayne were able to come to terms with the antagonism between them. The following Thanksgiving, Delilah spent the day and had dinner with Lindsey and Wayne.

- Timmy, Jeremy's foster brother, passed away from AIDS in 1994. Lindsey and Wayne Ross adopted him before he died. They also cared for and adopted Timmy's sister, who also died from AIDS.
- My Mom passed away from cancer two days after Delilah passed away. My Mom also died in an inpatient hospice, in a western suburb of Chicago. She had traveled here from Florida to receive her cancer treatments, so she could be closer to three of her children, but came down with pneumonia before the treatments even started.
- Hannah Hanley resigned from her position as Pediatric Nurse Practitioner at Jeremy's hospital in 1992. She moved to Wisconsin in order to help care for her aging parents. She currently works with children and families at her local hospital.
- Carolyn Mitchell retired from her job working with families with AIDS and child abuse and neglect in January of 1998. She has since become an Ordained Unity Minister. The social work position, which I held, was never filled by another master's level social worker after I resigned. Carolyn was either given a bachelor's level person or a student intern. The program has since dissolved at that particular agency, but is still going strong, continuing to serve these families, at another one.
- All of the children from the Jones family, (where Martin thrust quarters at my head,) with the exception of the two smallest children, were placed into foster care with the state. One of the teenage girls had a psychotic break when she began to have flashbacks of being raped by her oldest brother shortly after he was diagnosed with AIDS.
- The family where the mother threw the fork which stuck in her daughter's head was successful in earning all of their toddler children back from the state after complying with the state's requirements to get them back. This was the case where the sheriff escorted me to my car after I testified to have the children removed.

- Judge Morgan Hamilton continues to practice in the Circuit Court of Cook County, in the area of domestic relations.
- Statistics show that in the year 2000, there were 862,455 substantiated cases of child abuse and neglect in the United States. Illinois had 31,446 substantiated cases.
- After much research, I could find no data being collected on cases of AIDS/HIV and child abuse and neglect, although they do exist. I was told by several agencies that they do not correlate statistics for social problems with medical problems.
- Jim and I now have two beautiful children. Our daughter, Kathryn, was born three months after Jeremy died and our son, Stephen, was born in 1995. Stephen was named after Jeremy's lamb. Both Kathryn and Stephen have Jeremy's incredibly beautiful long eyelashes and big eyes, just like Jeremy promised me they would. (As Jeremy would say, better to give butterfly kisses!) Had Jeremy lived, Lindsey and Wayne were going to allow Jim and I to legally adopt him.

When Kathryn was two and a half, Jim and I took her to Toys-R-Us to pick out a "Jeremy" doll, because he was part of our family. We walked into the toy store and began looking around for a large, soft, African American male doll, that she could carry around with her. My hope of finding one made me have butterflies in my stomach.

We walked to aisle 21, the aisle with all the dolls in it, and looked up to see what was on the shelves. And voila! A large, soft, African American male doll, with soft brown curls just like Jeremy's, wearing blue overalls, with "My Buddy" embroidered on the pocket stood alone. We again gave thanks.

A year later, Kathryn, out of the blue, changed her Jeremy doll's name to "Simon," and neither Jim nor I had ever mentioned his name to her.

Kids are connected to the Source from birth. We all are. We've just become disconnected. It's time for us to reconnect.

If you ever have an opportunity to make a difference for just one person in need, do it. Don't be afraid to make a commitment and stick to it, no matter how hard it gets. Give away the love within your heart. It just might change your life... and someone else's forever. And together, we just may be able to heal the nations. Amen.

ACKNOWLEDGMENTS

To "Carolyn Mitchell," my other half on the job, thank you for your support. I love you sister.

To "Lindsey" and "Wayne," for taking Jeremy in and loving him as your own, I am grateful.

To "Hannah Hanley" for doing your part to love and care for Jeremy and Delilah, and for your support of me, I am grateful.

To Rosemary and Alan Bell, my sister and brother-in-law, thank you for your comfort and support throughout the whole experience, especially at the end. I am grateful.

To Reverend Sally Wales and her husband Bruce Wales, you saw us through to the end, and I am forever grateful. The spiritual knowledge that I gained through your classes gave me the courage and the knowing to keep going everyday, to face the darkness and unknown with complete trust in God and the Universe: To stand on the promises of God. Thank you, thank you for being my teacher and friend.

To all the caseworkers, supervisors, hospital staff, attorneys, and other people and agencies that played a role in Jeremy's life, thank you. Together, and with a lot of Divine Intervention, we each fulfilled our part and made a difference.

For helping me get started writing, I thank the Lisle Library Writers' Group. Very special thanks goes to Stephen Brockman, who truly took me under his wing, and helped mold me into the writer I have become. To Cliff and Barb Johns, who came into my life to assist me with the writing of the second half of the book, I am grateful. Thank you Karen Musgrave, for writing my introduction.

Thank you Mike Hamilton, for polishing my manuscript to, "Make it the gem it's supposed to be." To Mary Accetturo, for encouraging me to tell the spiritual truth in sections of the book that I was afraid to tell, thank you. To all the friends who helped edit along the way, I am grateful, especially Lorna Turner and Karen Osika.

Thanks to Shelly Sulski for helping me to format my manuscript for the publisher. To Deb Esposito and Shelly Sulski for getting our Angel Painting on CD and helping with the cover, thank you both.

To Kathryn Andries, for teaching her Discover Your Life's Purpose class and helping me to accept who I am, thank you. To Patrick Andries, for helping me to heal and surrender to my Higher Self, I am grateful, and thanks for your help with the cover, also.

Thank you Shellie Carter for sharing your *Angel Blessing® Cards* with me and proving what I already knew in my heart: Jeremy truly is an Angel!

And most of all, to our Heavenly Father, Mother God, through whom all things are possible, thank you, thank you. We did it! And so be it. Amen.

MUSICAL ACKNOWLEDGMENTS

The author is grateful for the role the following songs played in Jeremy's life:

("Composition"):

WIND BENEATH MY WINGS
Words and Music by LARRY HENLEY and JEFF SILBAR
© 1982 WARNER HOUSE OF MUSIC & WB GOLD MUSIC
CORP.
All Rights Reserved Used by Permission
Warner Bros. Publications U.S. Inc., Miami, Florida 33014

Philip Collins, *Against All Odds,* Phil Collins, EMI Golden Torch Music Corp. c/o EMI Music Pub., 1984.

Mick Jones, *I Want To Know What Love Is,* Foreigner, Somerset Songs Publishing, Inc., c/o Int'l Royalty Services Inc., 1984.

C. Austin Myles, *In The Garden,* Word Music, Inc., 1940.

BIBLIOGRAPHY

Buscaglia, Leo, Ph.D. *The Fall of Freddie the Leaf, A Story of Life for All Ages.* New York: Slack Incorporated, 1982.

Fillmore, Charles. *The Metaphysical Bible Dictionary.* Missouri: Unity School of Christianity, 1931.

Hodgson, Joan. *Hullo Sun.* England: The White Eagle Publishing Trust, 1987.

Tanner, Wilda B. *The Mystical, Magical Marvelous World of Dreams.* Oklahoma: Sparrow Hawk Press, 1988.

Robyn V. Accetturo, L.C.S.W.

Order Form

& How to Contact the Author

*Two agencies instrumental in providing services to Jeremy and other children and families living with AIDS are **Lutheran Social Services of Illinois, Second Family and AIDS Legal Council of Chicago.** Both agencies will be benefactors of a percentage of the profits for the sale of the artwork and T-shirts sold below.

Matted Prints of *Surely Goodness and Mercy* (the "Jeremy Angel")
Price: $45.00 + $5.50 shipping/handling
50% of the profits from sales will be donated to these two agencies*

Yellow or Forest green silk-screened T-shirts of My Wish For the Future... (Jeremy's picture essay in his own handwriting)
Price: $20.00 youth sizes S, M, or L + $5.50 shipping/handling
$25.00 adult sizes S, M, L, or XL + $5.50 shipping/handling
$28.00 for sizes 2X and 3X + $5.50 shipping/handling
Please specify quantity, color, and size when ordering.
100% of the profits for these T-shirt sales will go to LSSI, Second Family and AIDS Legal Council of Chicago*

*If a third non-profit sells artwork and T-shirts to host their own fund-raiser, then a portion of the profits will be shared with this non-profit agency, too.

Please, send check or money order made payable to **Baridi Press.**
Mail to: **Baridi Press   PO Box 3774   Lisle, Illinois   60532-9998**

If you wish to contact the author, you may write to her at **Baridi Press.** The author is available for speaking engagements and book signings. Speaking topics of interest include *Dance With An Angel,* Spirituality, Stress Management, and Meditation. If you would like Robyn to speak to your community group or organization, please write to her at the above address.

To order additional books of *Dance With An Angel* online go to
www.1stbooks.com/bookview/15721

ABOUT THE AUTHOR

Robyn V. Accetturo is a professional freelance writer and Licensed Clinical Social Worker. She has been in private practice as a social worker since 1991. She teaches meditation and progressive relaxation classes. She received her Bachelor's Degree in Psychology with Distinction from the University of Illinois at Chicago and her Masters Degree in Social Work, from the Jane Addams College of Social Work, at the University of Illinois at Chicago. She specialized in the area of mental health.

Robyn lives in a suburb of Chicago with her husband and two children. She is an active volunteer in her community and has been involved with several humanitarian projects.

Printed in the United States
87461LV00003B/103-120/A

9 781410 783981